1758

TRIBULATIONS AND LAUGHTER

By S. N. Behrman

Books

DUVEEN

THE WORCESTER ACCOUNT

CONVERSATION WITH MAX

THE SUSPENDED DRAWING ROOM

THE BURNING GLASS
(*a novel*)

Plays

THE SECOND MAN

SERENA BLANDISH

METEOR

BRIEF MOMENT

BIOGRAPHY

RAIN FROM HEAVEN

END OF SUMMER

AMPHITRYON 38
(*adapted from the French of Giraudoux*)

WINE OF CHOICE

NO TIME FOR COMEDY

THE TALLEY METHOD

THE PIRATE
(*from Fulda*)

JACOBOWSKY AND THE COLONEL
(*with Franz Werfel*)

DUNNIGAN'S DAUGHTER

JANE
(*from Somerset Maugham*)

I KNOW MY LOVE
(*from Achard*)

FANNY
(*with Joshua Logan*)

THE COLD WIND AND THE WARM

LORD PENGO

BUT FOR WHOM CHARLIE

TRIBULATIONS

AND

LAUGHTER

A MEMOIR BY

S. N. BEHRMAN

HAMISH HAMILTON

LONDON

First Published in Great Britain 1972
by Hamish Hamilton Ltd
90 Great Russell Street London WC1B 3PT

SBN 241 02171 5

PRINTED IN GREAT BRITAIN
BY T. & A. CONSTABLE LTD., EDINBURGH

For Harry Sions

Contents

Illustrations

Picture Credits

Courtesy of Glen Byam-Shaw: 29
Caricature by Will Cotton. Courtesy of Mrs. Harold Freedman: 48
Theatre Collection, The New York Public Library at Lincoln Center, Astor, Lenox and Tilden Foundations: 74, 192, 233
Photo by Sasha, London: 105
Courtesy of Serge Hovey: 141 (both)
Copyright Metro-Goldwyn-Mayer Inc. 1933: 150
From And the Bridge Is Love by Alma Mahler Werfel and E. B. Ashton, Harcourt, Brace & Company, New York. Copyright © 1958 by Alma Mahler Werfel and E. B. Ashton: 170 (both)
Photo by Pictorial Press, London: 207
Photo by Trudy Fleischman, New York: 230
Caricature by Al Hirschfeld. Courtesy of Mr. Hirschfeld: 240
Photo by Fabian Bachrach: 321
New York Public Library Picture Collection: 326

Acknowledgements

The author is grateful for permission to include quotations from *Collected Poems* by Siegfried Sassoon. Copyright 1918, 1920, 1948. By permission of George Sassoon. From *Amphitryon 38,* A Comedy and Prologue in Three Acts by Jean Giraudoux, adapted from the French by S. N. Behrman. Copyright 1938, 1966 by S. N. Behrman, Hamish Hamilton, London. *Lyrics on Several Occasions* by Ira Gershwin. Copyright © 1959 by Ira Gershwin. Reprinted by permission of Alfred A. Knopf, Inc. *George Gershwin*, edited and designed by Merle Armitage. Copyright 1938 by Merle Armitage and Walter Burroughs. Published by Longmans, Green and Company. Reprinted by permission of Mr. Armitage.

A substantial portion of this book appeared originally in *The New Yorker*.

I

Preamble

I T IS A STRANGE EXPERIENCE reading your own diary forty or fifty years after you've written it. I began mine while I was still an undergraduate in 1915. I have kept it up ever since. I don't know what first impelled me to start it — perhaps an unconscious impulse to salvage each day from oblivion. Many years later, having dinner with Felix Frankfurter in Cambridge, I confessed to him this obsessional avocation. "I wish," he said, "that I had done it. I would love to have a day-to-day record of my time with Stimson." Reading this diary — sixty volumes — which I have had to do to write this book, is very different from reading history; there the characters are all strangers and dead. Here, they are alive and present. Characters keep appearing whose very existence I had forgotten, and yet they keep reappearing, vivid ghosts, taut in their momentary preoccupations, clamped, as I myself was, in the imperatives of NOW. Reading through these pages, I can foresee their destinies; their futures are laid out, all the criss-crossed lines where my life intersected theirs. It is somewhat terrible to become possessed, suddenly, of all that foresight, a pointillism of time. They seem blindfolded, as I myself was.

I once asked Somerset Maugham whether he would ever write his autobiography. He replied, rather sharply, "No. Never." I asked why not. "Because," he said, "it is not possible to tell the truth." More copiously than Maugham, Mark Twain expressed himself on the impossibility of writing an autobiography. He agrees with Maugham, although for different reasons. I borrow from his own Preface while he stands morosely on the brink of the impossible:

What a wee little part of a person's life are his acts and his words! His real life is led in his head, and is known to none but himself. All day long, and every day, the mill of his brain is grinding, and his *thoughts,* not those other things, are his history. His acts and his words are merely the visible, thin crust of his world, with its scattered snow-summits and its vacant wastes of water — and they are so trifling a part of his bulk! A mere skin enveloping it. The mass of him is hidden — it and its volcanic fires that toss and boil, and never rest, night nor day. These are his life, and they are not written and cannot be written. Every day would make a whole book of eighty thousand words — three hundred and sixty-five books a year. Biographies are but the clothes and buttons of the man — the biography of the man himself cannot be written.

I suspect that Twain, who was an embittered man, with many shattering private griefs, didn't want to descend publicly into the abysms to which his private thoughts led him. I was told by Brander Matthews, when I was in his class at Columbia, that William Dean Howells, who had the run of Twain's house, walked into his living room shortly after the death of Twain's daughter. Twain had fallen asleep on the sofa; Howells' entrance woke him. Howells was horrified at what he had done: committed the unpardonable sin of snatching a sleeping friend from oblivion and impaling him abruptly on the sharp spikes of reality. He cried out: "Good heavens, Mark, did I *wake* you?"

There will be no abysm-dropping in this book, except for the descents made by others. What Mark Twain felt he couldn't do, I shall not presume to do. This will be a Memoir, a category much more relaxed and easygoing, vagarious and permissive. By this time — seventy-five plus — I have had just about all I can take of myself. I am a mild manic-depressive, difficult at times to distinguish from an acute one. To show how far it can go, I will relate a simple fact. Not long ago — February — I woke up and smelt the polluted air that comes

4

into my city bedroom. It was a mild morning; I thought that I sniffed, even through the sourness, an intimation of spring. Immediately then I felt the pain of past springs, the stifled, upthrusting longings of spring which have no resolution. I took lien, in February, on the cruelty of April. I thought: "This is going too far — to borrow angst from a problematical spring that I may not even live to see!" I had sensible arguments, but the still unborn spring nevertheless had its way. The sinking of the heart persisted. What is a sinking of the heart? Is there a physiological change? Can it be registered on a cardiograph? Has anyone a clue?

An odd quirk of destiny has put a great many people in my way. I want, in this book, to return to them. I want to revive their society; to share their tribulations and their laughter.

II

Ways and Means

To BE BROUGHT UP in a poverty-stricken household, to know nothing but poverty in childhood and adolescence, is not so bad while you are enduring it; it is quite tolerable in fact, at least it was in my case. It is in later life that it takes its toll. In the Providence Street ghetto in Worcester, Massachusetts, everybody was as poor as we were. The one rich man on the hill, who had a stucco house with a stained-glass window and who owned a Winton Six, was still devoured by the consuming passion to become the president of the Providence Street Synagogue directly across the street from us. He was illiterate in Hebrew and therefore had no standing. My father, on the other hand, who didn't have a penny, was learned in the sacred books and did have standing. There used to be an expression on the hill — "Does he know the little black dots?" — referring to the symbols for cantillation under letters of the Hebrew texts — and if you didn't know them, neither stained-glass windows nor Winton Sixes could save you. I realize now that the Providence Street community was a theological aristocracy in which money gave you no status. But I have been haunted by dreams of poverty all my life, through all the years since I have emerged from it. I dream that I am in hotel rooms without the money to pay for them. I dream that I am jobless and can't get a job. A pet, though disagreeable, dream is that I am walking, in a heavy rain, and carrying a leaden suitcase from Boston to Worcester. When I get to Worcester, there is nowhere to go. Everyone is dead. I go to the Bancroft Hotel, go up in the elevator, and walk down a corridor. Exhausted from the walk, my

6

shoes and my clothes soaking, I open a door, see a bed, and sink down on it. Then I see that the room is occupied. I must not fall asleep lest the occupant come in. I struggle to remain awake. I fall asleep. . . .

I went for two years to Clark College in Worcester, then switched to Harvard to study playwriting with George Pierce Baker. Harvard was idyllic then. Forty years later I was invited to come to Kirkland House for a week to "talk to the boys." The difference between the Cambridge I had known and the one I saw now was shattering: the difference between a small, manageable town and a swollen segment of the Boston-Washington conurbation. Exotics jostled each other in the streets — town and sari. For years after leaving Harvard I used to dream, in the inhospitable, jobless years I spent in New York, that I would wake up in Weld Hall, on the Harvard Yard. And yet the two years at Harvard were a clouded fantasy. I was haunted by the incessant query: What would I do when I got out, how get a job, how make a living? Providence Street got its licks in! My fears proved not to be chimerical; I did have a terrible time getting a job in New York — and in other cities as well.

I have a vivid memory of the June day when I sat in Soldiers' Field in Cambridge waiting for my degree. It is of John Singer Sargent, magnificent in his scarlet robe and bright yellow, nicotined moustache and beard, who rose to get his honorary degree, pinned on him personally by Abbott Lawrence Lowell. After Sargent and I got our degrees, I was assailed by a problem which, I am sure, did not bother Sargent, but which had for years been eroding me: What to do next? With the production of a successful play, which happened to me eleven years later, you acquire, overnight, a new identity and a public label. But this label is pasted on you, it doesn't obliterate what you are and have always been nor does it erase the stigmata of temperament. These I brought with me to New York where they were deepened by years of unsuccessful job-hunting. I went to every newspaper office in New York, even to Philadelphia and Baltimore. I had a half-dozen plays but I was allowed to keep them. In desperation and financed by my older brothers, I went to Columbia to get an M.A. in English. I joined a seminar in nineteenth-century French drama with Brander Matthews.

7

Matthews was a tall, thin man with wispy muttonchop whiskers. He was an established man-of-the-world, easy and anecdotal, the friend of Mark Twain, Theodore Roosevelt and William Dean Howells, in fact of everybody whom most people didn't know. We read a lot and heard a lot about the two most popular French playwrights of the nineteenth century, Scribe and Sardou. As an example of Sardou's skill as a technician — or was it Scribe's? — how quickly and easily he could establish his leading character as a sophisticated worldling, Matthews drew attention to a restaurant scene in which the protagonist enters and says casually to the headwaiter: "Good evening, Henry." This established, so dexterously, that the hero knew his way around expensive restaurants.

One day I made the mistake of bringing into class a copy of the *New Republic.* I had, actually, a contribution in it. Matthews looked at the *New Republic* and said, "I am sorry to see you wasting your time on that stuff." As a staunch Republican and intimate of Theodore Roosevelt's, he had to do his duty. Still, Matthews was a kind man. He gave a classmate and me cards to visit the Players' Club, which thrilled us, and me an invitation to hear Henri Bergson lecture in English. I was startled by the immaculateness and decorum of Bergson's English. When I reported this to Matthews, he said: "It is the English of a foreigner who doesn't know English — only the English classics."

The M.A. degree gave me a leg up. My newly acquired knowledge of nineteenth-century Parisian play techniques qualified me for typing up and classifying the want ads for the *New York Times.* The hours were from three in the afternoon to three in the morning. I worked on the widest machine I had ever seen; it was like driving a truck. It was then safe and lovely to walk to my room on West Thirty-sixth Street at three in the morning. I can't remember how it happened, but from the third floor of the Times Building I crept up to the tenth and got a job with Dr. Clifford Smyth, the editor of the book review section. I never learned how Smyth got his doctorate; maybe it was for marrying a daughter of Nathaniel Hawthorne. He sent me over one day to interview Siegfried Sassoon, who was here to read his war poems. I can't remember the printed interview, but this visit was the beginning of a friendship that long outlasted my job on the *Times.* After a few months, Smyth put me in charge of the "Queries and Answers" column. The flood of inquiries about obscure midwestern poets began to bore me. I got the bright idea of sending myself inquisitive letters. "What has become of Ambrose Bierce?"

It turned out that "Queries and Answers" was Mr. Ochs's pet column. He cherished it. He doted on the obscure midwestern poets; he found their view of life uplifting and salvationist. He put an end to my fascinating correspondence. The tenure I didn't have lapsed. I was prodded by the same old question: What to do next?

The involuntary leisure enabled me to spend a lot of time with Sassoon. He had a leisure problem too, very different from mine. He was lacerated by a private agony. He said that when he got an idea for a poem it took him very little time to write it. What made his situation intolerable was that he had the time to brood over this agony. After I got to know him better he confessed to me the source of his suffering. I think it did him good to have someone to confide in. It will scarcely be believed, but I was then so naïve and uninformed that it shocked me, though I did my best not to show it.

I recalled a remark of Charles Townsend Copeland's — in English 12, a writing course at Harvard — that poets wrote the best prose. I nudged Siegfried toward trying his hand at prose. I still have some pages, in his beautiful handwriting, of a novel he began that summer, which he never completed. The prose project kept our correspondence alive after he returned to England. The eventual result is an exquisite classic: *Memoirs of a Fox-Hunting Man.*

Siegfried told me his story. His antiwar poems were so searing that their publication led to a Parliamentary inquiry. What made the military scratch their heads in bewilderment was the perplexing fact that Sassoon's war record was recklessly heroic. He had twice been cited for bravery. But there is nothing beyond the military mind; it came up with a solution: that Sassoon was crazy — they called it shell shock. He was institutionalized. Had it not been for the accidental presence there of a great man, Dr. William Halse Rivers, a famous English psychiatrist and anthropologist for whom Sassoon's duality as a war hero and a militant pacifist was not in the least paradoxical, he should never, Siegfried told me, have survived that experience.

9

Siegfried Sassoon

Siegfried couldn't get over a feeling of strangeness in his present position as a famous war poet who had been summoned to lecture in America. In his youth, up to the outbreak of the war, his life had been devoted to horses and to hunting; all his friends had been sporting people. To them he was known, satirically, as "Old Sieg." If they knew, and many of them must have heard of it, that he had written antiwar poems, they must have written it off as an aberration and wondered when poor old Sieg would return to his true vocation, fox-hunting. Siegfried was sent to Marlborough for schooling. He had a hard time absorbing useful knowledge. Aware of this limitation, and in a gallant effort to make up for it, he spent a great deal of time, when he had to do papers, in illuminating the first letters of each paragraph. He supplied himself with pencils of all colors and with gold leaf, and devoted himself to imitating the lettering in medieval manuscripts. He found written on one of his papers: "Very beautiful the calligraphy, but alas, no content." Siegfried was plowed. He went back happily to his horses and his piano at which he spent hours playing Bach and medieval lute songs. During all these years he'd been writing poetry, a secret vice. That was his situation when he enlisted in the war. Up to then he had never felt deeply about anything. What he saw in the trenches made him feel. The *War Poems* were the result.

I was prepared to be frightened myself when I went to hear Siegfried read his poems in the Free Synagogue in Carnegie Hall. Siegfried was tall, lithe and extraordinarily handsome. He read quietly, without effect, without inflection. I remember still the stunned silence that followed the reading of one of his poems. I copy it from the little book of his war poems that he left me when he returned to England:

DOES IT MATTER?

Does it matter? — losing your legs?
For people will always be kind,
And you need not show that you mind
When the others come in after football
To gobble their muffins and eggs.

Does it matter? — losing your sight? . . .
There's such splendid work for the blind;
And people will always be kind,
As you sit on your terrace remembering
And turning your face to the light.

Do they matter? — those dreams from the pit? . . .
You can drink and forget and be glad,
And people won't say that you're mad;
For they'll know that you've fought for your country
And no one will worry a bit.

Except when he was away on his poetry-reading tours, I saw Sassoon constantly for the rest of that winter, and indeed through most of the following summer. He lived in Westover Court and he invited me to use these pleasant rooms while he was away. Westover Court was a real estate pleasantry of Vincent Astor's. In a book published thirty years later, *Siegfried's Journey,* Sassoon described the extra illumination in his room: ". . . my nocturnal outlook was dominated by the Putnam Building above which blazed the electric sign of Wrigley's Spearmint Gum. Flanked by two peacocks whose tails were cascades of quivering color, about a square acre of advertising space contained the caption: 'Don't argue but stick it in your face.' " It was the biggest sign in New York; it dominated Times Square. There was a story about it: a New Yorker was showing the sign off to a visiting Englishman. As the Englishman seemed to be insufficiently impressed, the native filled him in. He said: "There are three hundred thousand electric bulbs in that sign." "But, my dear chap," said the Englishman, "doesn't that make it frightfully conspicuous?" Westover Court was a very unlikely place to find in New York even then: four stories high, built around a court with a tree in the middle. On winter nights, when you came home late, the bare branches of this tree would be covered with night birds who resorted to it in lieu of a forest. Westover Court was a bachelor establishment with two-room apartments; it was like a dormitory in a New England college. Actors and artists and singers lived in it.

I was avid to learn about the English literary scene; Siegfried took me to the heart of it. The Georgian poets, hitherto names to me, were all friends of his. His love for some of them — Edmund Blunden and Wilfred Owen for example — was passionate. He read their works aloud to me; he talked for hours about their distilled virtues. I was delighted to hear him talk about Max Beerbohm, whom he adored. Whenever he talked about Max he chortled with glee; he imitated his light, penetrating voice and the stories he told illustrated the style, surgical and elegant, in which Max trepanned the pretentious and the pompous. Professor Rivers, who, as Siegfried always said, had saved his life, also made it possible for him to employ it. He told him he must get "an outside interest" and suggested the labor movement. Siegfried took his advice. He became actively involved. He was a friend of Harold Laski's and he was introduced by his publisher, Ben Huebsch, to labor circles here. There was no one to whom Sassoon was more devoted than to Ben, who was an activist in behalf of the American Civil Liberties Union. I was devoted to Ben too; I have never known a more lovable or kinder man. He came to my aid once by giving me a part-time job on the *Freeman,* which he published, and which was considered by many good judges to be the best-written magazine in America. We saw a lot of Ben and of Louis Untermeyer. Siegfried hated "Society"; he had an instinctive prejudice against the rich and resolutely turned down invitations which rained in on him from the well-heeled.

Siegfried's other passion was music. Ben Huebsch and Louis Untermeyer provided chamber music for him. We went to Carnegie Hall in the winter and to the Stadium concerts in the summer. One bitter February afternoon I took him uptown to meet the sister of a college friend, Emily Gresser, who was a concert violinist. The taxi trip provided an incident. Siegfried's legs were so long that he never knew quite what to do with them. He had been told by an officer that the best way to rest them in the trenches was to lie down whenever he could and prop them up as high as possible on whatever support he could find. He assumed this position in the cramped taxi. Soon a rift appeared in the plate-glass window separating us from the cabby. The cabby was furious. He stopped the cab and demanded ten dollars, the

13

price of the window. Siegfried embarked on a metaphysical argument with him, pointing out how difficult it was to fix responsibility, that the window had been weakened by bumps in the rutted road and that his boss who owned the cab couldn't own it because he, Siegfried, didn't believe in private property and why should the cabby? It was very funny, but alas, the cabby had no humor and Siegfried ended the argument by paying him the money. I wrote this dialogue up in a sketch called "Never Stretch Your Legs in a Taxi." It appeared in the *Smart Set*. It amused Siegfried.

We had a pleasant time at the Gressers'. Emily's father, a nineteenth-century Russian liberal, seemed to be awed at meeting Sassoon. He asked questions about his ancestry; Siegfried didn't seem to be much interested. Mr. Gresser ran to the bookshelves and brought over the S volume from the *Jewish Encyclopedia*. He confronted Siegfried with pages about his family, enlivened by engravings of turbaned ancestors. One dignitary, with an immense white beard and a magisterial expression, seemed to interest him particularly. He was sixteenth-century. Staring at his ancestor, Siegfried murmured: "Sweet character, isn't he?"

I got free tickets for a play by Edna St. Vincent Millay, and I induced Siegfried to come with me as there was no concert he wanted to go to that night. He and Miss Millay got on very well and saw each other a few times after that. Another time we went to see a play called *Over Night*. There was an engaging actor in it named Lynne Overman. In the first act, very tight, he goes to see some friends off on a boat to Europe. At the party in their cabin he gets drunker. The second-act curtain goes up on Overman fast asleep in an unoccupied cabin. There is a long pantomime. Overman wakes up. He looks around the unfamiliar environment. He sees a strange, oval-shaped window. He gets up, walks groggily to the window, and peers out. He is bewildered. He returns to the bed, picks up the telephone, and says: "Say, clerk, what's the idea of all this water?" Neither Siegfried nor I ever forgot that line. We used it in all sorts of situations that seemed incredible to us.

Siegfried kept asking me to come to England. I longed to go; I had never been abroad. I longed to see the London theatre and its marvelous comedians. I knew everything that was playing there and who was in it. I said I would try to come without any belief that I should ever be able to manage it. I was jobless and had a gnawing suspicion that I would never get a play on. I had too many now; it seemed pointless to keep writing more. In *Siegfried's Journey,* Siegfried describes our meeting in New York and how, when it came time for him to leave, we discussed the improbable project of my coming to London. "Somehow," Siegfried says in his book, "I couldn't foresee Sam as a successful writer." Neither could I. Nevertheless, it was fun to talk about it, as it is to wander about in any improbable fantasy. I asked, if the impossible should happen, where I might stay, as if there were no hotels in London. This lit Siegfried up. "You'll stay," he said, "where I once stayed — at 40 Half Moon Street. You'll be taken care of by 'Dame' Nellie Burton. You'll wonder how you ever managed before you met Burton!" I inquired about both. "Hazlitt lived there during his last days in London. Later Robbie Ross lived there," he said. "He was, like Rivers, my great benefactor. I can't tell you what he did for me, for everybody, in fact. He got Heinemann to publish my war poems. He apologized to me for helping me. 'Forgive me,' he said, 'but I am an incorrigible chaperon.' Arnold Bennett, who loved him, said to me: 'Our friend, Robert, is the most indirectly creative character I have known. He causes works of art and letters to occur.' Robbie was just on his way to Australia, to advise the museum people at Melbourne. The next night, just as he was leaving, he died. Gosse said that he wore himself out in deeds of active kindness."

Siegfried's speech came in little spasmodic geysers.

"Robbie — he loved to support lost causes — the stupendous thing about Robbie was . . . his loyalty . . . I've seen heroic acts on the battlefield . . . but I think loyalty is the greatest heroism, the noblest, it's a steady unheralded thing . . . it goes along without fanfare . . . it is unrecorded . . . unrewarded — except by those who remember it. And you know, Robbie, he was a great conversationalist — he'd stand there — I can see him now — in front of the fireplace in the parlor at Half Moon Street —"

Siegfried smiled in recollection.

"One night . . . we were playing a game . . . improvising epitaphs — what epitaph we'd want for ourselves . . . Robbie, you know, was always jumping in — flushing his friends out of troubled waters. For his own epitaph Robbie picked: 'His name was writ in hot water!' He was Oscar Wilde's literary executor. He was with him in Paris when he died. When Wilde's body was exhumed, the men were about to lift his body with their spades. Robbie stopped them — he got down into the grave and lifted the body in his arms . . . yes, Robbie was loyal."

To distract him, I inquired about my future London caretaker, "Dame" Nellie Burton. She had been, Siegfried told me, Robbie Ross's mother's lady's maid. It was Ross's mother who had owned the Half Moon Street house. When Mrs. Ross died, Robert inherited the house. He also inherited Dame Nellie. Dame Nellie inherited Robbie's friends, among others the Sitwells, Lord Berners and Sieg-fried. When Siegfried and Sacheverell Sitwell married, their wives became, in effect, Dame Nellie's daughters-in-law. Dame Nellie let the upstairs rooms. Lord Berners had rented one for a while. So had Siegfried. I asked for a description of Nellie. "I can't describe her," said Siegfried. "She's indescribable. She's Shakespearian. You'll just have to meet her. You see now, don't you, that you simply have to come to London!"

This remark made me feel that out of caprice, through some failure of the imagination, I was perversely rejecting the most beguiling of invitations.

And yet the chance did come, improbably and grotesquely and much sooner than I could possibly have anticipated — not through selling a play of my own but through a play which someone else had sold.

I saw Siegfried off when he sailed in August. Two film stars, Jack Pickford and Alma Rubens, who were standing against the rail on an upper deck, had the excited attention of the crowd. Pickford was so drunk he could hardly stand.

"In the morning," said Siegfried, "he's going to have hard work recognizing the water!"

There followed a series of sleazy jobs. Two of them I got by answering *Times* help wanted ads on *Times* stationery. This gave me the aura of a veteran journalist. One was from a Houston oil man who had gotten his photograph into the *Times* rotogravure section because he had flown his own tiny plane from Houston to New York. He hired me to publicize his oil wells in Burkburnett, Texas. I went to Houston and flew in his plane from Houston to Burkburnett. That flight and the return one induced a nervousness about plane travel that is with me still. When I got back to the Rice Hotel in Houston I got into a hot bath and stayed in it for hours; the tub was stationary. The man's name was S. E. J. Coxe. I inspected his holdings at Burkburnett but was unable to form a critical judgment. Coxe had a handsome office in Houston and a staff. His general manager was an impressive-looking, middle-aged, soberly dressed man who was a Christian Scientist and in God's confidence. I returned to New York with him. He took me to Christian Science meetings at which he gave testimony. Close as I was to the *Times* as an ex-employee, I couldn't get the Burkburnett enterprise on the front page or, indeed, on any page. The job lapsed. Another was given me by a seemingly sane man — an educated, serious man who belonged to a distinguished family. His older brother had an important government position in Washington. I got the feeling that he was jealous of this successful brother and wanted to outdo him in distinction. His idea was to send news abstracts to country papers throughout the United States which didn't have the AP service. I had to get to his office at three every morning to abstract from the early editions. He actually got some subscriptions but not enough to pay his office rent or me, though I was getting very little. Mr. Finch was a serious, well-intentioned man who wanted the whole country to be on the qui vive instead of the overindulged readers in the big cities. He was very sad when he had to acknowledge defeat.

During all these years I kept rising and falling on various locations in various plays. I was enticed by a scandal which racked Columbia University, not as horrendous as more recent scandals there, much more intimate and personal, but sufficient unto the day. It concerned Professor John Broadus Watson, the leading behavioral psychologist in the United States. He was fired from Columbia because of a non-academic relationship with one of his pupils, whom he later married.

Unfrocked, Watson joined the executive staff of the prestigious advertising firm of J. Walter Thompson where he spent the rest of his now affluent life conditioning the behavior of the consuming public. This seemed to me a social waste. I wrote a play about it called *The American Way*. The influence of advertising in American life — and this was before the day of radio and television — interested me profoundly. The first encouragement I got in New York came from Francis Hackett, then literary editor of the *New Republic*. He printed a "light middle'" of mine called "The Advertising Man," the piece I had tried to show Brander Matthews. It was reprinted not long ago in a *New Republic* anthology of its first fifty years. When the scandal broke out about Professor Watson, I felt I had a concrete and dramatic story to pin my feelings on: the confusion of standards which condemns a valuable citizen, because of sexual preference, to put his talents to second-rate and even antisocial uses.

The American Way brought Jed Harris into my life. My agent, Harold Freedman, sent it to him in Chicago where Jed was then press-agenting some show. Harris wrote me to say that he wanted to produce it and would, as soon as he could raise the money. But he couldn't raise the money. Moreover, he reported that the established managers to whom he submitted it with the offer to coproduce it with them, couldn't get excited about a play whose chief character was a professor. There was something about professors which seemed undramatic to them. A great many years later, in Hollywood, I urged Pearl Buck's *The Good Earth* upon Winfield Sheehan, the head of Twentieth Century–Fox. He sent for me after he'd read it. The book was before him on his desk. He shook his head. "Listen, Sam, nobody ain't going to take no interest in no Chinaman." And if there remained any residual prejudice against professors, *Who's Afraid of Virginia Woolf?* must have diluted that.

Jed did find the money for a play by John V. A. Weaver called *Love 'Em and Leave 'Em*. He asked me to be his play reader and press agent. I knew nothing about this highly specialized vocation. The dean of New York press agents, Richard Maney, an entrancing character and a very nimble writer, took me in hand. He tutored me. For a long time after, he kept telling people that I had asked him what a marquee was. He explained to me that it had nothing to do with the French nobility — that it was spelled differently. No one could have been greener than I, but, on the first Sunday, I got a lot of stuff in the papers. There were then fourteen papers in New York and also about sixty theatres. The theatre was the great entertainment medium for the United States.

Jed was an apparition in the city. There was a Svengali look about him. He was highly articulate; he talked about the theatre, about acting and directing, in terms of fine arts that had, so far, been only rudimentarily explored. He had a saturnine humor and was an infectious storyteller. He wowed everybody and was, for years, an obsessional subject of conversation. Plays and novels were written about him. Actresses swooned over him; they lived only to be directed by him and some even died as a result of it. At least one beautiful actress of distinguished family committed suicide over him. It added to his prestige and amplified his legend. His seductions were notorious. Every script came to him and any star he wanted. By the time he was thirty he had made a million dollars and had the New York theatre, which was then the American theatre, in the palm of his hand. Icarus, the velocity of his ascent catapulted him. Those in his orbit became his devotees and I was in his orbit. As his legend grew, so did his belief in it. In the end, this credulity undid him.

This phenomenal career started from a dingy playscript brought into the office one morning by Philip Dunning: *Broadway*. Dunning was a friend of mine and he asked me to read it. I did and Jed did. He decided at once to produce it. How to finance it? Jed made a suggestion. How about giving it to my friend Crosby Gaige? The pains of these years were mitigated for me by the friendship and hospitality of Crosby and Hilda Gaige. Gaige was a partner of the Selwyns, who had two theatres on Forty-second Street and one in Chicago. Crosby had a paneled office and a pornographic collection in the drawer of his Sheraton desk. He was tall, affable and enigmatic. Jed and I often wondered about his being in the theatre at all; his chief interest was in real estate and I suppose that was why the Selwyns found him useful. He was bookish; his hobby was collecting first editions by living English authors. He had "contacts" with them, among them Arnold

Bennett and Liam O'Flaherty. He had a beautiful country place, Watch Hill Farm, at Peekskill on the Hudson. Alexander Woollcott, Franklin P. Adams, Arthur Krock, George Kaufman and Moss Hart, the Lunts, Gregory Kelly and his wife Ruth Gordon, actors, actresses, newspaper publishers, were steady weekend guests — you could meet almost anybody at Watch Hill Farm. The croquet court was the scene of passionate tournaments.

Hilda Gaige was lovely and very dear. She was slender, with questing, blue-green eyes and shimmering chestnut hair. There was sympathy and affection between us always, and on her side an unwavering belief that I would emerge from press-agentry. She had a wonderful laugh. She was elfin — an adorable elf with a shadow over her. I wondered for a long time about the reason for the shadow. It came to me one day; it was her husband, it was Gaige. She was afraid of Gaige.

I brought Jed and Gaige together. Gaige read the script, though Jed said that Gaige had no equipment for reading a script, that his enthusiasm for it was simply an echo of his own. They made an arrangement to produce the play together, each to put up half the production cost. In about the third week of rehearsal, on a Sunday morning at Watch Hill Farm, Gaige took me for a drive. He told me of the financial arrangement he had made with Jed for *Broadway*.

"I put up my half right away," he said. "That's what we're going on now. But so far, your friend Jed hasn't put up his half. Not a penny so far from him."

Gaige made it clear, from his inflection of "your friend Jed" that Jed was my friend and not his, my responsibility, not his. But the play opened soon after and was an enormous success. Everybody connected with it tasted euphoria except Jed. He was eaten with resentment that Gaige owned half of it. On the surface things went on amiably between the partners. Jed liked Hilda and she adored him; she worshiped all creative genius. She took him to a tailor to dress him up to his new-found station. He was, she assured him, very handsome, and it would be apparent to the world once she had provided him with some decent clothes. He had always been a genius, but henceforth he would be a well-dressed genius.

I saw a great deal, in those days, of Arthur Krock. We had practically adjoining offices, he at the *Times* and I at Jed's in the Selwyn Theatre Building on West Forty-second Street. Krock was a theatre buff; he was teeming with ideas for publicizing Jed's show. He was fascinated, as everyone was, by Jed. He was a regular member of the Gaiges' weekend set at Watch Hill Farm. He was fond of Hilda and had what I thought was a critical intimacy with Crosby. A sentence in my diary for November 1926 reads: "A publicity idea of Arthur Krock's for *Broadway,* a picture-story series for the *Evening World,* sent me scurrying." The *Evening World* ran the story and Arthur was pleased to see his brainchild in the flesh. In the four decades since, I have not seen him at all. Having no longer to devise publicity ideas for *Broadway,* he has employed his consequent leisure to become eminent on his own.

It was at that time that my telephone phobia began. I have never since been able to dissociate the ring of the telephone from the imminence of danger. *Love 'Em and Leave 'Em* didn't require much tending but a big hit is demanding. Jed would call me up at two and three in the morning to berate me for something I had done badly or failed to do at all.

I got a telephone call one morning from Osbert Sitwell, about whom I had heard a good deal from Siegfried. Siegfried had asked him to get in touch with me. He was in town only for the day; he had to go to Washington. Could we meet for lunch? I said I'd love to, but that I had a lunch date with Jed Harris. Sitwell said he'd love to meet Jed. We made a date.

Sitwell was young, very handsome, full of vitality and good humor. He had the look of a Hapsburg prince. He told me at once Siegfried's news: that he was working on a prose book and seemed very happy and absorbed in it. I said I was glad to hear it. Sitwell was full of curiosity about the play Jed was doing on Broadway; he loved the theatre and listened with absorption to Jed's satirical account of the play and the actors and the "dictated" performances, dictated, naturally, by him. I asked Jed to tell Sitwell a funny story about a Jewish ham actor — a tragedian with a big voice and no talent. Jed loved to tell stories and went to it. Sitwell was delighted. He pronounced it

Heaven. Jed's success with the British aristocracy mollified him. He had been very angry with me that morning. The moment Sitwell was gone, he let me have it.

Though the New York theatre was a multitudinous enterprise compared to what it is now, it was also cozier. There were three or four extra-string critics on the papers since there might be that many openings each night. Production costs were not astronomical. There were ten or twelve accredited managers. Most of them invested their own money in their productions as did the Theatre Guild in its first glowing years. (Years later things had changed to such a point that George Kaufman told me that to finance a play of his he had to appeal to one hundred and four investors — all strangers.) There were marvelous actors who could play high comedy, a genre which has practically passed out of existence. For a time Philip Barry, Arthur Richman, Paul Osborn and I were the only American practitioners. There was Holbrook Blinn, an actor of such skill, subtlety and magnetism that I am sure he could have matched the famous English specialists in high comedy — Charles Hawtrey, for instance. There was Ina Claire. Richman and I were both lucky to have Ina in our plays. There were press agents who were beautiful stylists. There was Richard Maney. Above all there was Samuel Hoffenstein. He was press agent for Al Woods, an unwashed and illiterate one-eyed manager who had made a fortune producing melodramas. He would get on boats to Europe at the last minute without baggage or even a toothbrush, an instrument he never missed. He was a well-known character. Sam Harris was a character. So was William Harris. There was David Belasco, who was a clerical fake; there was Arthur Hopkins, who was a spirit.

I used to wait for Sundays to read Hoffenstein's pieces about Al Woods. They were based on the assumption that Al was a shy, scholarly man who locked himself in his office, deciphering palimpsests. Sam would invade Al's lucubrations with vulgar monetary information, how the Wednesday matinee had sold out, what this week's gross, barring accident, would certainly come to. At the mention of money Al shrank away. He would implore Sam with his eyes to leave him alone with his studies but Sam wouldn't go. The fun came from the fact that the cozy small town knew about Al. We didn't know, as we laughed over these pieces, that their author was to write *Poems in Praise of Practically Nothing*, the book that was found on Oliver Wendell Holmes's bed table when he died. There was Henry Miller. Arthur Richman was a friend of Miller's and used to stay with him in his house in Connecticut. Miller had a limousine with the biggest tonneau Richman had ever seen in his life, a special model. Driving into town one day with Miller, Richman said: "Do you really need a car this size?" Miller, melancholy, stared at the vast empty spaces: "I know," he said. "It's beginning to get on my nerves. It's like a Wednesday matinee in Baltimore!" There were playwrights and there were plays and there were plays by Eugene O'Neill, so that we had case histories even in that innocent time. The theatre in the thirties was organic, lively and multifariously cozy.

With the money pouring in from his half interest in *Broadway* Gaige took a magnificent apartment on Fifth Avenue. It had a walnut-paneled living room. I went up there to inspect it; Hilda showed it off to me. She was forlorn. She drew the curtains and lit the drawing room lights to show me how it would look at night. Suddenly she gave up. She sat down and stared at me.

"I can't," she said. "Do you think I'm terrible? I've got to leave Gaige. Haven't you known it?"

"I didn't know it was as serious as that."

"You'll be my friend, won't you? You'll see me through it, won't you?"

When I left her, on the way downtown, I saw it as an inescapable fact of life: walnut paneling could not patch up an unhappy marriage.

A new excitement rose. *Broadway* was going to London. Jed asked me to prepare a glossary to explain the esoteric Broadway argot for English audiences. I was longing to go. Jed vetoed it because, I think, he knew how passionately I wanted to go. I saw my hope of seeing London and Siegfried again crumble. Hilda knew how I felt about it. The idea of the trip had made a great change in her. She was wildly excited. She had a consuming interest in the English Royal Family. She read and read about them. She knew their homes, their relations, their habits. She forgot how unhappy she was. She was transformed. She asked me up to dinner with Gaige. At this dinner Gaige droned on, mostly about the eccentricities of my friend Jed. Halfway through Hilda couldn't stand it. She burst out at him.

"Why don't you tell him?" she cried.

"Oh, I've been working up to it." He addressed me. "You're coming with us," he said. "You're going to do that glossary in London."

He lifted his wineglass.

"Let's drink to the voyage. For Hilda and me — it'll be a second honeymoon. Won't it, darling?"

Over his wineglass he winked at me.

III

40 Half Moon Street

W E SAILED on the *Majestic,* formerly the *Bismarck,* an emolument of the First World War. The ship was immense, luxurious, confident. It had swimming pools and Ritz dining rooms. Few of the passengers gave any thought to its history or had any curiosity about it.

I looked up this journey in my 1926 diary. I was astonished at what I found; it was like reading someone else's. I had been a great admirer of Joseph Conrad; I had read most of him. It was not till I read this diary the other day that I was reminded that I met, on that journey, Richard Curle, one of Conrad's closest friends, indeed his literary executor, and that he talked endlessly about his hero. Curle, his name, his appearance, had vanished from consciousness, till he made this sudden and unexpected reentrance.

Philip Dunning, the co-author with George Abbott of *Broadway,* was on board. I worked with him on the glossary for the ignorant Londoners and helped him prepare his script for publication. He was a very decent man, in a state of shock over the bonanza that had overwhelmed him. Novelists with a first success have usually had years of writing experience behind them, short stories or journalism or other novels, but you can have a theatre success without such experience. Dunning had simply hit it, as you might strike an oil well or a mining lode.

The London company was on board, second class. We were constantly watching rehearsals. A fellow employee, Paul Streger, was there. He was ambitious to be a director and Jed had sent him to take charge of the company. This was a boon to me. At home, Streger and I and Herman Shumlin, another Jed recruit, had formed a triumvirate to console each other under the lash. Shumlin and Jed had grown up together in Newark, New Jersey. They were boyhood friends, before their lives really got started, and when they did, the friendship ruptured. It took each of us a long time to alleviate the traumas inescapable from employment by Jed.

From my diary I see that I was constantly trying to escape from the hectic social life of the ship and from rehearsals of *Broadway* to the privacy of my cabin to work on one or another of the three plays I had on tap. I wonder now how I could have worked on them with such intensity. Couldn't I see that they were dubious ventures? I couldn't. I didn't suspect how inadequate these plays were until they were produced. But you have to believe in what you're doing while you're doing it no matter how deluded that belief may be. The trouble is, that when you get older and your critical faculty sharpens, the generation of excitement over an idea becomes less and less frequent, until finally it is extinguished altogether. I once asked Maugham why he had stopped writing plays. "Because," he said, "I no longer get ideas for plays." He meant, of course, ideas in which he could believe. I read the other day a statement by a distinguished American playwright. She said that the reason she no longer wrote plays was because she no longer felt at home on Broadway. This is disingenuous. Broadway has nothing to do with it. It is because she has used up her material and she has nothing she wants to write.

Always on the scent for first editions, Gaige spotted the name of Richard Curle on the passenger list. He had been in America, lecturing on Conrad. I don't remember what Curle looked like, only that he was a morose man who seemed to be carrying a burden too heavy for him. He talked incessantly and with tragic intensity about Conrad. He had been with him on his last day; he had watched him die. Curle had arrived at Conrad's country place the night before. Conrad, who had been suffering from gout, was in bed, and they sat up to the early hours, talking. Conrad, Curle said, was a great talker and that night he was at his best. In the morning, after breakfast, the vein continued and Conrad, in wonderful spirits, insisted on driving Curle to see his new house, about eight miles away. He became ill on the way. They turned back. Two hours later he was dead. "On this ship — on this very ship," Curle said, "I met him at Southampton, on his return from his American visit. He was adored by your people. It was touching for me, deeply touching, after my talks about him, to have your countrymen come up to me — yes, they come up to me and they make me feel that because I loved Conrad . . . well, they looked on me as a friend because they loved him too."

Alone in my cabin after one of these séances with Curle I brooded too about Conrad's death. Curle had said that Conrad's mind was teeming with ideas which he longed to set down on paper and that he was eroded by the conviction that he never would, a conviction which Curle himself did not share because Conrad's conversation was so vigorous that he could not associate it with death.

Gaige invited Curle to dinner with us. I asked him an unfortunate question. I asked whether Joseph Conrad had ever written a play.

"He hated the theatre — despised it."

"Didn't he admire Ibsen?" I asked.

"He despised him. He called him 'an old fake,' " Curle said.

"So he never wrote one?" said Gaige.

"He did, as a matter of fact. *The Secret Agent*. Dramatization of his own novel."

"Did it succeed?" asked Gaige.

"Disaster. The whole thing nauseated Conrad. Nothing about the theatre he could stand."

"I hope," Gaige said to Curle, "that you don't share Conrad's aversion to the theatre. I'd very much like you to see the rehearsal of the play I'm doing in London. It will be valuable to my young friend here as he is preparing a glossary." He turned to me. "Whatever Mr. Curle doesn't understand you'll have to explain."

Curle, who felt perhaps that he had been too vehement about Conrad's contempt for the theatre, said he'd love to see the rehearsal. Hilda begged off. I sat with her for a few minutes. A steward handed her a cablegram. She tore it open. She was burbling with delight.

"Wonderful! Seats for the last performance — Gerald du Maurier. I never thought I'd get them! You'll come with me."

27

"What'll Gaige be doing?"

"Oh, he's seeing some English author. Imagine! Our first night in London — and *The Last of Mrs. Cheyney!*"

Hilda was as elated about Sir Gerald du Maurier as she was about the Royal Family. She never expected to see any of them. That too was to be vouchsafed her though she didn't know it at the time.

I had had, all my life, a nostalgia for England. On the boat train I had a thrill of recognition when I found that we were in Surrey. I knew Surrey, its fields and its sheep and its houses, from the photographs in *Country Life* which I used to study in the periodical room of the Worcester Public Library. I never missed an issue either of that or of the *Illustrated London News*. The streets of London were strange but familiar too. In a deep sense it was a return. I had grown up, on Providence Street in Worcester, in the nearly constant companionship of two British subjects, William Shakespeare and Charles Dickens. When the taxi turned into Half Moon Street I recognized it and felt cozy in it; it was exactly my idea of what a London street should be. The parlormaid who admitted me took me upstairs to my room. She told me that Miss Burton was expecting me and would soon summon me for tea. I drew the curtains and looked up and down the street. I was pleased to see, at the end of it, the shop of Trumpers, the hairdresser, because Siegfried had told me, with a certain fine edge of reproof at the self-indulgence, that Osbert Sitwell went to Trumpers sometimes twice a day. I was in a state of scarcely controllable excitement. I was in London! I had dreamt of it, tried, with some success, to imagine it. I had gone innumerable times to see friends off who were going to London, but that I would ever be among them was not conceivable. Here I was. There, actually, was Trumpers, an appointed servant of His Majesty's.

Presently there was a light tap at the door. It was the maid. Miss Burton was in the parlor, awaiting me for tea. I went downstairs.

Siegfried had not prepared me for The Presence which greeted me. Dame Nellie was short, almost spherical, with a large expanse of face and innumerable chins. She had prominent blue eyes, an encompassing smile, and an expression of benevolent innocence. She was highly

"Dame" Nellie Burton with "Siegfried"

decorated, spangles and ornaments of odd shapes were pinned to her bodice. She had a mass of gray-brown hair piled up in a minaret; semiprecious, pale lights gleamed from the minaret too. It was a congeries of ornaments and unclassifiable styles, but somehow I was soon aware that Miss Burton securely dominated her effects so that she had a style of her own. There was a quickening reassurance in her directness; you felt that she was a force of nature, that nothing could swerve her from a decision or a loyalty. She became a fixture in my life at that very moment and remained so forever.

She welcomed me warmly. I asked how Siegfried was.

"Oh, you know 'im. 'Is usual — broodin' an' moodin'."

A tall, middle-aged, ectoplasmic, lemonish man made a tentative appearance. Miss Burton introduced him.

"Mr. Fleming. 'E's in rear double. I'm sure you'll 'ave plenty in common!"

Miss Burton held a chair for me. Mr. Fleming sat opposite. Miss Burton took command at the head of the table and began to pour. It was an immense tea; I had never seen such a lavish tea: plovers' eggs, meat sandwiches, bread and butter with strawberry jam, crumpets, scones, and a heavy cake which looked like a Christmas cake.

"Mr. Fleming," said Miss Burton, "is a Theosophist!"

Mr. Fleming's head, perched on a long neck, nodded vehemently as if pulled by an elastic. I had not yet heard Mr. Fleming say anything.

From where I was sitting I was looking directly at the fireplace. I began to populate this room with the artists who used to come in late at night for advice and encouragement from Robert Ross — poets, artists, composers, playwrights. I saw Ross, a keen-eyed, subfusc figure standing in front of this very fireplace, coining epitaphs.

But Miss Burton was dredging around for subjects which Mr. Fleming and I had in common.

" 'E is, in fact," Miss Burton was saying, determined that Mr. Fleming should not be underrated by a visiting American on whose previous conditioning you could not count, "a very 'igh-placed Theosophist."

Mr. Fleming, very busy at the crumpets, made a deprecatory gesture and shook his head.

"We do a bit o' crystal-gazing 'ere and there, don't we, Mr. Fleming?"

Mr. Fleming, agog with plovers' eggs, nodded.

"And would you take it amiss if I told Captain Sassoon's friend, 'oo appeared to us one day in the crystals?"

Mr. Fleming shook his head.

Miss Burton leaned a bit across to me with a stentorian whisper.

"Madame Blavatsky."

I felt I was under false pretences with Mr. Fleming and Miss Burton. Theosophy was not in my realm. I didn't know what it was. I didn't know who Madame Blavatsky was. Miss Burton made things worse by adding a cubit to Mr. Fleming's stature in theosophy.

" 'E 'as," she said, "the very 'igh regard of Mrs. Besant. In fact . . ."

Miss Burton cupped her mouth with her hand.

"Not only," she said portentously, "did Mrs. Besant come 'ere to see Mr. Fleming but she brought . . ." her voice dropped as if she didn't want herself to overhear, "she brought Messiah!"

The parlormaid came in and whispered to Dame Nellie.

"Oh yes." She spoke to me. "Captain Sassoon on the phone for you. Brenda will show you — in the 'all."

I followed Brenda into the hall. I told Siegfried I had to go to the theatre. I promised to come to his flat in Campden Hill Square right after. I made my excuses to Dame Nellie and Mr. Fleming, went to my room to dress, and took a taxi to the Berkeley, where the Gaiges were staying. At dinner I told Hilda about the wonderful new experience I'd just had: meeting Dame Nellie. She made me promise that I would bring her to Half Moon Street. We took a taxi to the theatre. While the cabby held the door open for us, he sighed. He looked very melancholy. He said:

"It is indeed the last o' Mrs. Chynee!"

Hilda adored the play; she was starry-eyed. She missed no scintilla in the somewhat narrow panoply of Sir Gerald's public behavior. But it made me restive. I was impatient for the streets of London. I wanted to roam them, to possess them. The last thing I wanted to see that night was a play; I resented the play for keeping me off the streets. I longed to see Siegfried and Campden Hill Square (how idyllic that sounded in itself!). From there I determined to walk back to Half Moon Street no matter how late or how far. The play over, we joined in the fervent farewell ovation given to Sir Gerald by his admirers. When I said good-night to Hilda, I told her I was going to see Sassoon. She longed to meet him as well as Miss Burton. I promised to arrange both.

In the taxi I looked for the street signs. I was aware, suddenly, of the joy of not being encrusted in numbered streets. To go up Broadway or Fifth Avenue is like tracing a trial balance; there is no mystery in arithmetical sequence. The streets of London had caprices of their own; they took no dictation from the rigidities of arithmetic. Boston has a bit of variety but neither the scope nor the majesty. I tried to memorize the streets as I passed them to facilitate my intended walk back from Siegfried's apartment. The taxi began going up. Campden Hill Square was a plateau. As I climbed up the stairs to Siegfried's apartment I heard, on the piano, Bach's Chromatic Fantasy and Fugue, Siegfried's charming welcome ode because he used to play it all the time at Westover Court. I used to tease him over his "fumbled fugues."

After we had greeted each other, I saw the ironic half-smile which curved his lips, presage for a joke, preferably at my expense.

"Osbert told me about meeting you in New York. Jed Harris made a great impression on him. He was very taken with him."

"Oh, Jed makes a great impression on everybody! He's a fascinating character."

I sat on the sofa. Siegfried pulled up a chair. He offered me a cigarette.

"You look well, Sam. How long has it been?"

"Four years. I was glad to get Sitwell's message about your book."

"Yes." He pointed to a mass of pen-written manuscript on his desk. "I've been struggling. I find I can't do it unless I shut myself off completely. Ghastly life."

"I got a bad report on you from Miss Burton."

"What did she have to say about me?"

"She says you're broodin' an' moodin'."

Siegfried slapped his knee hard with his hand; he always did when he was greatly amused.

"Leave it to Burton! No one can sum up the truth in a few words the way she can."

"But explain to me about Mr. Fleming — I am a little confused about Mr. Fleming. Does Burton believe in all that crystal-gazing stuff?"

"I'm sure she thinks it's all flimflam. She's a realist if ever there was one. About Fleming — she says: 'Mr. Fleming, 'e belongs to the spirit world, 'e's a man of the spirit but 'e likes 'is food regular.' She's a great character-part. You ought to write a play about her!"

We both sat for a moment, in a marvel about the phenomenon of Burton. Siegfried said:

"What's new with you — about your plays? Any luck with 'em?"

"Harold Freedman's got the Theatre Guild to take an option on one of them."

"What does that mean?"

"They pay me five hundred dollars for six months. They're supposed to produce it by spring."

"This spring?"

"Hopefully."

"That would be wonderful."

"I have a feeling they won't."

"Why?"

"I always have a feeling they won't. I don't mean the Guild particularly. They. Whoever they might be. They won't."

"The unseen enemies, the unfurled disasters?"

"Exactly. Meantime here I am where I want to be. In London. And I am, I'll have you know, a lexicographer."

I explained to him about *Broadway* and my job to translate its dialogue for the English. He was amused.

He looked at the clock on the mantel shelf. It was after two.

"You must be tired. I can always go back to that thing." He pointed to the pile of manuscript.

"What are you calling it?"

"*Memoirs of a Fox-Hunting Man.*"

"I'd love a look."

He got up and picked up a chapter.

"About fifty pages. Take 'em along to Half Moon Street. They'll put you to sleep."

He fixed the fifty pages into a manila envelope.

"Fine," I said. "I was going to walk but with these I'll take a taxi."

"You'd better. It would be a considerable walk. You'll find a taxi rank — bottom of the square. Will your lexicography permit you to have lunch?"

"Of course," I said. "My staff does the heavy work!"

"Naturally. Friday, I'll take you to my club."

We said good-night on the landing. Campden Hill Square was asleep, an expanse of darkness. I walked to the corner and found a taxi. It was cold. I let myself into Half Moon Street with the key Miss Burton had given to me, found my room, with the bedside lamp on, undressed, and got into bed. I was startled. There was something warm, alive and furry in my bed. I jumped out to investigate. It was a flat, hot stone, covered with a fur wrap. It was a mercy. I said a prayer of thanks to Burton, stretched out comfortably and immersed myself in Siegfried's memories of the, to me, least likely of enterprises, fox-hunting. I'd never heard of anyone in Worcester, Massachusetts, who engaged in so bizarre an occupation.

I was entranced. I slipped mesmerically into Siegfried's calligraphically penned fifty pages, scarcely an erasure in them. I had never read anything which brought so close the feeling of the earth, its scent and taste, its contours, the zest of open air, the voices of birds and animals, the lives of foliage, hedges, flowers, the excitement of chase, the community of horses, dogs, huntsmen and grooms galvanized in a single impulse, their consciousness merged in sky and forest. In Worcester, somehow, though it was surrounded by nature, there was, at least around me, no cult of nature! There was also in Siegfried's impassioned pages involvement with golf and cricket. I came nearest to him when he wrote about cricket because it reminded me of the involvement of my crowd on Providence Street in our baseball games on the lopsided, gravelly sandlots where we played scratch games. But the chief delight was Siegfried's humorous sensitivity to the people of his world: the grooms, the farmers, the clergymen and the noble lords who mastered the hunts. What struck me was the homogeneity, the classlessness. The Cult of the Horse was the cynosure. When I finished the fifty pages I fell into a dream. What must it be like, I wondered, to have been born as Siegfried was born, in the English country, in an established hierarchy, with these fields and wealds and streams and forests to roam and hunt? Mr. Gresser, the father of the girl violinist whom I had taken Siegfried to see, had told me when I next saw him that the Sassoons were the oldest Jewish family in existence, that, compared to them, the Rothschilds were upstarts. I began to muse on this. My family was as old as Siegfried's; there are no age differences in any human families. My existence was my birth certificate, as immemorial, if you could but know, as anybody's. What Mr. Gresser must have meant was: the oldest recorded Jewish family. When I asked my father about his father and his father's antecedents, I couldn't find out very much. My father himself didn't know. He came out of darkness, out of mystery. The tradition of ancestry he knew was anonymous, impersonal. There were no people in it, no individuals, nothing idiosyncratic. There were historic concepts. Carnage. Persecution. No people. Victims. No games. Escapes. I fell asleep, as Siegfried had predicted, over his pages. I scanned a sentence before I put the light out: "Rooks would be cawing in the vicarage elms, and Butley, with its huddle of red roofs and square church tower, was a contented looking place." Worcester looked neither contented nor discontented, just somnolent. I fell asleep trying to effect a transfusion of locales. "What must it be like . . . ?"

The next morning, just before noon, Jed telephoned. He had arrived the night before from Paris. He had called me; I had not been home. He had just called the Gaiges — they were out shopping. There was something in the way he said this that boded ill. By this time I knew him so well. They were out shopping on his time and, even, at his expense. I could tell that he resented their presence in London; the detail that Gaige had financed the entire production constantly escaped him. He was in a bad mood. So was I. I had, just an hour before, received a devastating cable from Harold Freedman. It was open before me. It read:

GUILD UNABLE TO PRODUCE PLAY THIS SEASON. THINK CAN
GET THEM RENEW OPTION. MAURICE WERTHEIM WANTS TO
SEE YOU ON RETURN. NO HURRY. BEST HAROLD.

Jed asked me to meet him at the Strand Theatre, where *Broadway* was to open. I said I'd be there. I took the cable back to my room to ponder it though there was nothing much to ponder. It had killed two dreams, the intertwined one was of the moment when I could tell Jed that I was quitting. It was a dream the three of us shared: Herman Shumlin, Paul Streger and myself. We lived for the moment when we'd give up our jobs. I decided I wouldn't tell Siegfried about this cable; it would distress him. I wouldn't tell anyone.

I found Jed at the Strand with Captain Troubridge, the manager of the theatre, and John Balderston, the London correspondent of the *New York World*. They were both eating out of his hand. Jed was in wonderful spirits, fed by his conquests, and perfectly charming to me. Balderston had dramatized, very successfully, Henry James's unpublished and unfinished novel, *A Sense of the Past*. Balderston called his play *Berkeley Square*. It was running in New York with Leslie Howard, an enchanting performance which I'd seen, and in London with Jean Forbes-Robertson. Everything was milk and honey. I owed Captain Troubridge and Balderston a lot just for being there. They didn't know what they had saved me from.

I was to see a great deal of John Balderston and his attractive wife, Marion, on this and subsequent visits to London. Balderston worshipped Jed. Indeed, Jed's effect on people was extraordinary; the forward thrust of his personality, the physical embodiment of his total self-belief, was hypnotic. He simply knew that he was destined for mastery, that his success with *Broadway* was merely the first rung of a career that would be omnipotent. And it was so — for a long time it was so. No one in the theatre, now or since, has so magnetized attention on a managerial personality as Jed did for a decade. He was so articulate about the plays he produced that he gave the effect of directing them, even though he engaged directors. I once asked the shrewd and observant Harold Freedman whether the current supermagnate might not, ultimately, go the way Jed went. "Oh no," he said, "he's a much better businessman." Jed became bewitched by England and the parliamentary system. One day, sorting out his ambitions, he said to me: "You know, I think of settling down in England. And you know, if I did and if I went into politics, I think I could have the same career Disraeli did."

I repeated this one day, as a kind of joke, to John Balderston. To my surprise, with perfect gravity, Balderston said:

"I have no doubt whatever that Jed could."

My friendship with Siegfried enabled me to shuttle between Captain Troubridge's office in the Strand Theatre and press-dealings there, and the elite of the London literary world to which I had no valid admission fee. Siegfried invited me to go with him to a tea party at Sir Edmund and Lady Gosse's. The cable from Harold Freedman and the rejection of my play by the Theatre Guild made me more than ever conscious of having no admission fee. There was a great crowd; I heard storied names: Edith Sitwell, Geoffrey Scott. What was I to do? How was I to survive? I felt completely out of my depth, a yokel who had stomped into a Parnassian séance. Gosse was talking about "my substantial political victory in Italy." Was Gosse running for office in Italy? Was it a private joke? Then Gosse rose to greet me, a tidy man with a booming voice. His gray hair was parted in the middle; he wore a patch over one eye. Siegfried told me later that he changed the patch from eye to eye as it suited him, thereby anticipating the inspiration of an American advertising man by half a century. He went on to tell of a transatlantic crossing he'd made to America after the Civil War. The passengers all ate at one long table; he told of the super elegance of an American lady. There was a great salmon in the middle of the table. " 'Do you mind, Mr. Gosse,' she said, 'if I assist the salmon?' I wondered what she thought she could do for the salmon that the salmon couldn't do for itself!" My life was saved by Lady Gosse, who spoke as softly as her husband boomed. She took me into her confidence about an indiscretion of Lord Haldane's. She told me of a great party at the Duchess of York's and Lord Haldane's inspiration for getting out of it. He made a tour of the drawing room admiring the pictures; he admired and admired till he found himself out in the hall. "Wasn't it wicked of him?" she said, smiling delightedly at me behind her hand. I'd have liked to sit with Lady Gosse forever. Siegfried took me away, though, to show me an early Sargent portrait of Gosse and a wonderful Swinburne caricature. We returned to the tea table. I sat beside Miss Sitwell. I got fixed on her fingernails. Her hands were beautiful, the nails abnormally long and of a strange color, pale silver, the color of a fish's belly. Gosse was talking of her verses in a just-published book. He made a critical comment about one poem. Miss Sitwell bridled. Gosse rolled over the bridle. To console Miss Sitwell I asked her whether she would care to go to the opening of *Broadway*. She said she'd love to go. Siegfried and I took her home. In the cab she expanded on Gosse's effrontery; I was somewhat astonished at the ferocity with which she attacked him. "He rapped me on the knuckles," she said, "as if I were a schoolgirl!" Then she remembered that I had invited her to the opening of *Broadway*. She asked Siegfried if he would take her. Siegfried said he would.

Broadway opened at the Strand Theatre two nights later. The house was full, the audience dressy. I sat with Jed's wife, Anita. I saw Siegfried and Edith Sitwell. I saw Richard Curle with Hilda. I saw the Balderstons. I saw Arnold Bennett, a hero of mine because I greatly admired *The Old Wives' Tale*. *Broadway* is a gutter play about the lowest forms of human life, set in a degraded cabaret frequented by rival bootlegger gangs with guns at the ready. I wondered how this genteel audience could relate to it. When I looked at Curle I wondered again: "What would Joseph Conrad, who despised Ibsen, think of this? Better than Ibsen, probably." What was Arnold Bennett thinking? I was never to know because he does not mention this first night in his published diaries.

John Gassner, Sterling professor of the drama at Yale, included *Broadway* in an anthology of twenty-five American plays, chosen and edited by him. He says that it is "sensational theater and a cultural vestige of considerable interest to us. It is 'Americana' that we may not care to display abroad as an example of the best in American civilization, but its robustness is of a kind that only America has displayed in the theater. Salty and loud, it is a testament to some sort of vitality and to democratic élan gone berserk."

I have read the play recently — *Broadway* is a good play. It is as realistic as a metronome. There isn't a grain of sentimentality in it. The story is tight and holds the audience. The two murders are as casual as stepping on fleas. Eugene O'Neill once said that he wished the human race were destroyed by the atomic bomb. The vision of life offered by this play would make you see the bomb as a cleanser.

I saw Siegfried and Miss Sitwell in the intermission. Miss Sitwell said she was having a lovely time. Gaige, Hilda and Curle joined us. Miss Sitwell and Siegfried begged off coming to the Gaiges' party. Jed was threading the lobby, eavesdropping on comments. Hilda waved to him. He waved back but did not join us.

At the party everyone felt that the play had gone very well and would be a hit. Balderston telephoned and had St. John Ervine's notice read to him. "It's a money notice!" he announced. At one in the morning Jed said he was leaving and asked me to come to his suite with him; he was also staying at the Berkeley. When we got there he called room service and ordered coffee. He was quite amiable.

"One thing about you I'll never understand," he said, "how you can spend so much time with the Gaiges."

"I like them very much," I said. "Gaige has always been very kind to me. I love Hilda."

"A lot of good that'll do you."

He was smiling. He had anticipated this conversation. He had decided to play it friendly.

"I've bought a play. *Coquette.* I'm putting Helen Hayes in it. That'll give you a nice little job when you get back."

"Not me. I'm quitting."

"Hecht and MacArthur are working on a terrific play for me. Chicago newspaper life. *The Front Page.* What I've seen of it is terrific. You'll have a ball with that. You'd be very foolish to quit. I've read your plays. You'll never get anywhere with them. They're thin."

"The Guild doesn't think so."

Jed looked at me pityingly. He was silky.

"Poor deluded boy. Why do I call you boy? You're at least ten years older than I am. I don't like to break it to you. But I'd better, to keep you from making a mistake. You know I'm a master of espionage. My spies are everywhere. I know what's going on in every office. The Guild will never do your play. They have other plans. You'd better stick with me."

"There's one thing you don't understand about me."

"There are many things I don't understand about you." Jed sipped his coffee. "Your devotion to the Gaiges, for instance."

"You keep harping on the Gaiges. It slips your mind that Gaige has financed this whole production. You never put up your share. Is that why you hate Gaige?"

"You're a stooge for Gaige. You're in love with Hilda. Just because she hates Gaige doesn't mean she'll give you a break. Get on to yourself."

"I'm on to you."

He got up, walked over to me and said quietly; "If there were no penalty for homicide I'd kill you."

I couldn't resist quoting a line from *Broadway:* " 'Ain't you the brave guy, though?' "

I left. I walked down the hall to the lift. I was blind with rage and frustration. Jed was right about the Guild. Harold Freedman's cable was the proof.

I wondered whether Gaige's party was still on. I had left my over-coat in their suite. I went back there and rang the doorbell. Hilda opened the door. She looked very tired, dead beat. She managed to smile at me — wanly.

"Party's over. Gaige has gone to bed."

I apologized for intruding on her.

"I'll just pick up my coat and run."

"Please don't. Sit for a minute and talk to me. I feel sort of — what did Jed have to say?"

I followed her into the drawing room. I sat wondering how I could edit Jed's remarks to make them presentable. She sat opposite me in a big armchair, her hand over her face. I decided how to edit Jed.

"Oh, he's very high. Full of plans. He's got Helen Hayes for a new play he's doing and he's crazy about another one by Hecht and Mac-Arthur. It's all about Chicago newspaper life. He . . ."

I saw then that Hilda wasn't listening. She was crying. She had given up, her head in her arms. I got up. I wanted to do something for her, to say something. I felt that the best thing I could do for her was to leave her alone. I went to the corridor, picked up my coat, and left. I walked to Half Moon Street. Second honeymoons, I reflected, were no more solace than walnut paneling.

The next morning I went down to what Max Beerbohm called "the street of the ship-shops" and got myself a second-class cabin, again on the *Majestic,* sailing next day. I rarely make a decision without regretting it. This was not a decision; it was a compulsion. Freedman had cabled me not to hurry, yet I was hurrying. Jed knew this about me and was counting on it. That's why he had told me in detail his inviting prospects. But while these conflicts were warring in my incorrigibly vacillating mind, I went through all the motions, paid for my ticket, and put the seal on the compulsion. Siegfried had told me that he was leaving to visit Thomas Hardy and I went at once to Campden Hill Square. I told him I was going back to New York and that I had quit Jed. He was sorry about the former and glad of the latter. Then he began talking about Hardy. He venerated him beyond every living writer. He described the village of Dorchester in which he lived, his simple house, surrounded by trees, the friendship with his beloved sheep dog, Wessex. He conveyed the simplicity and the greatness of his idol. He showed me some of Hardy's letters to him; the qualities he adumbrated were in the letters.

" 'True Thomas,' Gosse calls him," Siegfried said.

He told me he was leaving London. There were too many distractions there for the work he wanted to do. He was going to look for a suitable country house he could buy and where I could come to stay. On the chimera of this next visit, we said good-bye. I must let him know about my play; he would let me know about the house. On these mutual promises we parted.

On the way back to Half Moon Street I wondered: "What must it be

41

like to be going to the Hardy country, on such a bright morning, to be welcomed there by its creator and proprietor!" At Half Moon Steet I found a message from Hilda. I called her. I had left her, early that morning, weeping. Now she was excited. She told me that Gaige had left for Paris, but that wasn't what she was excited about. She was excited because Captain Troubridge had called her from the theatre to tell her that the Prince of Wales was attending the performance that evening. She must, of course, go, and I must take her. I had intended to spend the evening packing, but I promised. I sought out Miss Burton to tell her my problem. She brushed it aside. She was sorry I was leaving. So would Mr. Fleming be. " 'E 'as taken a shine to you," she said. As for the packing, she had always packed for Robbie's mother and, she didn't mind telling me, "she 'ad more to pack than you 'ave. She always said: 'No one can get so much in so little as you can. 'Ow do you do it?' she'd sy. I never let 'er watch me!"

I granted Burton similar privacy. I took my briefcase down to the study, took out my notebook, and tried to work for several hours. But my thoughts kept wandering to the simple, tree-surrounded house in Dorchester, to True Thomas and his sheep dog.

Captain Troubridge provided us with seats in a box and we saw the Prince of Wales plain. He was, as a matter of fact, extraordinarily handsome and debonair. Hilda drank him in. She was a bit ashamed of doing so but we were at a considerable distance — the Prince sat in an orchestra seat — and we both noticed that the audience left him in peace, no one ogled him.

Hilda was upset when I told her that I was leaving the next day, but she didn't try to stop me. She knew how unhappy I was working for Jed and approved my quitting him. To dispel the gloom she said: "And I haven't even met Burton. Tell you what — I'll pick you up and take you to the boat train. I'll come early so I can meet her."

The next morning Burton knocked at my door. "Mrs. Gyge." She started downstairs. I followed. I was a bit apprehensive about her meeting Hilda; she had one day said to me: "I 'ave to sy — I don't like women very well — they're fair to the eye an' rotten to the core. I'm speakin' general. An' that way I don't like 'em. I won't use their tricks." Nevertheless, she welcomed Hilda with enthusiasm. Mr. Fleming was standing at attention in the parlor. He was presented to Hilda. He took to Hilda. It was the first time I'd heard Rear Double say anything:

"I don't believe, Mr. Behrman, you've ever seen my room. I have some mementos I would like to show you before you leave. Won't you both do me the honor?"

Hilda and I said we'd love to. We all three followed him upstairs. He ushered us into his room. It was a large, very commodious room, somewhat dark, with shaded lamps. There was the smell of incense. The effect of the room was Oriental, Indian — buddhas; brass vases, heavily scrolled; ivories. There were three large photographs, elaborately framed, in what looked like teakwood.

Burton pointed out to us the photograph of a dark, lowering lady with a deadly serious, grim expression.

"Madame Blavatsky," said Burton.

As if compelled by her hypnotic expression we all stood before Madame Blavatsky. Mr. Fleming breathed her name, staring at her reverently.

"Dear Madame Blavatsky. Dear Presence. She was often here, wasn't she, Burton?"

"Indeed she was!" confirmed Burton. "In and out."

Emboldened, Mr. Fleming ventured on eloquence, even braggadocio. "She — I think I may say so without exaggeration — she loved this room. She paid me a compliment on this room — one that I shall cherish forever."

Hilda asked what it was.

"She said that this room — it is a compliment that rightfully belongs also to you — dear Nellie — she said that my room reminded her of Scriabin's room in St. Petersburg."

This interested Hilda.

"The composer Scriabin?"

"No other."

"Did Madame Blavatsky know Scriabin?"

Mr. Fleming spoke with patience, without condescension.

"She was the greatest influence of his life. All his greatest music was inspired by her. As she has been the greatest influence and inspiration of my life."

He turned suddenly to me.

"May I ask — do you know Evangeline Adams?"

"The seeress?"

"Yes. I want so to go to America to see her."

"That may be difficult. The greatest people in America, politicians, financiers, they all fight for appointments with her."

Hilda gave me a satiric look.

"Do you?"

"Oh, no. I couldn't afford it. She's very expensive."

Fleming insisted: "However I would appreciate it if you could arrange it."

I assured him that I would do my best; I would let him know.

Mr. Fleming then stood, in a votive attitude, before the photograph of an incredibly graceful and handsome young Indian.

"I hardly need say who this is."

But Burton did.

"That's Messiah," she said crisply. "Looks it, don't 'e?"

On the way down Hilda turned to Burton:

"Oh, Miss Burton, it just occurs to me — wouldn't you and Mr. Fleming like to see *Broadway?* It's a great success. The Prince of Wales saw it last night. He seemed to enjoy it."

"Oh, that *would* be a lark. Wouldn't it, Mr. Fleming?"

Mr. Fleming nodded — for him, vigorously.

Miss Burton hugged me good-bye. Hilda promised to call her about the tickets.

In the cab I complained to Hilda about the job Fleming had saddled me with. She laughed. She thought it was very funny.

"It's no joke. How can I possibly compete for Evangeline Adams's time with Morgan partners?"

"Arthur Krock'll swing it for you," she said.

"Wonderful idea. The *Times* can do anything!"

I hadn't told Hilda about Harold Freedman's cable. I hadn't the heart. At the train she said:

"Where will you be when you get back?"

"I think I'll go to the Delaware Water Gap. There's an inn there that stays open all winter. I've gone there before. Very cheap."

"Leave word at the apartment — address and telephone number."

"I will of course."

"Good-bye, darling. I just want to tell you a little plan I have — have had for a long time for you. Your play will be a great success — I know it will. The minute it happens, I'll find you a nice apartment. I'll furnish it for you. You'll leave those mangy hotels you live in and walk into your charming apartment — your first home."

I ran on to the train.

On the way to Southampton, my thoughts were full of Hilda. I saw her beautiful blue-green eyes when she said good-bye to me. They were misted, not for this parting, but for her own sorrow. I remembered the sadistic conjecture Jed had flung at me. I was thirty-three. Hilda was at least ten years older. Jed couldn't have been more wrong; I am sure he knew it.

In my more circumscribed cabin on the *Majestic,* I sat down and lit a cigarette. I tried to face the future. On a stupid impulse I had made myself jobless. I was again prey to the perennial erosion: What next? Well, anyway, I had advanced. I had a heavy commission from Mr. Fleming. Despite the difficulties that this commission presented, I felt that doing a job for Mr. Fleming would be more pleasant than working for Jed Harris.

IV

"Don't Mention
My Name"

I N 1925, I WAS INTRODUCED by my old friend and collaborator,
J. Kenyon Nicholson, to the well-established and esteemed literary
agent, Carl Brandt, of Brandt and Brandt. Nicholson was from Indiana
and a friend of the Hoosier novelist and essayist Meredith Nicholson,
no relation, who took an interest in Ken Nicholson, or Nick, as he was
known. Nick was an extremely personable young man and Meredith,
the author of an immensely successful novel, *The House of a Thousand Candles,* thought that his own agent, Carl Brandt, might help
him. Nick and I had, from the start, this in common: we didn't want to
write literature; we wanted to write plays. Carl Brandt introduced us,
therefore, to Harold Freedman, whom he had just engaged to start a
drama department for him. Carl told me, long afterwards, that he
couldn't for a considerable time understand why he had engaged Harold Freedman for a selling job. In the first place, no one he had ever
met was less theatrical, in approach and style, than Harold. He spoke
almost inaudibly and with great difficulty; every sentence was inter-
larded with "ers," he was practically inarticulate. He was also Scottish.
His family had emigrated from Scotland when Harold was a boy and
settled in Pennsylvania, where they had a go at farming. That didn't
work out. His parents and three brothers moved to Washington and
started a paper and wood ware business, which still exists, and be-

came very successful. Harold came to New York and enrolled at Columbia, where he majored in chemistry with a side glance at drama. After his graduation he joined the Washington Square Players, which was the matrix of the Theatre Guild. It was hard for his friends to imagine Harold as an actor but he was for a time. The connection proved valuable though, for himself and his later clients, because he did a lot of business with the Theatre Guild. Among his early clients were Robert Sherwood, Maxwell Anderson, Philip Barry and myself. It was a useful connection for the Guild too; at a moment when it found itself in a financial doldrum, Philip Barry provided it with Katharine Hepburn and *The Philadelphia Story.*

Harold carried reticence to the point of mania. Secrecy, for him, was a way of life. He regarded the commercial Broadway theatre as a kind of stock market, where careers could be made or broken by the drift of rumor. I had been with him for a long time — he had sold many plays for me and written many Hollywood contracts — before I knew where he lived. If we were going uptown in a taxi, he would get out at a street corner, so that I wouldn't know which house he lived in. I was with him for a month in London once. I saw him constantly, as he was arranging a contract for me with Alexander Korda. I didn't know till I returned that his wife, May, who by that time was a friend, had been there all the time. This foible became a kind of trademark for Harold. Stories about it were rife. Guthrie McClintic was fond of telling how Harold called him one day and said he had something to speak to him about. Guthrie asked him to meet him on the stage of the New Amsterdam Theatre, where he was rehearsing. Harold came, as arranged, at five o'clock. Guthrie dismissed his actors and called Harold over. Harold made sure that the last of the actors had gone but he still seemed insecure about transmitting his secret. He looked around nervously at the vast gloom of the New Amsterdam stage, lit by a single ghost light. Guthrie saw that Harold was nervous; who could tell what spies were lurking in the shadows? He took him into Marilyn Miller's dressing room. Harold closed the door, which Guthrie had left open. By this time Guthrie had begun to lose his temper a bit. He demanded communication. Harold leaned close to

Harold Freedman as portrayed by Will Cotton

him and began to communicate, but, as Guthrie told it, "his voice was so goddamn modulated that I couldn't understand a single word he said!"

My own favorite is an office legend at Brandt and Brandt. Carl Brandt had employed a young man of prepossessing appearance to come in and learn the business. He had been a football star in college, was very good-looking, genial, and a snappy dresser. He stayed about a year and decided that he would do better in Hollywood. He did. He married film stars. On his last day at Brandt and Brandt he went around to say good-bye to everybody. He came into Freedman's office, put out his hand, and wrung Harold's with Rotarian fervor. He said what a pleasure and privilege it had been to know Harold and to study his working methods. To show his gratitude he made a large offer: "Now, Mr. Freedman," he said, "is there anything I can do for you in Hollywood? I'll be only too happy to do it."

Harold's whispered answer was distinct: "Yes," he said, "don't mention my name."

Harold's secrecy fetish became a kind of trademark for him. In an odd way it generated confidence. Though he drove them crazy the film executives and the local managers trusted him. In Hollywood, visiting a friend, I met an august film tycoon. He asked me whether I had an agent. I said I did and told him who. He was abashed. "Oh," he said, "have you got an agent!" Harold was religious. He had high ethical standards; he expected the people he dealt with to live up to them. When they didn't, he remembered it and found opportunities to even the balance. The delinquents, poor dears, found themselves living up to standards that they had never professed. In time Harold's stable of the leading playwrights here and in England made his position very powerful. Terence Rattigan had an almost filial devotion to him. He represented John Osborne. In a coffee shop one day I was asked to join Herman Levin, the producer of *My Fair Lady,* Harry Kurnitz and Martin Gabel. Levin was very funny on the subject of the martyrdom involved in dealing with Harold Freedman. The pivot of his grievance was in Freedman's inhuman choice of a summer place, an unmapped location, called Deer Isle, Maine. Only Freedman would choose a remote place like that in which to spend the summer. First there was the difficulty of getting him on the phone. It was always busy. Harold was always talking to Rome or to London. Then, when you did get him, there was the problem of understanding what he said. Conversation with him, said Levin, was to be cradled in hesitation. I used to visit Harold summers in Deer Isle. It was indeed a difficult place to get to; after you thought you had arrived you still had several hours more to travel. Harold would be on the phone all day and into the night: to Ischia, where Terence Rattigan was on a holiday, which meant that he was working on a play; to Manchester, England, where a play of Enid Bagnold's was opening; to San Francisco, where Ina Claire was living. There is an amusing caricature of Harold by Will Cotton which shows him, enhaloed in a circle of telephones, all of which he is answering simultaneously, his eyes looking in every direction. Harold did not represent actors but he cosseted them. I had written a play called *Biography* which urgently needed a star. Finding one presented a problem to which Harold devoted himself. I was in the Belasco Theatre one evening. In the intermission I found Harold waiting for me. He had come there to give me the glad news that he had persuaded Ina Claire to play *Biography*. He performed a similar service in the case of another play of mine, *No Time for Comedy,* which urgently needed a brilliant leading man to play opposite Katharine Cornell. He provided Laurence Olivier. It was an enjoyable moment for him when he was able to tell me that he had persuaded Noel Coward to play Alfred Lunt's part in *The Second Man* in London, and a decade later, that I could count on Rex Harrison for Olivier's part in the London production of *No Time for Comedy.*

It has been urged against Harold that he preempted the functions of management, that he was a frustrated producer. He was not; he was a functioning producer. He had all the fun without having to bear the ultimate responsibility. He is one of the few men I have known who was doing exactly what he wanted to do and had no wish for extension. He was powerful and he knew it. He was pleased with being a one-man business. He could have sold out to the corporate agencies for a very large sum but he was never in the least tempted. He enjoyed the way of life he had made for himself. He lived in the Volney Hotel on East Seventy-fourth Street for thirty-five years; he built a house in

Deer Isle because he had lived in a boardinghouse there on his holidays while he was still in Columbia. He loved the theatre. He loved plays. His loyalty to his clients was unflagging. When they died, this loyalty seemed to intensify; he worked unceasingly to keep their plays in motion. He had a very shrewd notion of the capacities and the limitations of all the producers. He did all he could to supplement their limitations. These were sometimes so wide that they made Harold, force majeure, the virtual producer. But he never wanted to be one. I once said to him: "You know more about the theatre insides than anyone. Why don't you write a book about it?" "Because," he said, "I can't write." When he got difficult plays on — Mrs. Chase's *Harvey,* Enid Bagnold's *The Chalk Garden* — he savored the joys of successful management. The vast success of Mrs. Kerr's *Mary, Mary* almost made him complacent. In my own case, he persisted with *The Second Man* though it had been rejected by every management in New York, including the Theatre Guild, which finally produced it.

An odd quirk of Harold's relationship with managers was that in many instances he liked them and they liked him; but he became their deadly enemy when a play he had sold them was in production, when their limitations, from his point of view, began to show. The source of the quarrel could be major or minor — publicity, what Harold thought an inept casting, a dress or shoes worn by the ingenue — but the intensity was fixed and it was maximal. An instance was his relationship with Bob Whitehead. They liked each other. Bob told me once that he couldn't imagine the New York theatre without Harold Freedman. Bob had a play of mine in rehearsal. We had a conference about it in my apartment. We took a taxi to the theatre. As we were going down Park Avenue we saw Harold in another taxi. We waved to him but got no response — it happened to be in the middle of a feud. At the next traffic light, though, Harold dismissed his cab and crowded into ours. He did not return our salutations. He was very grim and sat staring straight ahead of him into a hopeless future. Whatever Bob and I had been talking about was swept clean from our minds. Bob made a hopeless gesture, indicating Harold:

"The House Detective!" he said.

Harold's sudden death affected his older clients grievously and, for

51

all I know, his younger ones also. Is it proper for an agent to build up so potent an influence over his clients that they feel crippled when he dies? Whether it is proper or not his clients were certainly grateful for it while he was alive. Irene Mayer Selznick, in a letter to her friend Enid Bagnold, after Harold's death, spoke of it with indignation: "How dared he!?" she demanded. Playwriting is an impossible craft and an impossible career. It is no wonder that a lifelong practice of it made a Nihilist of Eugene O'Neill. It can't be kept up, not even by a genius such as Shaw. I think myself that *The Millionairess,* written in Shaw's old age, is a very poor play. It is a bleak revelation of Shaw's obsession about money which darkened his old age and the lives of those who were devoted to him. There is no one who can be so ravenous about money as a Communist. Even *Geneva,* written when Shaw was younger, is so far off the beam that G.B.S. makes Hitler in it a mere acolyte of the all-powerful Mussolini.

I apologize to the shade of Harold Freedman for not complying to the request he made of the Hollywood-bound young man in the Brandt and Brandt office, but his life had been so closely and incessantly intertwined with mine that to omit his would be to defoliate my own. From the day in 1925 when he began to sell my first play, to the last day of his life, when he called me at five-thirty in the afternoon to advise me on a perilous project I threatened to embark on, he was omnipresent. In this last conversation he asked me to think over the suggestions he had made; he would call me in the morning to check. In the morning he was gone; he had died in his sleep. For those of us who are not geniuses, but who have talent in various degrees, Harold's existence, his solicitude and his patience were abiding graces of stimulus and solace.

When I got back from London I found Nick established in a nice job. Because we had written three unproduced plays together, he had been chosen to teach dramatic writing at Columbia. He was also established in a grisly roominghouse on West Thirty-sixth Street. As I was jobless, I moved into it. Nick now had academic friends, girl pupils attracted by the looks of the Professor, though they were repelled by the looks of the Professor's quarters. The horrified glances of our friends at what they beheld after climbing four flights of uncarpeted stairs made Nick and me feel that we should put up some kind of ameliorative sign. I happened to read a novel by Gilbert Cannan about an English pacifist who was being sent to jail for his unpatriotic utterances on the eve of the First World War. His friends gave him a farewell dinner. He made light of his impending incarceration. "As for my going to jail," he said, "think nothing of it. After all, one must live someplace." The last four words struck me as a possible motto for our apartment. Nick agreed. We had them printed on a strip of cardboard, signed Gilbert Cannan and tacked it up on the wall. The next startled visitors had it pointed out to them; it appeared to acclimate them. Nick and I wrote a series of stories about our fellow boarders; some of these stories were printed in the *Smart Set*. We planned to make a book of them and have often since regretted that we didn't. We were interrupted in our Balzacian labors by two accidents. A play written by Nick on his own, *The Barker,* was produced and was an immediate hit. It had Walter Huston as its star and it presented, for the first time, to a famished American public, the alluring figure of Claudette Colbert. Not long after, the play I had written on my own was produced and was also a success. We took down Gilbert Cannan's sign until we should need it again. Some forty years later, I was invited to the White House, to a mass dinner for the French Minister of Culture, André Malraux. I sat next to Mrs. Auchincloss, the mother of our hostess. I had a play then on tour with Charles Boyer. Mrs. Auchincloss inquired about it. She was, she said, greatly interested in the theatre; she had, in fact, once written a play herself. Not to be outdone, I expressed an interest in her play. She said: "Do you happen to know Kenyon Nicholson?" I said I did. "I wrote the play for him." she said. "I was his student at Columbia. He directed it, but it wasn't very good, I guess. But I'm so glad you know him. A wonderful man, isn't he?"

I went to see the wonderful man on his well-stocked farm in Lambertsville, New Jersey, and recalled to him his early directorial experience. He called my attention to his peacock and his cows.

The three plays Nick and I had written together were now, due to their distinguished authorship, promptly produced. They failed. One of them was produced by Winthrop Ames, a grandee whose family had a town named after it in Massachusetts. Still, the production of these three plays, the innumerable rewrites, the rehearsals, the tryouts, kept Nick and me and Harold Freedman busy for quite a spell. Winthrop Ames was a director of great sensitivity. He kept asking me to rewrite the second-act curtain line of the play he was producing, the title of which I have forgotten. Nick was busy rewriting one of the others. I wrote nine curtain lines for Ames. He didn't like any of them. Neither did I. I never saw the play except in Mamaroneck.

Nick and I took these failures lightly. It is easier to stand failure in the lee of a success which, by that time, Nick and I both had. I was swimming in plays. Novels were sent me to dramatize and plays by fledgling authors (how narrowly I was now removed from them!) for the same reason. I don't know how I came to get it but a little novel anonymously published in England captivated me. It was *Serena Blandish,* "by a Lady of Quality." Whoever she was she certainly had it. The book is enchantingly written with irresistible style and humorous invention. It also has a tough awareness of the metallic facts of life.

I asked Harold Freedman to secure me the rights. I had gone to work on it even before he got them. I went to a Treadway Inn in Williamstown, Massachusetts, and slaved away at it. I am an authority on the Treadway Inns; I've fought it out in all of them.

Jed Harris, whose mind it had slipped that my plays were thin, went for *Serena Blandish.* He decided it was a starring vehicle for an uncannily skillful actress, Ruth Gordon. I have said earlier that the New York theatre then was cozier than it is now. Aleck Woollcott cozied it up. He idolized Jed Harris. Jed said to him once: "Why don't you face it, Aleck, you are in love with me." "I am afraid," said Aleck, "that you suffer from delusions of grandeur." Noel Coward arrived with his revue *This Year of Grace.* "I've simply passed out over Jed Harris," he told me. He applied to Jed the sobriquet "Destiny's Tot," and this stuck to Jed for quite a long time. Jed was equally lambent about Noel. "He's a one-man theatre," he said. "There's simply nothing in it he can't do." I loved Noel's revue. I couldn't see too much of it. I was sitting one night in Noel's dressing room while he was making up. An old friend of his and an acquaintance of mine, Joyce Barbour, came in to weep on Noel's shoulder. She was in distress; she draped Noel in a long inventory of calamity. She had just been released from a big Broadway musical show in which she had hoped to open. Her fiancé, Richard Bird, had just been released from a show on the road. On account of an Equity ruling they both had to go back to England since they couldn't try for another job here for another six months. The stocks she and her fiancé owned had taken a sickening drop — it was 1929! — so they hadn't the wherewithal to go back to England. She stopped for breath. Noel looked up at her, smiled brightly, and said:

"And you're not getting any younger you know, either, dear!"

When she'd caught her breath, Miss Barbour laughed harder than any of us.

But I have jumped a bit ahead of my story. My first chore on my return from London was to have lunch with Maurice Wertheim, one of the directors of the Theatre Guild. There were six of them — Lawrence Langner, Theresa Helburn, Lee Simonson, Helen Westley, Philip Moeller and Maurice Wertheim — and they were a very unusual group of people. They were all, in the best sense, amateurs, that is to say art lovers. No individual or group since has done for the American theatre what the Guild did. They brought the New York theatre into the twentieth century. They demolished the cliché that nothing in the theatre can be accomplished by committee. They accomplished everything that way. They produced Eugene O'Neill and Shaw, even to the eccentricity of devoting three evenings to *Back to Methuselah*. They taught an audience to come to the theatre at four-thirty in the afternoon, go to dinner, and return for the rest of the play. Moreover, they made them like it. At this moment they had four hits, two of them by Sidney Howard. They had produced plays by Georg Kaiser, Franz Werfel and Stefan Zweig. They were very successful; they had long since lost their amateur standing. They maintained it within themselves.

It was now, though, about two years since my first interview with Theresa Helburn at the Guild Theatre on Fifty-second Street. A little thing, she sat behind her glass-topped desk in a small office. Underneath the plate glass was a great ruled chart spotting each Guild production all over the United States. Someone once said that Terry was the ablest executive in the United States, that she could have run General Motors. She could. She was also a poet. This I didn't find out till I had won her confidence. She showed me then a poem of hers reprinted in an anthology of American verse. It is a moving poem, dedicated to her mother.

Terry smiled at me and said:

"Well, we like your play."

I thought there I was, but I didn't know Terry — not for a long time. I was to learn that she was not self-indulgent. She didn't put on plays just because she liked them. It had to be a passion. And even if she were impassioned, she was helpless unless her colleagues were equally impassioned. She would sigh and reflect on the intractability of people: how difficult it was to move them to passion. Now at last Harold Freedman had gotten them to promise that they would do my play for a spring tryout. Maurice Wertheim invited me to lunch at a place I had never been to, the Bankers' Club at the top of a building down Wall Street way.

I had always found Maurice warm and friendly. I got from him vaguely the feeling that he would like to be hail-fellow-well-met but that he didn't quite know how. This was appealing. His appearance was the totality of correctness: beautifully dressed, of course, and manners in the pink of courtesy. He was good-looking; he had a short, flat-surfaced nose; he looked like a middle-aged kitten, a kitten with worries. I knew of course that he had been sent by Terry to break the news to me that they had to postpone my play and that he didn't at all like the assignment. Mr. Wertheim began to explain. They were, at the Guild, suffering from an embarrassment of riches. Their plays were too successful. Therefore the actors playing them were tired; the Guild had overworked them. They had overworked the Lunts, who demanded a well-deserved holiday. Here was the nub: the Guild wanted the Lunts for my play and the Lunts wanted it too — Alfred had told him personally that my play offered him the best comedy part he had ever had in his hands — but the Lunts were adamant about going to Europe in the spring and if they did my play, they could stay in it only seven weeks.

I said that I'd rather have seven weeks with the Lunts than seven weeks without them.

Maurice said he quite saw my point of view. Did I see his?

While I was struggling to get his point of view, he began talking to me about another play I had, *Meteor.* The Guild was greatly interested in that too.

I felt that Maurice was grooved to postpone *Meteor* too, but I didn't argue the point since they hadn't bought it yet.

By this time, though, I was having a good time with Maurice and found myself liking him very much. I got a curious impression from him — that he was harried by anxiety. It had nothing to do with anything he had to tell me; it was about something which he was on the verge of telling himself. It was an anxiety about himself. He began talking about his daughters. He wanted me to meet them. They were the dearest children in the world. He could hardly bear it he loved them so. His daughter Barbara! She was on the *Nation.* He thought that was wonderful. They thought highly of her there. The glee with which he reported this gave me the clue to him, at least I felt *a* clue. Maurice didn't enjoy being correct. It locked him in, it stifled him. What he really wanted was to kick his heels up. Having a daughter on the *Nation* was kicking his heels up! It was Bohemia! It was not correctness he wanted; it was Bohemia he wanted. I knew that he was married to the daughter of a distinguished family. I had been, several times, to his beautiful house, but never met Mrs. Wertheim. Was she, too, the epitome of correctness?

I left him without knowing the fate of my play but with a nice feeling that I now had a friend who belonged to the Bankers' Club. Maurice wanted me to come for a weekend at his country place in Cos Cob. I already had the Gaiges' place, Watch Hill Farm, but could one have too many? Maurice wanted me to meet the young star on the *Nation.* I wished to meet her too. We parted the best of friends. I took the subway uptown to my Bohemia: Jed Harris and Noel Coward.

For a change, Jed and I were going to see *This Year of Grace* again.

In the subway station at Times Square I ran into Marc Connelly. He was excited. He had something to tell me. He walked with me to Jed's office. He'd read a book by Roark Bradford, *Ol' Man Adam an' His Chillun,* which had completely captivated him. He had already begun to dramatize it. He began rhapsodizing about it: a Sunday school picnic, colored children, all the characters colored including the Massa Lawd, who pays them a visit, "firmament — plenty of firmament." I'd never heard Marc so excited about anything. It did sound entrancing. I told him so. I said I'd speak to Jed about it.

"He'd be wonderful for it," said Marc.

At that time Jed was considered a kind of magician, who couldn't produce a failure. It remained for me to impair that myth. I told Marc to go back to work and repeated my promise to speak to Jed.

At dinner in Dinty Moore's, I told Jed about my meeting with Marc. I told him the idea of the play, that it sounded just up Marc's street and altogether entrancing. Jed was skeptical. Marc had a reputation for dilatory work habits.

"Marc'll never finish it," he said flatly. "He can talk a play but he'll never write it."

"I think he will. He's very hot on it. With some encouragement from you I'd bet on it."

"You know Marc!"

"Call him up. Offer him an advance. It'll turn the trick. I'm sure of it."

Jed thought a moment. "What's his number?"

I gave him Marc's number. Jed went to the telephone booth. When he came back he told me, with satiric intonation, that Marc said he had enough done so that he could finish the play in six weeks.

"I told him that was too fast — to take three months. What'll you bet that's the last I'll hear from him?"

I wouldn't bet.

V

Ladies on the Green

ONE SUNDAY NIGHT I went to some kind of benefit at the Theatre Guild. There I ran into Marc Connelly. I hadn't seen him since the day I met him in Times Square. I asked him how he was getting on with Jed and *Ol' Man Adam an' His Chillun,* by now retitled *Green Pastures.* Marc looked grim.

"It's all off," he said, "with Jed and me. Here! Read this letter Jed sent me."

He handed me the letter. I read:

"Dear Marc, I have given it a lot of thought and come to the conclusion that I cannot go on with your play because you appear to be taking too great an interest in the production."

I was astonished. I looked at Marc.

"That's all you have to read," he said sardonically. "The rest just compounds my felony."

I finished the brief letter and gave it back to Marc.

"Too bad," I said. "What are you going to do?"

"Find another producer. Have got one reading it this minute. I'm not worried. It's the best thing I've ever done."

He smiled, his natural sunniness restored. "I've dug up a dream actor to play De Lawd. He's from Heaven, naturally, as that's his home!"

We parted.

I went home troubled by this. I was troubled by the possible effect of this letter. The success of Marc's play, as with all plays, was problematical. That was not the point: Jed was rolling in successes, but wasn't it reckless to write a letter like that to a well-known and functioning playwright? I sat down to write my diary, a spinsterish habit, fixed, like brushing my teeth; I noted the meeting with Marc, conveying my tribulation about it. My concern about Jed rather surprised me. Was I fond of him? Whether I was or not, I was fascinated by him. At his best — in my last meetings with him — he was irresistible. No matter what you might say, Jed was a primal force, an artist. He was not, as so many producers are, an assembler, an exporter-importer; he was an innovator.

The next morning the phone rang. It was Maurice Wertheim. He was less modulated than usual. He seemed excited.

"Well," he said, "we've had a board meeting. You said you'd rather have seven weeks with the Lunts than seven weeks without them. We're giving you seven weeks with them. Starting April eleventh."

I could tell that he was elated, even triumphant, at being the transmitter of this news. I thanked him.

"Call Terry right away," he said. "See her today."

I said I would. I called Harold Freedman to report. At two o'clock I went to see Miss Helburn in her office. Miss Helburn, her hair lavenderish, greeted me warmly. She had a disarming smile.

"I am in a crisis with my husband," she said. Her eyes twinkled.

I had met her husband, Oliver Updyck. He wrote books on syntax with mandatory titles like *Get It Right!*

"Have you been indiscreet?" I ventured.

"Oh, Oliver wouldn't mind that. It's much deeper than that!"

I could see that she had saved it up to tell me.

"My difficulty with Oliver is that he's a gentleman. He can't help it. He was brought up that way."

"Did you offend his code?"

"Exactly. That's it exactly. So you can see — it *is* serious!"

She waited. She was enjoying herself.

"It's over Lee Simonson," she said. "Now you know Lee, don't you?"

"I've met him several times. I liked him very much."

"Of course. You would. He's charming. Very intelligent. And, as you know, a fine artist. But between us, a fearful temper. I hope you'll work with him. You're bound to find it out. Well, Oliver and I have an agreement. He doesn't care for the theatre very much. He's discovered it's not entirely populated by gentlemen. So we have this agreement: he's not to cross my theatre line; I'm not to cross his syntax line. I couldn't anyway — don't know enough. I often don't get things in the least 'Right.' It drives poor Oliver crazy. Well, yesterday Simonson looked in on me at Terry Top — that's my little place in Westport. We were having a disagreement about a production and Lee began to yell and scream at me, simply because I wouldn't agree with him. Oliver was upstairs in his study struggling with syntax problems and heard every word. Nothing Lee didn't call me. When Lee left, Oliver ran downstairs. His face was white. He was shaking with anger. 'It was all I could do,' he screamed, 'to keep from coming down here and knocking his block off!' 'I'm glad you didn't, Oliver,' I said. 'Lee's block is valuable.' My calmness infuriated him. He expected to find me as angry as he was. 'Don't tell me you're ever going to see that son-of-a-bitch again!' 'Of course I am, Oliver,' I said. 'As a matter of fact this afternoon. We're having a meeting about Sam Behrman's play.' This was too much for Oliver. He saw that it was beyond him, that the distance between us was too great. At lunch he didn't speak to me. In fact he hasn't spoken to me since. You hit it exactly. I did offend his code. What do you advise me to do?"

"Ask your husband to send his book to Mr. Simonson. Tell him to inscribe it. Mr. Simonson's written books. Surely he's made mistakes in syntax. Couldn't your husband, gently but firmly, call these mistakes to his attention?"

Terry laughed.

"Perfect," she said. "Just what I'd like Oliver to do. Of course he won't."

With this great domestic worry off her mind Terry turned to my play.

It had not been easy, she said, to get Miss Fontanne, who had just played triumphantly the star part in *Strange Interlude*, to play a small and subsidiary part in my play. Her wish to give her husband the chance to play the leading part had helped. They were going ahead and were happy about it. Should the play get over, the Guild wouldn't necessarily have to close it when the Lunts left. They could recast it and, with the help of Gray's Drug Store, a cut-rate theatre-ticket emporium, possibly run all summer. I asked how you could possibly recast the Lunts. It wouldn't be easy, said Terry smoothly, but it might be contrived. Who would come to see a play in which the Lunts were not, I inquired dolefully. The vast audience which had never seen them, she said, as well as the selecter audience which had missed them in their brief engagement. She made it seem that the brevity of their engagement was an advantage since it increased the audience which hadn't seen them. She was extremely adroit.

I went to a pay phone to call Harold Freedman. He laughed when I told him how Terry had transformed the horrid prospect of replacing the Lunts in a play with four characters into a rosy vista. He knew Terry very well and appreciated her. The moment I left the phone booth I ran plump into Lee Simonson. He greeted me robustly.

"You've seen Terry? Then she's told you! I'm delighted. I love your play. I wish I were doing the set for it. Congratulations!"

I thanked him. Simonson was a medium-sized, dark man with a black moustache. He vibrated with energy — he gave the effect of a projectile about to be shot out from something.

"We were all happy yesterday when we settled it finally on your play. You have a strong ally in Wertheim. Phil Moeller will direct it beautifully. We feel that you are our author."

He dived across the street into the Theatre Guild. I wanted more than anything to get into my room on Forty-ninth Street to collect my thoughts. Once there, I sat and thought. Well, here it was! Meeting Simonson gave me a clearer notion of the Theatre Guild. He said he wanted to do the set for my play. Why didn't he? He was one-fifth of the producer. The whole, evidently, preferred Jo Mielziner, who did it. Terry! I couldn't get over Terry. She was very sophisticated, with lively humor. I had an intuition that her colleagues were children to her. She humored them. In the succeeding years, as the Guild did many of my plays, this first impression was confirmed, constantly and entertainingly illustrated, established.

My phone rang. It was Jed.

"When in the hell are you going to get on with those *Serena* re-writes?" he demanded. "The play is in poor shape. I don't have the nerve to send it to actors!"

I told him that I was going out of town tomorrow to work on it, something I had just decided.

"I've got a great idea for Martin," he said. "Aleck Woollcott thinks it's a stroke of genius. A. E. Matthews. Do you know him? He could charm a bird off a tree. The part's so goddamn marmoreal — Martin's such an inhuman bastard — Aleck says Matty'll take the curse off it."

I added my congratulation to Aleck's on Jed's stroke. Mollified, Jed went on, forgetting that he was ashamed to send the play to actors:

"And I've got a great idea for the Countess — Constance Collier. Aleck thinks that's great too."

I joined Aleck.

"Constance says she'd love to play it. All I need is a SCRIPT!"

I promised to get him one. I repeated that I was leaving first thing in the morning.

"Where you going?"

"Woodstock, Vermont."

"That's hell and gone out of the way!"

I said that was why I had chosen it.

"Guild's trying out your play, I hear."

"Yes. In April."

"How long will the Lunts be in it?"

"Seven weeks."

"You're an idiot. So is Harold to let you do it. If you'd saved the damn thing for me I'd have given you a regular production. I've been casting it. Thought of putting Lou Calhern in it. He'd be perfect for it. How stupid can you be — you and Harold both. Call me tomorrow from that swamp in Vermont."

He hung up.

I had discovered Woodstock through an accident while staying, as a paying guest, at Aleck Woollcott's satrapy, his island in Lake Bomoseen, Vermont, about a half hour from Rutland. He had found the house and the island and fallen in love with both. He bought them. As it was inconceivable to Aleck to stay anywhere alone, he developed a scheme: he would fill it with his friends and charge them ten dollars a day, since he could not himself afford to entertain on such a scale. I went up for a week, which was about all I could afford. When I got there I found Ben Hecht, Charles MacArthur and Harpo Marx. It was very pleasant. Aleck presided at all the meals, which were good, and talked. It was all he asked; I have never seen him as happy or in such good form as he was at Bomoseen. He was possessive; he didn't like any of his guests to go to the mainland. The island was small and a bit claustrophobic. I had a longing to tread the streets of Rutland once and asked him how I could manage it. He heaped scorn on me for entertaining such a vulgar impulse, but when he saw that I was firm, he explained derisively to the other guests:

"He wants to go to 'The House of All Nations' in Rutland!"

A half hour or so in Rutland made me quite willing to return to the island. Aleck was excited about starting a series of pamphlets on public questions — he bemoaned the absence of pamphleteering in this country and wanted to enlist Ben Hecht for this. "Broadsides!" he would cry. "What this country needs are broadsides! — to arouse controversy!" It was all good fun; Aleck was very fertile in invention; he kept things humming. At the weekend two ladies arrived: Cornelia Otis Skinner and Eleonora von Mendelssohn. On Saturday Miss Skinner wanted to take a drive to show Vermont to Miss von Mendelssohn. Aleck consented to this. I went with them.

Miss von Mendelssohn was a German actress of great beauty. She had been a member of Max Reinhardt's company at home and had appeared in several plays in New York. While we were driving through the beautiful countryside, on a perfect day, Miss von Mendelssohn became suddenly ill. Greatly concerned, Miss Skinner directed the driver to go to Woodstock where her father lived. He would get a doctor on whom she could rely. I was quite excited at the prospect of meeting Otis Skinner. He was a great hero of mine. I had seen him in the Worcester Theatre as Colonel Philippe Brideau in a play adapted from the French, *The Honor of the Family*. I had never forgotten his swashbuckling entrance, late in the first act. Things were not going at all well for the family but the Colonel had such immense authority and decision that you knew he would turn the tide. It began to turn with his entrance. While I was an undergraduate I saw him at the Colonial Theatre in Boston as Haj, the beggar, in Edward Knoblock's *Kismet.* I remembered him lying on his stomach by a pool, holding an undesirable character under the water and vaingloriously defining himself: "To the Caliph I may be dirt but to dirt I am still the Caliph!"

We drew up in front of a modestly substantial house on a tree-lined street. Mr. Skinner opened the door for us. He and I went to the car to help Miss von Mendelssohn into the house. I was engaged in a piece of business with my hero. I felt as if I were following a stage direction. Indeed I was, Mr. Skinner's. He was very definite and decisive in his direction and immensely gentle. I was surprised at his size; I had remembered him, from the stage, as gigantic. He was an elderly, worn and thoughtful man of medium height. He looked like a university professor at the end of an exhausting seminar. I remembered what an Englishman, W. Graham Robertson, who had been a friend of Henry Irving's, had said to me when I asked him whether Irving was tall: "He was tall when he wanted to be." Mr. Skinner must have wished to be tall on the two occasions when I had seen him. The doctor arrived. I wandered to the back porch. I looked down at the river that ran along the back of the house. I followed the river. Just a few houses above, it curved away and ran under an iron bridge. The backyards, between the houses and the river, were all garden. It made me think of England. I walked back into the living room. Mr. Skinner was talking to his daughter. He got up when I came in.

"I've been looking at your river," I said. "It's so beguiling."

Mr. Skinner's face lit up with pleasure.

"I'm glad you like it," he said. "We love it."

"Could I — do you think . . . ?"

"Take a ramble? Of course. Do. It'll soothe you. The doctor is with your friend. He's very good. Don't worry. He'll have her right in no time. Do take a stroll."

Cornelia encouraged me too. Mr. Skinner took me to the front door.

"Follow to the bridge. Cross the bridge. Then follow the river to the next bridge. We are rich in bridges." He smiled. "But come back to us!"

I had never encountered so benignant a presence.

As I walked down the street I could hear the river. Some of Mr. Skinner's neighbors had very large houses indeed. To the right of me ambled the village green. Beyond the green I saw a great wooden porch-enclosed building. The Woodstock Inn. It was built in the eighties and looked it. Ladies were sitting on the porch in rockers. The street curved to the left to the bridge. Crossing the bridge I stopped and looked back over the gardens fronting the river, including Mr. Skinner's. Looking the other way I saw the uptown or upriver bridge. I walked toward it, about half a mile. The houses on this side were less manorial, just nice houses among trees and flowers. The road curved and was intermittently hilly. On the left, covering the side of a hill, was the village churchyard, well populated but spacious. When I got to the next bridge I stopped there too. The river was turbulent here; I looked down on its cavorting. Walking up the incline from this bridge, I passed a series of very handsome houses and a beautiful church. Who were the well-heeled people who owned these houses? Presently I found myself treading a sidewalk. The residence-street had become a business-street: very leisurely, a drugstore, a market, a specialty shop. Some of these had benches in front of them for the weary. When I got to the end of this street I found myself back on the green and facing the Woodstock Inn. I saw that the town had no railroad station. I saw why Mr. Skinner had chosen it to end his days in. For the next thirty years the Woodstock Inn was to be my working home. The walk I had just taken was to become my fixed walk, day and evening, for all of those years. In the next decades, for instance in Hollywood, I was to be seized with longing to be in Woodstock and to be walking those bridges.

When Jed hung up I put in a call to the manager of the Woodstock Inn to make my usual reservation: Room 202. What a succession of managers I have dealt with since — I have outlived so many of them.

I arrived in 202 after a long trip by bus to White River Junction from where I took a taxi to Woodstock. The village had done nothing to make itself accessible; you had to be single-minded to visit Woodstock. But I found a bridge table in 202 for my typewriter; the manager had kept his promise. There was also a message from Harold Freedman. I called him. He had had a letter from the author of *Serena Blandish,* the Lady of Quality. She was very upset by the nomenclature of several characters. In my first draft of the dramatization of her book I had called one Roderick, with the comment from another character that his name conveyed rugged strength which did not altogether conceal the hard fact that he was a poor weakling. I had called another — out of fanciful reaching for a highborn English name — Ottoline. Roderick, she wrote Harold, happened to be her husband's name and Ottoline, that of one of her friends. She was very upset. Harold must write her that I would change these names. I changed them on a pad beside the telephone while I was talking to Harold. I told Harold to write her the deed was done. I still didn't know who the author was. I asked Harold to tell me. He said he would another time and hung up.

I walked the bridges daily and sat in my large room, full of light, going over the packet of notes I had gathered in the preceding months on the play: from Jed, from Aleck, from Richard Burton, whom Jed had engaged to direct it. The months went by. The seasons merged. I became attentive to their transition. I thought I would like to live here the rest of my life to anticipate and revel in these changes. The autumn was glorious; the winy air and the colors. With the fall the Inn filled up somewhat with people who came to inspect the foliage. The autumn passed; the snow came. I had friends in the village: the drugstore man — New York papers, cigarettes, magazines, telegrams; the lady in charge of the Woodstock Library, a tiny, ivied, old brick building next to the Inn; the barber; the chauffeur supplied by the Inn, who kept the shoe store. He was a native and a charmer. He told me of the bitter rivalries among the local hierarchies; they were intricate and fierce. He had an animus against a special hierarchy which he always referred to as "The Ladies on the Green." These ladies owned the beautiful houses which had made me wonder at their opulence on my first walk through the village. They were very rich, they came from Chicago, Boston and Detroit. They were a power, in fact they were *the* power. A Hollywood company had proposed shooting a film in the village. Everybody was very excited, the drugstore man, the Inn people. Everyone thought how great it would be for the village. But the shoe man was skeptical. He had told them, at their Rotary meetings, not to let themselves get excited. "The Ladies on the Green," he insisted, "will never allow it." And indeed they didn't. The film offer was refused. Another town grabbed it. You could do nothing against the Ladies on the Green. They were ruthless. They had the power. They objected to the film on the score of its morality. As he repeated this my chauffeur snickered scornfully. He knew them all; he knew their private lives and their diversions. Who were they to talk about morality? Situations like this made him cynical and bitter. The only thing you could do, he said, was to love your family and make as good a living for them as you could. You would get no help from the Ladies on the Green!

Jed called me frequently. He was very amusing, in good humor because things in the theatre were all going his way. I would read him scenes written in longhand; he would ask me to type them up and send them. He would tell me all the gossip and stories about Aleck's avid interest in *Serena Blandish*. Aleck greatly admired Ruth Gordon; the fact that she was going to star in the play made his interest in it more than avuncular. Jed's comments on the works of his rival producers were trenchant. For most of them he predicted early closings. Then he would, without false modesty, enlarge on the felicities of his own current productions, *The Royal Family* and *The Front Page*. Some of the highest-praised performances in them he would dismiss with the lethal words: "Dictated performance." He left it to you to guess who dictated them.

The snow got so heavy it was no longer practical to walk the bridges. This was a deprivation, but I could still visit my barber, whose shop was on the second floor of a building down the street from the Inn. He was a grizzled oldster, very wiry and full of general comment. I complained to him about the snow and the bridges. "This is nothing," he said. "Come last Christmas you should have seen!" He pointed to the window. "Snow come up to there. Come lunch time I jest walked out that winder. Saved me the stairs."

On New Year's Eve Maurice Wertheim called me up to wish me a Happy New Year and to invite me on a yachting cruise. He had chartered, from Claude Graham White, his yacht, the *Ianara,* for an August cruise along the coasts of Norway and Sweden. He was inviting ten people. Would I like to come? Never able to think on the telephone, I said yes, since my vocabulary becomes restricted to this one word when I am asked anything on the telephone. As soon as Maurice hung up I knew that if my play failed I would be in no mood for yachting trips. Well, August was still a long way off. Lawrence Langner called me. I had had various conversations with this protean man. He was Welsh, dark and handsome. He came, when young, from Cardiff and started out as a patent lawyer. By this time he had his own firm, perhaps the leading patent law firm in the United States. He was one of the founders of the Washington Square Players. He wrote plays and books and had the courage to engage in acrimonious differences with Bernard Shaw. He held his own. On Broadway he was known as "the Persian." This was because he was so volatile that he was intangible. He was thought slippery; the truth is that he was absentminded. He couldn't remember names or even identities, so that the forgetfulness which the insidious thought to be evasions were, as I came to see, genuine and innocent lapses of memory. Many years later, at the opening of *Jacobowsky and the Colonel* at the Shubert Theatre in New Haven, I was standing with him and Miss Helburn in the lobby of the theatre. Looking around the lobby Lawrence said: "Oh, there's Gene O'Neill's son, teaches Greek at Yale. I want you to meet him." He hailed O'Neill, who came over. Lawrence said: "Oh, Gene, I want you to meet . . ." He presented me but couldn't remember my name. We had been working together for twenty years. I supplied my name and things went along. I told this story when I spoke at his funeral and it got a titter of recognition from his friends in the audience. His mind was teeming always with large ideas. He was a remarkable and very decent man with a strong, mystic faith in an underlying impulse toward justice. In the headlong rush of his activity he found the time to build and start the Shakespeare Theatre in Stratford and the West-port Country Playhouse. When Lawrence died, not long after Miss Helburn, the Guild died too.

. Lawrence spoke to me about casting. What would I think of Margalo Gillmore for the ingenue? As I adored Margalo, both on stage and off, I said that would be fine with me. Lawrence wanted to speak to me about something else but it had slipped his mind for the moment. He would call me up later when he remembered it.

I worked in Woodstock on *Serena* till the middle of March, when Miss Helburn called to tell me that I'd better come back to New York for rehearsals. Here it was at last! To celebrate I commandeered the local philosopher and shoe man to drive me to the Hanover Inn on the Dartmouth campus for a festive dinner. I had already stolen away there several times for a treat. The food at the Hanover Inn was excellent; they served hot corn bread which was delectable. I enjoyed strolling around the Dartmouth campus and visiting the well-stocked library. I was startled, on my first visit to the library, by the Orozco murals, a searing mélange of color pulverizing the capitalist system, particularly our educational system as practiced at Dartmouth. The colors are so vivid, the drawing so bold, that I wondered how the students could go on pandering to an educational system so vicious: a skeleton in cap and gown being interred by a capped and gowned faculty; a cadaverous figure, looking very like Woodrow Wilson, on his hands and knees pawing ravenously at a heap of gold coins — the whole mural a procession of money-mad scavengers, money-grubbing, all in this demure, denominational New England college with its white church spire presiding over all. I tried to imagine an American artist being invited to Moscow to paint Stalin luxuriating in a bloodbath, to regale students at Moscow University. It was beyond imagining. I reflected that the Orozcos in the Dartmouth library were a sign of security after all.

On the day I was to leave for New York I was delighted to get a call from Alfred Lunt. A gourmet and a chef himself, he inquired how the food was at the Inn.

"Simple," I said, "but bad."

He sympathized. He had been going to a cooking class and he felt more authority than formerly. He would make it up to me when I got back. He would give me a bang-up dinner. He'd bought a suit in London to wear in my play. It rather shocked Aleck. "He calls it," he said, "my purple suit." He said he practically knew his part already, not from studying it but from reading it.

"I am doing it," he said, "just to say one line in it."

I asked what the line was but he wouldn't tell me. "It would spoil it for me," he said, "if I told you."

Alfred had always fascinated me — both on the stage and after I had got to know him personally. He had tremendous strength shadowed by tremendous vulnerability.

"Lynn and I rehearse our scenes all the time. Lynn'll be magical in it. We love it but probably they won't like it!" His voice swerved off at the dismal prospect of what "they" would do to it. I had noticed before that Alfred referred always, and darkly, to an invisible and malevolent force which existed, seemingly, for the sole purpose of destroying him. I had teased him about this before.

"Who are 'they'?" I asked. "The Ladies on the Green?"

"Ladies on the Green? How charming! Tell me about them."

Alfred fell in love with the Ladies on the Green. A villager himself, he loved small-town intrigue and small-town gossip.

"You must get Lynn to tell you her story of the Lady on our Green in Genesee Depot."

This was the prelude to a series of conversations I was to have with Lynn and Alfred over the next four decades. They have wildly humorous imaginations. Their feel for human idiosyncrasy is instinctive and unerring; their gift for echoing it uncanny. Their repertory is practically endless, encompassing their vast experience — offstage and on — with an international assortment of people from the Genesee Lady on the Green to Winston Churchill. I brought to see them, not long ago, in their tiny exquisite house on East End Avenue, a well-known Broadway director, to discuss with them a project in which we were both interested. They were at the top of their form and in radiant spirits. They couldn't undertake our project, but they captivated the director, who had never met them before. At the same time he felt a maddening frustration because of the revelation they gave him of what our project might have been had they consented to engage in it. In the cab on the way home he said bitterly: "There simply *are* no people like that around anymore."

VI

The Lunts

THERE IS REALLY NOTHING IN THE WORLD so heady for a writer as theatrical success. It is instantaneous. It is unmistakable. That must be why so many novelists yield to the temptation to have a go at it. But it is (in spite of what many practicing novelists say) much more difficult to write a good play than it is to write a good novel. Many novelists have found that out. The author of a well-received novel never knows whether his book, even if it sells, is also read. Nor does he know where his reader yawns, at what page he may have decided that he wants no more of it and throws it away in disgust. The novelist's audience is invisible; the playwright's right there with him. With a successful play the author is reviewed every night and the playwright can tell what kind of review he's getting. Robert Sherwood, who wrote a novel, complained to me that it was reviewed under the heading "Other Books," and that was that. Sinclair Lewis was a friend of mine. Somehow, though I'd read most of his novels as they came out, I'd never read *Babbitt* till long after it was published. While I was reading it, with excitement and admiration, I was also reading a play he had just written (we had the same theatrical agent) and which he was backing with his own money. It is a quirk of my temperament that I am always lost in admiration of people who can do things that I can't do — like mathematics or writing novels. Reading *Babbitt,* I felt distress that Lewis should abandon a field in which he was a master for one in which he was inept. His play was no good at all and I knew that he would lose every cent he was putting into it. Just the day I'd

73

Alfred Lunt and Lynn Fontanne in *The Second Man*

finished *Babbitt,* I went to dinner at 21. I was hailed by Lewis. He was having dinner with the company that was rehearsing his play. He came over to my table. He was swimming in euphoria. I decided to be severe with him.

"Look, Red, I've just read *Babbitt.* It's — well, you know how good it is. Tell me, why should a man who can write a novel like that bother with plays?"

Lewis saw that I was serious. He sat down.

"Listen," he said. "Do you know what a novelist's life is like? I sit up there in Vermont for a year writing a novel. When it's finished I write to my publisher to tell him I've finished my book. He, to be nice, says he'll come up to see me. He comes up. That's it. Hell, I'm gregarious. I like PEOPLE!"

With a schoolboy's grin of delight he went back to his table in an ecstasy of gregariousness. The blueprint of disaster which those in the know had diagramed for his play was fulfilled. The last time I ever saw Lewis, before he went to Italy, where he died, he told me what that particular venture had cost him. Gregariousness came high.

I was received once, in Cambridge, Massachusetts, by William James, the son of the philosopher and the nephew of the novelist, in the mellow house in which his father had lived and died. Mr. James was a painter, a tall, courtly, gentle man. He sat me down on a sofa in the parlor. He must have been briefed that I knew my way around the New York theatre. In those days I did. Mr. James seemed troubled; I sensed that there was something he wanted to say but that he was too shy. Finally, it came out. "Tell me," he said, "Uncle Henry's plays — do you know his plays?" I said I'd read one. "Tell me," he said, "plays are made from his books — and they succeed — but Uncle Henry's own plays — tell me, what is the trouble, can you not . . . ?" He couldn't go on with it. He made me feel that one of Uncle Henry's plays was that very minute trying out in New Haven and why, instead of sitting with him in Cambridge, wasn't I in New Haven seeing to it that Uncle Henry's play was doing the right thing? I told the incident to Willie Maugham, who was in New York at the time. He said: "Do you know why Uncle Henry's plays don't succeed? I'll tell you why. I've read them all. They're lousy, that's why they don't succeed!"

The heady experience I have described above, of being present at a successful first night, came to me in April 1927, when the Theatre Guild produced *The Second Man*. The Guild had rejected it the year before. My agent, Harold Freedman, was thorough: he wouldn't rest till it had been rejected by every other producer in town. He then brought it back to the Guild, to give them a fresh experience. Mr. Freedman's hearing was highly selective. He never heard the word "No." The play had an extracurricular advantage working for it; it had only four characters and one set. The Guild did well by it: the four characters were played by Lynn Fontanne, Alfred Lunt, Margalo Gillmore and Earle Larimore. Jo Mielziner did the set.

I owe this play to the most tenuous and untraceable of accidents, to the chance reading of a sentence. I have never been able to remember where I read that sentence. It was quoted somewhere, perhaps in a newspaper, perhaps in some literary review, from a letter of Lord Leighton's. The sentence reads:

". . . for, together with, and as it were behind, so much pleasurable emotion, there is always that other strange second man in me, calm, critical, observant, unmoved, blasé, odious."

I wrote a short story, based on Leighton's second man, which appeared in Mencken and Nathan's *Smart Set*. One winter, stuck for an idea and jobless, I dramatized this short story. It took me three weeks to write the play and three years for Mr. Freedman to sell it.

It wasn't till I went to London, for the English production of *The Second Man*, with Noel Coward, in 1929, that I found out who Lord Leighton was. I met a lady who'd known him, who in fact knew everybody, Sibyl Colefax. London is very hospitable to new playwrights; Sibyl was the first new friend I made there and she remained my friend till her death. She'd been very excited, she told me, when she read the excerpt from Lord Leighton's letter in the theatre program; she had never seen it; she wanted to read it all; she demanded to see the whole letter. As it had not been written to me I couldn't supply it. But she told me how completely even this excerpt expressed Lord Leighton's eroding self-dissatisfaction. He was, by the end of the century, wildly successful; he had everything: very good looks and vast success as a portraitist. He had been president of the Royal Academy. But this excerpt from his letter confirmed a suspicion she had entertained herself about him, that he wasn't taken in by his success, that, like the protagonist of my play, he knew that he was second-rate. He was not deceived; he *knew*. His career could be summarized as Harold Nicolson summarized Lord Curzon's: "He had successes but no success." A quarter of a century later I was to run into Lord Leighton again. This was in the Villino Chiaro, Max Beerbohm's little house in Rapallo. We were going through Max's book of caricatures, *Rossetti and His Circle*. Suddenly there was Lord Leighton. I said to Max: "But he's the man who gave me my first play!" "I'm glad he did that," said Max. "He gave me this caricature. He was one of the hollow men." The caricature is a masterpiece. Lord Leighton is handsome, elegantly bearded, monocled and cravatted to perfection. Rossetti is lying on a sofa; you see only his slippered feet. Leighton is haranguing Rossetti's feet; they are so relaxed that you are sure their proprietor is asleep. You are sure also that Leighton doesn't much mind; he is listening to himself. He is trying to induce an "up and do" attitude in Rossetti:

"Think not for one moment, my dear Mr. Rossetti, that I am insensible to the charm of a life recluded, as yours is, from the dust of the arena, from the mire of the marketplace. Ah no! — I envy you your ivory tower. How often at some Council Meeting of the R.A. have I murmured within me that phrase of Wordsworth's, 'The world is too much with us!' But alas, in all of us there is a duality of nature . . . you smile, Mr. Rossetti, yet I am not disemboldened to say to you now, as I have often wished to say to you, in the words of the Apostle Paul, 'Come over and help us!' Our President — I grant you in confidence — is not of all men the most enlightened. But I, in virtue of what is left to me of youth and ardour, conjoined with the paltry gift of tact, have some little influence at Burlington House. Come now! — let me put your name down in our Candidates' Book."

I was awfully green when *The Second Man* went into rehearsal. We were to open "cold" without a road tour. We rehearsed on the top

floor of the Guild headquarters on West Fifty-second Street. The day
before we started I had a long talk with Philip Moeller, my director.
He was a member of the Guild board and directed most of the plays I
did for the Guild for the next twenty years: four for the Lunts, one for
Jane Cowl, three for Ina Claire. I was lucky to have Phil Moeller; he
suited me perfectly. He was an elfin character, restless and volatile,
impassioned for art. His great love was music; he studied scores and
he was animated, when directing a play, by ideas of counterpoint and
harmonic structure. In one scene of *The Second Man* he had Lynn sit
at the piano and play a haunting passage from *Der Rosenkavalier,* and
this was a time before that music had become threadbare with repetition. He wrote plays himself. One, *Mme Sand,* was critically, if not
popularly, well received. He was quirky, mercurial and impulsive. He
blurted out what was on his mind without thinking. This sometimes
caused outbursts of temper between himself, his actors and his authors. He never retreated; he relied on Miss Helburn and Mr. Langner
to patch up these differences. Mr. Langner sometimes made things
worse but Miss Helburn was infallible. There was an innocence about
Phil Moeller. He lived alone, saw very few people. Miss Helburn used
to be exasperated with him because he never went to the theatre. He
cared about nothing but music and painting. When anything pleased
him he became incandescent.

The Guild headquarters was a transformed private residence. The
top floor where we rehearsed must have been the ballroom. The stage
manager had chalkmarked the floor, indicating the doors and windows
and the staircase and the gallery, since the hero lived in a duplex. On
this area Phil Moeller deployed his four actors. I sat in a chair on the
sidelines to watch. I was fascinated to observe how, for these virtuoso
actors, the stage space became embodied, transfigured by inches, each
turn, each approach, each retreat. They had to consider how their faces
and bodies looked from all directions and from all angles. Half the
time I didn't know what they were doing or why. As for the words,
they began to sound like so much gibberish. At one point, during a
murky passage, Miss Fontanne came up to me. "I suppose," she said,
"it all sounds like nothing to you." I admitted that it did rather. "You
see," she said, "we're not thinking of the words now, just the move-

ments, but I promise you — it'll be all right." She smiled at me and squeezed my hand. I have never forgotten this little errand of mercy. Alfred Lunt's readings — and not merely on the first day — were very casual, only sporadically vital, and in the main, disinterested. I had no idea what his performance was to be like till the opening night. Some days Miss Fontanne advised me not to come at all. I took her advice.

And then suddenly it was over. The play opened. I sat in the first row of the balcony and got a headache. It was the last time I went to an opening of my own in New York. Harold Freedman came up each intermission to tell me how he thought things were going. I realized as I watched that first performance that I'd had not the remotest idea of what Lynn and Alfred could or would do. The illuminations of the script provided by the actors dazzled me because I had not perceived them during the rehearsals. Lynn's part was a small one but now in the performance I heard overtones that I didn't know were there. For example, I had written a line for her about another character who bored her: "He never has anything interesting to say." What I heard was: "He never has anything interesting to say — never — never — never — never — never," a perfectly graduated diminuendo of "nevers," conveying an endless vista of boredom, the last "never" faint — but audible! — faint with the claustrophobia of boredom. It took Theresa Helburn's strategic expertise to get Lynn to play this part, but I think she was assisted by Lynn's instinct that the man's part would be very good for her husband. Alfred, all the way through, had the audience mesmerized; he did what he wanted with it — made it laugh and made it listen. In his last scene on the telephone when he calls up the character played by Lynn to win her back, at the moment when he says: "Thank God you're laughing!" the audience laughed. Later in his dressing room Alfred told me what a lifesaver that laugh had been.

Just before the curtain fell I saw an element in the play which I had not written, certainly not consciously; the dramatization of a terrible moment, a watershed moment, when you face nullity. The nonhero has been abandoned by the older woman who loves him and by the young woman whom he, had he been less practical, might have loved. He has just seen the younger woman out the door. My stage direction reads: "He leaves the door, goes to the telephone." That walk, that walk from the door to the telephone, shafted a light on the play and the character which I had not foreseen. It was a moment of self-confrontation, of complete awareness. Why hadn't he taken a chance? Why hadn't he tested himself? Perhaps he was better than the louse he knew himself to be? Alfred's eyes, when he picked up the telephone to get back what he didn't want, went insane.

By arrangement, Harold Freedman picked me up before going backstage. We took a turn around the block. We were both under the spell of Alfred's terrifying little walk to the telephone. He'd made Calvary out of an innocent stage direction.

The reviews, with one exception, were enthusiastic. The exception was Woollcott in the *World* who said I was like an outsider peering through the plate-glass windows of an opulent house to observe how the well-bred inhabitants behaved. I was solaced for this by a featured article in the *Nation* by Joseph Wood Krutch, who was all out for the play. One of the daily reviewers said the problem of selection facing the Pulitzer Prize committee would be greatly eased by this production. But the committee spurned an easy out; they preferred the hard way. Nor have they ever deferred to me since, though I have nudged them about twenty times. I was solaced also by the fact that the play sold out at every performance. The second week I got a telegram from Alfred in Worcester, Massachusetts, where I had gone to see my mother: "We sold out last night with thirty standees. That's pretty good for Good Friday." My first royalty check exceeded a thousand dollars. I stared at this check with incredulity.

What would *The Second Man* come to if it were beautifully produced now? It would probably seem very old-fashioned and, as Jed Harris used to enjoy telling me, "thin." But for a time it had, and gave me, a lively reputation. Again, decades later, during the war when Harold Ross asked me to go to England to describe London in wartime, I went to see Somerset Maugham, then in New York, to ask for advice. He gave me a letter to H. G. Wells. In it he introduced me as the author of *The Second Man*. Since then, just a few years ago, I wrote a fan letter to Frank Swinnerton because I had greatly enjoyed a reminiscent book of his. He answered with a charming letter in which he said that he was happy he had entertained me because I had entertained him with *The Second Man*. He wrote as if he had seen the play a week before. Actually, he had seen it in London when it was done by Noel Coward in 1929.

The seven weeks with the Lunts went by all too quickly. Miss Helburn set about to recast it. In a cast of four there were two replacements, actually three because Earle Larrimore replaced Alfred. Donald McDonald replaced Larrimore and Emily Stevens, Lynn. Emily Stevens, a niece of Mrs. Fiske, was a profound actress herself, as she had demonstrated when she played Hedda Gabler. She had enchanting humor — when she read the play, she said of Lynn's part: "Why, the woman is a perpetual exit!" She thought, and I agreed with her, that she was being treated rather shabbily. She had to wear Lynn's clothes. They didn't really suit her; they had to be recut and restitched for her. It was humiliating and sad-making — a bad patch on what had been a happy experience. But Miss Stevens was game. She stuck to the part and to the hand-me-down clothes and was distinguished. She couldn't help it.

The first night of the new cast I went to the theatre early to see Miss Stevens and the others. I came out front about eight o'clock. There was nobody there. I said to Miss Helburn: "This is pitiful. Couldn't you cancel this performance?" "They'll come," said the indomitable Theresa. They did. By 8:20 the house began to fill up. When the curtain rose, it was full. I was astonished. "Where do they come from?" I asked Miss Helburn. "Gray's Drug Store," she told me, looking very self-satisfied. It was like that till September when the Guild opened its new season.

ii

Those few hours in the Guild Theatre on April 11 changed all my circumstances for the rest of my life. I was deluged with offers. My diary lists them. Frank Crowninshield, the editor of *Vanity Fair*, asked me to write twelve pieces for him, to run a year. *The Second Man* was accepted for London and Noel Coward agreed to play it. I began to get film offers; they came rapidly. I put them off because none of the ma-

terial that was offered appealed to me. At about this time I met Harold
Ross. I loved him from the day I met him to the day he died. He asked
me to write for the *New Yorker,* then two years old. I wrote a profile of
George Gershwin. It was the beginning of a long and fruitful associa-
tion that continued after Ross's death with his successor, William
Shawn. In time my concentration on my work for the *New Yorker*
became so intense that it caused Harold Freedman concern. He telephoned me one afternoon while I was working with Shawn on a
profile of Lord Duveen. He asked me what I was doing and I told
him. I had been engrossed in these pieces for what seemed to him an
interminable time. He ventured into humor: "I was walking in Central
Park," he said, "and I saw an old man sitting on a bench. 'What are
you doing?' I asked. He said: 'Workin' on Duveen.' "

It was a vertiginous time. I found myself in a millstream of gregariousness in New York and in London: incessant contact with great
theatre stars, with rich people and social people, at posh hotels, at
parties, and on yachts. But through it all I never shook off the plain-
tive counterpoint of my origins, the memory of my parents, their
religion and their poverty. An odd illustration: late one night in
Copenhagen harbor on Maurice Wertheim's yacht, I'd been unable to
sleep. The captain had invited me to join him on deck when I felt like
it. I dressed and went up. He was a most agreeable man. I stood beside
him as he steered the elegant, slim white craft through the shipping in
the harbor. There was a moon; the scene was serenely beautiful. But I
was not present. I was unaccountably in my father's insolvent grocery
store in Worcester, Massachusetts. A show had been advertised by an
itinerant huckster in Mechanics Hall. Most of the boys in the Providence Street Grade School were going. I longed to go. I asked my
father if he would give me the admission price — fifteen cents. He
looked at me with pain in his eyes. He had to refuse. I saw how keenly
he wanted to give me the fifteen cents. He told me he was forced to
close the grocery since it was doing so badly. I left the captain and the
moonlit shipping and went back to my cabin. I remembered Disraeli's
eternal dichotomy: "The Privileged and the People form Two
Nations."

I sit here now, aged seventy-seven, turning these remote and incredible pages—the breathless notations of my diary of those years. I am mourning the death of a beloved friend in Hollywood, fifteen years younger than I, whose obituary I have just read in the *Times*. Why was he sent and I spared? We can only fall back on the inscrutable pseudonym which we paste on the central mystery — Chance — which tells us nothing.

iii

In a sense, the rest of my playwriting life was devoted to the Lunts, though I had only one more success with them, the adaptation, which they commissioned me to do, of Jean Giraudoux's *Amphitryon 38.* There was one original play, *Meteor,* and two foreign adaptations: *The Pirate,* by Ludwig Fulda, and *I Know My Love,* adapted from Marcel Achard's Paris hit *Auprès de ma blonde.* It was not easy, with the Lunts, to distinguish a hit from a failure because whatever they did attracted a large audience. Bob Sherwood had written a doggerel:

> *If you want a play to run many a munt*
> *Get Lynn Fontanne and Alfred Lunt.*

On the road, of course, they could do no wrong: business would be astronomical for as long as they cared to tour. *The Pirate* and *I Know My Love* gave me and them great trouble: my adaptations of these plays didn't stack up. I went to Paris, in 1946, to see *Auprès de ma blonde.* The idea behind this play was a good one: that a very happy married couple arouse envy and hatred from those around them, even in their own families. Yvonne Printemps played the lead in the Achard play. I was struck by the disparity between our audience and the French, by the second-act curtain line of Achard's play. The husband's younger brother falls in love with Yvonne and commits suicide. When she hears the awful news, Yvonne brings the curtain down with the line: "Oh God, why didn't you make me ugly?" I couldn't imagine a heroine winning sympathy with a line like that in America; the line seemed a little self-conscious. Alexander Korda urged me to adapt this play for America; the Guild got the Lunts for it. What appealed to

Lynn and Alfred was that the play took this couple from youth to old age and through the Second World War. They saw in it a parable of their own marriage. It ran the gamut; the Lunts were eager to make the run.

The Pirate was in a different realm: a romantic satire set in a tropical scene. It gave Alfred a chance to walk a tightrope into his lady's chamber. The wife, Manuela, dreams of the exploits of the romantic hero, a pirate who dominates the surrounding waters. It turns out that her fat husband is the pirate. By the time we got to Philadelphia with this play the Lunts and I were at an impasse with it. Sometimes Alfred and I would battle over a line which I liked better than he did. He continued to say it, but would misread it intentionally so that it fell flat. Then he would turn to me and say with impish triumph, "See, I told you it wouldn't play." But in Philadelphia we came to strong differences about the whole second-act curtain. There seemed no way out but to close it. I would submit a rewrite; Lynn would say: "I don't think Alfred will like this." It was not always possible to know where the source of the discontent resided. At this point an old friend, the violinist Efrem Zimbalist, came to see the play. In the intermission I told him how upset I was. He told me not to worry so much, and to ease my mind told me the following story:

Zimbalist and his first wife, Alma Gluck, the singer, had been great friends of the Lunts. I had known Alma — she was a renowned artist and an entrancing woman. One day Lynn came to her in a state of agitation:

"Alma," she said, "I've got to meet Rachmaninoff!"

Alma was surprised. She said it would be easy to arrange. She wondered why.

Lynn explained: "Nothing like this has ever happened to me before," she said. "I was walking up Fifth Avenue. Rachmaninoff came out of Dunhill's. Something about him — I don't know what — captured me. I followed him. He went into the Savoy-Plaza. I waited till he came out. Then he walked over to Madison. There I lost him. Alma! You've got to do this for me. I've got to meet Rachmaninoff!"

Alma said nothing would be simpler; Rachmaninoff came to her house often to play cards with her husband. He was dour and silent.

Alma would sit reading while he and her husband played cards. After an hour Rachmaninoff might say: "Zimmy, vot is population Odessa?" Zimmy would hazard a guess and that would satisfy Rachmaninoff for the rest of the evening.

This did not discourage Lynn. She wanted to meet Rachmaninoff.

The arrangement was made for the following Sunday evening. Lynn appeared, looking marvelous in a Worth gown. Alma was standing at the piano with her husband and Rachmaninoff. The latter was anxious to get to the card table but Alma held him off. She introduced Lynn.

Lynn looked at the pianist. She turned to Alma.

"That's not Rachmaninoff!"

Alma was taken aback. The great man's features were so well known from the innumerable photographs that were appearing constantly in record advertisements. She took Lynn aside.

"Lynn, dear," she said. "Don't you recognize him? Of course it's Rachmaninoff."

Equally positive, Lynn said: "That's not the man I followed!"

I don't know why Zimbalist told me this story. Perhaps he wanted to remind me that Lynn's certitudes were highly personal, sometimes based on imaginary facts. The story does illustrate the insulated lives led by Lynn and Alfred; they were a part of the great world wherever they went but they lived in their own theatrical fantasies. These fantasies grew from the parts they were playing at the moment.

Alfred's performance as the eighty-year-old Bostonian in *I Know My Love* (I had shifted Achard's play to America) was remarkable. I remember his walk across the stage during which he glanced down at a telegram he was carrying without interrupting his conversation with his son — it was uncannily lifelike. Alfred's details for his performances were like the observations of a great novelist. Peter Brook, who directed the Lunts in the last play they did in New York, Dürrenmatt's *The Visit,* told me a wonderful story about Alfred. In one scene, Alfred, down and out, is sitting on a bench in front of a railroad station. He asked Brook how it would be if, to convey his sorry state, he took off one of his shoes and shook some pebbles out of it. Brook said that would be fine. After some thought, Alfred asked: "How many pebbles, do you think . . . three . . . four?" Lynn told me that in one scene, where she is sitting upstage and overhears a scene in which the doomed Alfred tries to shield himself against the encroaching suspicion that walls around him, Alfred was so touching that she could hardly bear to listen to it.

Very few Americans return to live in their hometowns after they have made a great success in life but Alfred did — to the improbable habitat of Genesee Depot, Wisconsin. He sent his mother, Hattie, to Europe for a holiday. He saw her off on the *Queen Mary*. Hattie had a look around. She complained to Alfred: "I don't see anyone here from the Depot!" Their Genesee house expresses the Lunts entirely: their tastes, their histories. There are porcelain stoves from Scandinavia; ceilings fabulously painted by an artist friend; on the piano, in glass, lies a huge cigar given to Alfred by Winston Churchill; there is a set of imaginative drawings made by Alfred for *Macbeth;* a photograph of himself in *Meteor* looking very like Jed Harris. The only conventional room is the handsome and up-to-the-minute kitchen, where Alfred experiments endlessly with his second art: cooking. It is a very comfortable house to stay in. The meals are often gala, with a constant obbligato of Lynn's stories and imitations — of the Lady on the Green in Genesee and the titled ladies of London. There are not, in the world, two people more self-sufficient than Lynn and Alfred. It has been said of Lynn — or used to be — that by an act of will she converted herself from a rather awkward though interesting-looking young girl, into one of the great beauties of the stage, so radiant that she could play a mortal woman alluring enough to bring to earth a god from heaven. This made her ready to play Alkmena, the heroine of Jean Giraudoux's *Amphitryon 38,* which was to come years later.

iv

Lynn Fontanne used to say when I first began writing plays for the Lunts, that it was really her husband that I wrote for. There may have been something in this because I was fascinated by Alfred's style and personality in the first play I ever saw him in, an adaptation from the

French, called *Banco.* He captivated me. He had total command, not merely physically but mentally. You saw his brain digesting the lines and the situations and finding them funny. There was glee in his voice, in his expression, in his gestures. I went to see *Banco* time after time. I saw that Alfred changed his readings, changed his performance all the time, but he never changed his point of view, which was comedic. It was the comedy of intelligence. He was not always amused by the same things so that you got different facets almost at each performance. I felt that he was a creative actor and that it would be an easy step for him to play a creative artist, if you could write such a part for him. In my first play I wrote the part of a writer whose intelligence far transcended his talent. It was a disarming stroke of luck to get Alfred Lunt for it. It was generally admitted by the critics and by the public that in this play Alfred gave the greatest comedy performance then visible.

There are two actors who can, by coming on the stage, transmit the suggestion of genius. One is Alfred Lunt. The other is Laurence Olivier. Ibsen, in *Hedda Gabler,* keeps telling you, through the mouths of his characters, that Eilert Lövborg, he with the vine leaves in his hair, is a genius, but Lövborg does nothing to support this claim. Of all the characters in *Hedda Gabler* he is the dullest. You feel nothing in Lövborg but mediocrity. Producers worry who is going to play Hedda. They should be worried about who is going to play Eilert Lövborg. I have wondered how the play would seem if Lövborg were played by Lunt or Olivier.

The next play I wrote for Alfred was *Meteor.* He thought that Jed Harris was the model for it — he made up to look like Jed — but actually he wasn't. Charles A. Beard, in the *History of American Civilization,* which I was reading when I wrote this play, dilates on the extraordinary profusion of millionaires who appeared at this time: 1920 to 1929. The character was a young man with "ghetto" vitality from the meanest background who pinned a grandiose name onto himself — Raphael Lord — and who persuaded himself that he had the gift of clairvoyance.

The first reading of *Meteor* took place at Ford's Theatre in Baltimore. The reason for this was that the Lunts were in the middle of an unusually successful tour in an adaptation of a European comedy called *Caprice*. After Baltimore we followed *Caprice* to Philadelphia and Boston. The *Meteor* rehearsal tour — sandwiched between the performances of *Caprice* — was as dolorous as the *Caprice* performances were lightsome. "They," said Alfred, referring in his customary manner to the brigade of hostile critics who dogged his efforts, its collective will made up in advance to discredit him, "they won't like me in *Meteor*." He meant that they wouldn't like *Meteor* and here he was as prophetic as Raphael Lord, the character whose peculiar obsession he was wrestling with every minute he wasn't playing *Caprice,* which "they" received rapturously eight times a week. I was rewriting all the time. I wrote reams in the hotel rooms of Baltimore, Philadelphia and Boston. There was one thing I was aware of powerfully: the climate of the time was such, the proliferation of private fortunes, the vision of "success," meaning money and power, which hung over everything like a canopy, made Lynn's speeches, the ones I wrote expressing a humanitarian point of view, sound prissy and abstractionist. It couldn't be got right. We, the management, Terry Helburn, Lawrence Langner, Phil Moeller, were stuck with Raphael Lord's obsession, just as he was. One day, rehearsing in the beloved and now vanished Hollis Street Theatre in Boston, Phil Moeller broke down. The rehearsal had to be stopped. Afterwards Lawrence Langner said: "If Phil hadn't broken down, Alfred would have. It was a good thing."

On the day of Phil Moeller's breakdown I spent the evening in my room rewriting with the hope of sparing him other breakdowns in the future. The Lunts rang me when they got to the hotel after their performance in *Caprice*. I went to their suite for a light supper. It was Christmas Eve. Lynn suggested we take a walk up Beacon Street to hear the carols. The three of us sallied forth. It was a mild evening; the Common was covered with snow but the streets were navigable. Beacon Street was a few minutes away. We began to pass the wreath-hung houses; through the windows we saw Christmas trees being festooned and lit. We stopped in front of a hospitable window. "How enviable these people are with just Christmas and presents and no play on their hands," said Lynn.

"I'd like to get my hands on some of those presents," Alfred said.

I misunderstood him. Lynn corrected me:

"Alfred means to wrap them," she said. "He has a wonderful knack for wrapping presents."

We passed groups singing carols. Lynn and Alfred remarked how much Beacon Street reminded them of London. We walked up to the State House and then returned to Commonwealth Avenue. On Commonwealth, Alfred stood still in the middle of the sidewalk in front of a brightly lit brownstone.

"What was it," he asked Lynn, "the exact point where Phil broke down?"

Lynn answered promptly.

"It's in our Second Act scene where I say: 'There may be a lot of cant spoken in the name of altruism. Just the same, there is such a thing as altruism.' "

Alfred picked it up.

" 'There may be, but I can't pretend to feel it. Moreover, I see no need for it. I expect to make a decent place of Ariandos — bathtubs and gardens, but I do it as an economic measure. I do it because it will save me trouble and insurrection in the future . . . most of all I do it because it's a terrific job and I'm the only man alive who could pull it off.' "

Lynn and Alfred had forgotten where they were and were rehearsing. I moved a bit away from them to give them a sense of privacy.

Several passersby had joined me and stopped to listen. The Lunts were so absorbed in each other's readings that they didn't notice. Alfred was saying:

" 'Lenin's motive wasn't altruism but revenge on the Czarists who shot his brother — the first Utopian who knew how to handle machine guns.' "

A burly man, alcoholized, in a muffler with a soft felt hat pulled down over his eyes, had pulled up beside me and stood listening. When Alfred mentioned Lenin, he began to splutter.

"Who is that guy?" he asked belligerently.

"A friend of mine," I said.

"Well, who is he to shoot his mouth off about the Abe Lincoln of Russia? He's a goddamn reactionary!"

Lynn and Alfred didn't like irrelevant conversation while they were rehearsing. Alfred shot me a warning look. I went up to them and suggested their rooms might be better for what they were doing. I began to walk the two reactionaries toward their hotel.

A light snow had begun to fall. Great flakes began to settle on Lynn's fur coat.

"Look at them," she said, showing off the snow flakes on her sleeve, "how big they are, how soft and perfect — like buttercups."

But Alfred was still ruminating over his immense plans for Ariandos.

When I got back to the hotel I found a message to call Harold Freedman. He told me two bits of news: Guthrie McClintic, to whom he had given a comedy I had written, called *Brief Moment,* wanted to produce and direct it. Also, Winfield Sheehan, the head of Twentieth Century–Fox, was in town and wished to see me. He had a film proposal that he thought would interest me. Fox had bought Molnár's *Liliom* and wanted me to write the screenplay at twelve hundred and fifty dollars a week. I asked him to make an appointment for me with Mr. Sheehan week after next.

Going to sleep I began to recollect *Brief Moment.* I had written it in a long breath some months ago. I was deep in worry over *Meteor.* Anyway, *Brief Moment* presented no special problem: no one in it had the faculty of clairvoyance or was bloated in self-belief. Actually the hero of *Brief Moment* felt himself a failure. That was a chilling thought too. I prayed for sleep but it eluded me.

v

Just ten years later, I adapted for the Lunts Jean Giraudoux's haunting play *Amphitryon 38.* Like all good comedies, *Amphitryon* is, in essence, a tragic play, since comedy is the saving grace which makes life bearable. A French dictionary beside me, I began. Giraudoux arose on *"une terrasse près d'un palais."* He is laconic; he doesn't say whose terrace, or whose palace, and as I had no equipment for furnishing places like that, I was equally laconic. But Alfred got an idea which changed all that. Terraces in the vicinity of palaces seemed dull to him, especially as he, Jupiter, is on at the opening. "I want to go up," he said, "with me and Mercury lying naked on a cloud and watching Alkmena on earth from there." Godlike, Alfred anticipated the nudist future by a good many years. I had never written an "At Rise" on a cloud before, but when you are working for two great stars, you adapt yourself. Besides, I thought it was a thrilling idea. I arose as follows, getting a lift myself from the elevation:

A cloud above Olympus. Jupiter, the master of the gods, and Mer-cury, his half-son, are lounging comfortably on this cloud, their phos-phorescent eyes focused for the moment on the domesticities of a terrestrial couple, Alkmena and her husband, General Amphitryon. Jupiter's long beard is a firework of golden curls; otherwise he is naked, as is Mercury. They are lying on their stomachs; they face the terrestrial audience; their arms and faces are their own; their backs, legs and buttocks belong to the scenic designer.

The new At Rise necessitated a slight dialogue change also. I had to improvise a bit for Mercury:

Jupiter, you astonish me. If you're in love with this mortal, why don't you employ the facilities you have as a god? Why waste an entire night, ravished with longing, bouncing about on a cloud, sniping at her shadow when you might so easily, with your ordinary god-sight, see her as she is through the walls of her chamber?

Amphitryon 38 we rehearsed in Chicago, in Baltimore, in Boston, in Genesee Depot and in London, where the Lunts took Edward Knob-lock's house in Cadogan Square for the summer. They gave me the top floor, where we rehearsed. You couldn't *be* with the Lunts without rehearsing. Mr. Giraudoux would have been surprised at the amount of time that was spent in reorchestrating the harmonics of the dialogue scenes between the two of them, the tiniest capillary changes, re-canalizing the flow of the scenes. They had played together so much that Alfred, who was very musical, knew exactly what he wanted, the tone and the lift of every second, the diminuendo of every suspension.

The opening in San Francisco was fun. I have never enjoyed an out-of-town opening more. When the curtain went up on the nude, recumbent gods, a wave of delight swept over the audience. Alfred, with his long beard, curled golden fillets, looked like the master of the gods; had Jupiter caught sight of him, I am sure that he would have made up to look like him, especially for public appearances. It was a gala evening. In the intermission I heard a decolletéed woman, with a sigh of deep satisfaction, say to her companion: "Well, everybody from Burlingame's here tonight!" A few days later the Langners took me to see the Eugene O'Neills, who were then living not far away. I told them how cooperative our opening-night audience had been. "Oh, yes," O'Neill said, "it's the best audience in the world. They come to enjoy themselves. Singular motive, isn't it?" He confronted Mr. and Mrs. Langner. "I warn you. I don't care what it'll cost you, but from now on you'll have to open all my plays in San Francisco."

The play opened in New York at the Shubert Theatre. Following my by-this-time rule, I didn't go to the opening. It was easy not to go; I knew it couldn't possibly come up to the San Francisco opening. Giraudoux, who had a high post in the French Foreign Office, was on a world tour in his official capacity. He was, luckily, arriving next day. I was to take him to the theatre and introduce him to the Lunts. Giraudoux was tall, lean, and had a narrow face with keen eyes. He was courteous but, somehow, formidable. His play had run for a year in Paris, in a tiny theatre with about three hundred seats. I walked him into the auditorium of the Shubert, which was packed. I could see that he was astonished by the vastness of the theatre and by the crowd. "It's a large room," he said. We stood at the back and watched the stage for a few minutes. "Is there another room upstairs?" I said there was indeed and walked him up to the balcony, also packed. I could see that he couldn't resist the fascination of the packed, suspended other room. I watched him. He edged cautiously down the outer aisle till he came opposite the first row. From there he could see both rooms and their occupants. He ran up the steps to rejoin me. He looked disturbed, tense, unhappy. I asked him what was the matter. His English was not

THE THEATRE GUILD presents the

ALFRED LUNT & LYNN FONTANNE

PRODUCTION OF GIRAUDOUX'S COMEDY

AMPHITRYON 38

ADAPTED BY S. N. BEHRMAN

The Lunts in *Amphitryon*

at the ready. I wondered about this because I knew that he had, in his youth, been to Harvard. He asked me what I thought the receipts at the theatre would come to this week. I told him, $24,000, which was capacity for the Shubert at the then price scale. He looked horrified. He computed it in francs. *"Mais,"* he said, *"c'est astronomique, c'est . . . !"* It must have come to millions in francs. It sounded like it; I had never heard so many francs. He looked woebegone.

"But," I said, "aren't you pleased?" He shook his head.

"I shall have difficulty with my income tax."

"But you can deduct this trip as an expense."

He shook his head, looking sadder than ever. He sighed.

"Unfortunately," he said, "my expenses are paid by the State."

Amphitryon 38 is an ideal comedy. Alkmena's husband, the General, whom she adores, is the square of all time, the essence of squares; you could use him to compute the square root of anything. Having just issued a peace proclamation, Amphitryon goes off to war. He explains to Alkmena how he has achieved his reputation as a conqueror:

AMPHITRYON

Well, first of all I surround their left wing with my right wing, then I divide their right wing — using only three quarters of my left wing — and then with the remaining quarter of my left wing I dart in among them —

ALKMENA

I see. A kind of battle of the birds.

AMPHITRYON

. . . And that gives me the victory.

ALKMENA

How many victories have you won?

AMPHITRYON

One, just one.

ALKMENA

Well, tell me, Amphitryon, have you killed many men?

AMPHITRYON

One, only one.

ALKMENA

How economical you are, dear. Was he a king? Was he a general?

AMPHITRYON

No, he was a simple soldier.

ALKMENA

So modest — modest to a fault, my dear. Tell me, did you, in the process of his destruction, did you allow him one instant in which to recognize you and be aware of the distinction you had just conferred on him? Did you, sweetheart?

AMPHITRYON

Yes, I did. Blood pouring from his mouth, he looked up at me and managed, with his last breath, a faint respectful smile.

ALKMENA

He must have been very happy! Did he tell you his name before he died?

AMPHITRYON

He was an anonymous soldier — there are quite a few of them.

ALKMENA

I see! You know, darling, when you breathe, your armor loosens at the fastenings, and your tunic gives your skin a tint of dawn. Breathe, Amphitryon, breathe — deeply — and let me savor, in the darkness of this night, the glow of your body. Stay a little longer (*presses closely to him*). Do you love me?

AMPHITRYON

Yes. I have to wait for my horses anyway.

On its surface, Amphitryon is a sex comedy; you never know whether Jupiter has slept with Alkmena or not since he could have done so without her knowing it. But he is human enough not to want to do it without her knowing it. Farce is heartless; comedy knows all, feels all, understands all. It is a hairsbreadth removed from tragedy, not the tragedy of death but the abiding one of life. In the last act Alkmena, the mortal, and Jupiter, the god, are sitting cozily on a sofa, talking things over. Jupiter has been making her large promises: clairvoyance, forgetfulness, happiness.

JUPITER

I shall obliterate the past; shall I also reveal to you your future?

ALKMENA

No! No!

JUPITER

It will be a happy one, believe me.

ALKMENA

I know what a happy future consists of. My beloved husband will live and die. My dear son will be born and live and die. I shall live and die.

JUPITER

Since I cannot share your mortal life with you, will you not, for an instant, share the life of the gods? Since your whole past is about to sink into oblivion, do you not wish to see, in one flash of clarity, the whole world — past, present and future — and to comprehend its meaning?

ALKMENA

No, no. I'm not curious.

JUPITER

Do you not wish to see humanity at its labors, from its birth to its final dissolution? Do you not wish to see the eleven great beings who will constitute the finest ornaments in history: one, with his lovely Jewish face; another with her little nose from Lorraine?

ALKMENA

(*tempted for a moment, sighs*) No! No!

JUPITER

And since you are about to forget everything, do you not wish to understand the illusions that constitute your virtue and your happiness?

ALKMENA

No. — No.

JUPITER

Nor, at this last moment, what I really am to you?

ALKMENA

No — forgetfulness, Jupiter; I beg of you — forgetfulness —

JUPITER

And I beg you, Alkmena; do not abandon me; do not leave me with nothing on my hands but my divinity.

ALKMENA

I must — as you must abandon me to my humanity.

This play requires from the actress who plays Alkmena the rarest of qualities: radiance. Miss Fontanne had it.

VII

"Everyone Sang"

REHEARSALS of *The Second Man* in London were starting earlier
than originally planned. I had got a letter from Dame Nellie
Burton telling me regretfully that she couldn't put me up at 40 Half
Moon Street just then because she was full up. At the same time I got
a call from Carl Brandt telling me that he had taken a little house in
London and that I would be welcome to stay in it as he would be
traveling on the Continent. He invited me to lunch with him at the
Century Club. The Negro waiter seemed to be a great friend of Carl's.
I remarked on this. "Oh," said Carl, "a year ago I returned from
Europe and found Jim gone. I was desolate. I inquired. They told me
he'd gone to the University Club, probably because he had been offered
more money. Well, one day to my joy, here he was back again. I said
'What's the matter, Jim? Didn't you like it at the University Club?'
'Well, I'll tell you, Mr. Brandt,' said Jim, 'I found the conversation
over there kinda triflin'.' "

Carl and I exchanged travel notes. He was leaving for London too,
in fact that night. I was leaving on the *Mauretania* a week later. He
had taken a charming little house in Chester Place and had to leave for
Berlin on the day of my arrival. He offered me the little house for the
ten days he would be away.

"It will give you a chance," he said, "to have a look around and
decide where you really want to stay." I accepted his offer.

My last week in New York was hectically crowded between casting
ideas for *Meteor* and *Serena Blandish*. The casting of the main part of

Serena was still unsettled, and Miss Helburn told me that the directors to whom she had offered *Meteor* were not enthusiastic about it. There were endless discussions about these two plays. It was also a time of party-giving, even costume parties. I went to one given by Pauline and Elza Heifetz, the sisters of the violinist Jascha Heifetz. I had been introduced to the Heifetz family by my friend, Samuel Chotzinoff, at that moment Heifetz's accompanist. The Heifetzes were an entrancing family. The dominating figure was the mother, Anna Heifetz. She was a large, handsome woman, who had piloted the whole family to this country from St. Petersburg. Jews were not allowed to live in St. Petersburg, but Mrs. Heifetz got a special dispensation for the family because her son was enrolled in the Royal Conservatory of Music — the star pupil of the famous violin master Leopold Auer. Recalling those early days when Jascha was in the Conservatory, Mrs. Heifetz told a story about his having been ill. She put him to bed for a few days. Another pupil asked to see him. The boy came to the bed where Jascha was lying and made a sudden request: "I want to see his feet," he said. Curious about what was in the boy's mind, Mrs. Heifetz lifted the blankets and revealed her son's feet. "Why," the boy exclaimed, "they're just ordinary feet!" "What did you expect?" Mrs. Heifetz asked. "I thought he would have gold feet," said the disillusioned visitor.

Mrs. Heifetz's husband, Reuven, was a violinist and Jascha's first teacher. He was also an unhappy character in a perpetual state of resentment. He disapproved of his daughters' plastering their lips with cosmetics. He objected to his wife's spending money, from his point of view, unnecessarily. He didn't think that America gave enough thought to the violin. He would stand in the wings at Carnegie Hall and give last-minute advice to his impassive son: "Jaschinka, don't forget what I told you about the second finger."

Jascha had by then played innumerable concerts in Russia, Europe and America, and was an established phenomenon. He said one day to an American newspaperman: "I've made my own living and supported my family from the time I was six years old." "I suppose," said the newspaperman, "that up to then you were just a parasite."

Anna Heifetz was a remarkable woman — hardheaded, detached,

unsentimental, but she was full of humor and fun. When she dressed up to go to concerts or to the opera, she looked like a duchess, or the way a duchess might like to look. Her daughters captivated the town. Pauline, as the eldest, came in for most of this attention. Alexander Woollcott was crazy about Pauline's tawny complexion. Many young men strove to take her out. She said afterwards that they always took her to prizefights and football games — things she was not really very interested in.

At the Heifetz costume party Jascha was a complete and dashing Mexican officer, Alexander Woollcott a somewhat excessive cardinal, Charlie MacArthur a Parisian taxi driver, George Gershwin an Italian diplomat, Helen Hayes a little schoolgirl, which she was. Josef Hofmann sat in a corner telling lewd stories. Hofmann's licentiousness was brought to Mrs. Heifetz's attention. She rose above it. "In my house," she said, "an artist like Hofmann can speak what he wants to speak."

I arrived at 43 Chester Terrace just as Carl Brandt was leaving by train for Berlin. He introduced me to Miss Abbott, a spinster of about fifty, who would do for me. I should be, he assured her, much less trouble than he was. I was quieter. Miss Abbott received this information with a bobbing skepticism. I found myself alone in the drawing room and in an armchair in front of the fireplace. It was a tiny room with a tiny fireplace in what seemed to me the tiniest house I had ever seen. The fire took itself very seriously; it crackled and fumed as if its responsibilities were too much for it. Outside of these flourishes the house was perfectly still. It was heaven. I don't think I have ever been happier than during the days I spent in that midget house. Miss Abbott was part of this perfection. She never spoke; she bobbed and smiled. I called up Siegfried. There was no reply. I thought I'd look in on Miss Burton to see if I could find out about him. I was already so fond of this miniscule house that I hated to leave it. On the sidewalk I took in Chester Terrace. All the houses on it were tiny, demure. I became immediately unfaithful to my first love, Half Moon Street. Nevertheless I went there.

I found Miss Burton in deep conference with Mr. Fleming. I received a rapturous welcome from Miss Burton, laced with lament for being unable to take me in at this time. Mr. Fleming was more reserved; he seemed more lemony than ever. I remembered suddenly that I had not asked Arthur Krock to arrange an appointment with Evangeline Adams for him. I confessed that I had simply, in the stress of things, forgotten to do it. Mr. Fleming was understanding but supposed that it was not yet too late. They asked about my play. When I said that Noel Coward was to be in it they were both enthusiastic. Miss Burton said that she knew and admired Mr. Coward, that he used to come often when Robbie was alive. Siegfried? Burton thought he had gone to Max Gate to be with Thomas Hardy "at the end." She believed that Hardy was dying. The moment of gravity was not allowed to settle. Miss Burton swept it away in personal gossip.

She had been to an astrologer, a marvelous diviner, Miss Victoria Sadee. She meant no disrespect to Miss Evangeline Adams, but she felt herself that Miss Sadee had everything that Miss Adams had, in fact more. The understanding, the penetration of that woman was beyond belief. On Burton's first visit — imagine, her *first* — Miss Sadee had said right out: "Though you are mother to many, you have borne none." "Mr. Fleming could hardly believe it when I told him, is it not so, Edward?"

Mr. Fleming admitted that it had seemed to him remarkable. I conveyed that I was myself quite impressed. Miss Burton went on:

"The wisdom of that woman. 'Though you have lived with many men,' she said, 'you are not immoral.' Truer word was never spoken. I asked her advice: should I marry Siegfried, should I marry Osbert Sitwell? She advised against it. She was firm: 'You are not meant,' she said, 'for double 'arness.' While she was syin' it, I knew it was the truth. In single 'arness I shall remain!"

She crossed her arms and stared defiantly at me to convey that this was her last word on the subject and to impress me with the fact that I must never reopen it in case I should be tempted to ignite Siegfried or Osbert with false hopes.

A maid came in to announce that her mistress was wanted on the telephone. Miss Burton rose at once. "Wouldn't it be a lark if it was

Siegfried?" she said to me as she left the room. I was left alone with Mr. Fleming. He said nothing; neither did I. We sat, congealed in silence. I finally ventured a sally:

"Do you know Chester Terrace," I ventured, "where I am now living?"

"Only by reputation," said Mr. Fleming charily.

I didn't know what to think. Had Carl Brandt been sold a den in iniquity? It couldn't be. That dear little street — those chaste little houses.

Miss Burton returned. She was all smiles. "It *is* Siegfried," she said. "'E 'ad a feeling 'e'd find you here. 'E wants to speak to you. You remember the phone?"

I did indeed. Siegfried sounded very far away. He was at Max Gate. Thomas Hardy had died a few hours before. I gave him my address and telephone number. He didn't know when he'd be returning to London. It depended on Mrs. Hardy. His voice was shadowed, faint. He hung up abruptly. I returned to the parlor. Miss Burton was triumphant.

" 'E was just syin' to me — do you by any chance know — I said I more than know. 'E's right 'ere. It was as simple as that!"

I invited Miss Burton and Mr. Fleming to my first night and got away with becoming speed. From the taxi window I saw the great newspaper hoardings stating that Thomas Hardy was dead. I got back to 43 Chester Terrace. I telephoned Noel. He wanted me to come to the Playhouse Theatre at ten-thirty the next morning to meet the company. He sounded bright and cheerful as ever. I couldn't help contrasting his voice with Siegfried's.

The next morning at the Playhouse Theatre I met the company: Miss Zena Dare, Miss Ursula Jeans, Mr. Raymond Massey and Basil Dean, the director. Noel was in great form. He'd been, the night before, to the Pantomime and he did an imitation of Miss Florrie Ford, the principal "boy." He described her: beyond middle age, corpulent and with a garish voice and a garish smile. He became Miss Ford; he became the principal boy. He sang Miss Ford's song: "If your fyce wants to smile well LET IT."

Miss Ford's smile was cosmic. Noel "let it" amply before all of us.

Basil Dean had to exert authority to get his little company going on to the reading of the play. I was struck by the fact that there was no aspect of the theatre that didn't vitally interest Noel; Florrie Ford and the Pantomime, as much as Shaw or Shakespeare. Anything theatrical engrossed him. I went out front to listen to the first reading. They went so lickety-split in some of the dialogue that I couldn't understand them; it was like listening to a play in a foreign language. Noel must have felt this because he called out to me: "We're probably going too fast for you but don't worry about the tempo — our audience will understand us." The third act began with Noel reading some pages he had just written, crushing them up and throwing them in the wastebasket while he stigmatized them: "Trash, trash, trash." When he'd read this, he confided to us, "Don't be surprised if there's a little burst of applause when I say that." Noel was referring to the fact that the last two plays of his own in which he had appeared had been booed; they had both been disastrous failures. Presently it was over. I went to lunch with Noel and Mr. Dean.

As I remember now the most serious problem was finding a place to rehearse which was not too cold. Once we rehearsed in a shabby series of rooms over a vegetarian restaurant. It was so bitter cold that I said to Noel: "It would be more appropriate for Owen Davis's *Icebound*." "Quite," said Noel. "I'll suggest it to Dorothy Dickson — she's doing *Icebound*. Nothing fazed Noel. He went through that rehearsal with care and precision, as if the circumstances were idyllic. I invited him over to Chester Terrace. I was sure Miss Abbott would provide a cup of tea. On the way he began questioning me rather seriously about my origins and early background. Was my family rich? I told Noel all and it seemed to provide him with a certain satisfaction. "So you came from the wrong side of the tracks too? With no help from anyone. Good!" I felt that if Noel had found out that my circumstances had been comfortable, he'd have been quite disappointed, as if it would have violated his credo to find that anyone with talent could be well-born.

We sat before the fire talking shop. I asked Noel whether he knew the author of *Serena Blandish*. I'd had a letter from her in which she said nice things about my dramatization.

"Enid Bagnold. Indeed I do. Enchanting creature. You will fall in love with her. She is, unfortunately, at the moment in love with Jed Harris. He went out to the country and read your play aloud to her. He's a very good actor and the reading did the trick. She's on the hook."

"Well, it's not surprising. Jed has great charm when he wants to exert it."

"No, not a bit surprising. But mark my words; it'll be the usual process: first the high temperature — then the rash."

"Have you quarreled with Jed?"

"Not at all. We just don't speak to each other. The truth is, you know, I am harder and more sophisticated than Jed."

"Does he suspect it?"

"I don't think so. What he is bound to learn is that I can go all the way from winsome to determined without change of tempo."

With his unfailing instinct for an exit line, Noel departed, leaving me laughing.

It was the weekend. I spent it reading the tributes to Thomas Hardy in the London papers. On Saturday I got a telegram from Siegfried, asking me to meet him at the Reform Club for dinner on Sunday night. He was changed — thinner and with a look in his eyes that showed a heightened awareness of the pain of life. I had never seen the Reform Club before; its colonnades and staircases were not majestic; they were intimate. Siegfried explained to me that he'd stayed the weekend at Max Gate because Mrs. Hardy had asked him to. She would be busy now with the arrangements for Hardy's funeral in Westminster Abbey. He described Hardy's last day, his last hours, how Siegfried and Mrs. Hardy had taken turns at reading poetry aloud to him — Browning and Fitzgerald. His interest in poetry and literature was unflagging to the end. He insisted on sending his check for dues to the Authors' Society. This was his last chore.

I asked Siegfried how his work was going. He had a poem in the current *Mercury*. Had I seen it? He would send it to me. But I felt that he was under a great strain; he had been finding it a terrific struggle to work, to achieve the solitude necessary for it. There were categories of

Noel Coward

people, he said, who lived for fun. They kept urging him to share their excursions, but he always refused and often with nothing to show for it. He had begun to wonder whether his way of life was not altogether wrong.

We were sitting in the library now. It was very still. He went on about the terrific inner struggle in him — to get work done.

"It's what you want," I said, "you'll get it done."

He began to talk about me.

"You can become a first-rate comedy writer — which the world needs — but can you do it with everybody tearing at you?" He warned me to hoard my time and my energy — to put it into my work. I was touched and flattered that he took me so seriously. I responded by telling him that nothing could prevent his becoming — he already was — a Name in English poetry. When we parted I think we both felt better.

"I've wanted to have this talk with you," he said.

"So did I."

We shook hands on it.

The next day I went to tea at Hyde Park Gate with Enid Bagnold. She was in bed, convalescing from an illness. I met her husband, Sir Roderick Jones, the head of Reuters. Jones apologized for being there, said he wouldn't stay, but that he wanted to meet me too. I tried to make him feel he was not an intruder. Miss Bagnold wondered how I had come upon her book. I couldn't really remember but it had delighted me so I couldn't keep my hands off it. I asked her why she hadn't put her name on it. She said that her father was an army officer, retired, and that he had objected to her publishing it; he was fearful of its effect on the British army and even on Reuters. Jones interjected that he thought Reuters could survive it but his father-in-law didn't think so. Simultaneously with the book, she had also started a baby; they were both finished at the same time. "It was nice," she said, "to produce something that I could claim publicly." But it also amused her to publish her book anonymously. It was fun to go to dinner parties, hear her book discussed with no one suspecting that the author was sitting right there. H. G. Wells, who knew the original *Serena,* had said that the trouble with the universe was that there weren't more girls like Serena in it! At this point Jones left saying that he and his wife were giving a lunch party for me and that we would therefore meet soon again. Enid, relaxed, told me that she was completely fascinated by the theatre, that she actually read plays, counting the words on each page to help her catch the trick of how it was done. She asked me whom I'd like to meet at their luncheon party. As a kind of joke, I recited a list of the great figures in English literature. Enid fixed a place, Sovrani's, a new restaurant on Jermyn Street, and the date, the day after my opening. The next day, lunching at the Ivy, a very handsome, modish woman came to sit at the next table. She looked vaguely familiar. We stared at each other for a few moments, exchanging suspicious glances. When I was sure, I said, "Oh, hello, Lady Jones. It's the first time I've seen you out of bed."

I began receiving, almost daily, books, novels and plays from Elizabeth Bibesco. She was the daughter of the recent Prime Minister, Herbert Asquith, and the wife of Prince Antoine Bibesco. I saw a good deal of both of them. In later life I have come to rail against my ignorance; instead of talking to Bibesco about plays and movie sales, I should have questioned him about Marcel Proust, who was a great friend of his. I now have a handsome edition of Bibesco's correspondence with Proust. But I was plunged too abruptly into this complex and highly sophisticated society. I didn't really know anything about it; I skated along on thin ice as well as I could. Bibesco used to come into my hotel room and question me endlessly about the theatre situation in New York. Once he asked to read *The Second Man*. I gave it to him; he asked me whether I would allow him to make a French adaptation. I said I would. He was excited and happy but I felt somehow that I would never read his adaptation. Elizabeth Bibesco was a wonderful talker and certainly a prolific writer. She talked to me about the arts, her girlhood, which she spent talking with Aldous Huxley and Bertrand Russell, and about American politics, about which she knew a great deal. "My father," she said once, "is very knowledgeable about the political situation in Ohio." I always felt a deep malaise in her, and that her writing and the fluctuations in her brilliant and esoteric conversation led everywhere but to self-satisfaction. She took me to dinner at the Savoy once with her mother, Margot, and her brother, Puffin, later the famous film director. I had read Margot's memoirs in America. She was very pleased that I knew them. Her voice was soft. She had great natural dignity. Puffin had it too; it was only in Elizabeth that I felt pursuit by the furies. Elizabeth's kindness was immeasurable; one wished that she could share in it.

Siegfried gave my social life a steep turn to the left by taking me to Harold Laski's. He lived in a modest little house in Fulham. It was a very gloomy day but gloom was dissipated by Professor Laski's high humor. He was very fond of Siegfried and had given him lifts in his effort to find occupations that took more time than writing poetry. Professor Laski was then in the process of preparing and publishing the *Holmes-Laski Letters,* a correspondence which had been going on for some years. Mrs. Laski teased him about it. Smiling, she said to Siegfried and me: "You should see him when he gets a letter from Justice Holmes. He runs upstairs into his room with it and shuts the door. He's like an undergraduate who's just got a letter from his sweetheart."

Laski, to whom pupils came from all over the world (Nehru and John F. Kennedy, for example) started off by telling me about a countryman of mine. He had him to dinner and after dinner they went into the parlor where we were now sitting. The American asked: "Professor Laski, how do you live?" " 'Well,' I said 'you've had dinner, haven't you? Didn't you have enough?' But that's not what he meant," Laski said. "The son of a great millionaire, he simply couldn't take in the scale, the house, the absence of servants, the general penury." He was very funny about it.

Laski asked Siegfried how he was getting along at the *Daily Herald,* where Siegfried was literary editor. Laski took an incisive interest in everything: in comment on current fetishes, he said: "Give me the price of two dreadnaughts and I'll change the face of England." As the money was not immediately forthcoming, we settled down to less exigent conversation. Laski asked Siegfried to tell us about Hardy's funeral in the Abbey. Siegfried said what he found unforgettable was a meeting between Kipling and Bernard Shaw, who hated each other. Due to an uncertainty in the seating arrangements, they found themselves facing each other. The person in charge ventured an introduction. Kipling's face was purple. He looked at Shaw with aversion. Still he was being introduced. "How do you do, sir?" he managed to sputter out as if he were greeting Lucifer.

"How do you do, sir?" Shaw replied urbanely.

Laski was delighted. He went into a brilliant disquisition on Shaw and Kipling, the Boer War, India, Little England and Big England, the kind of spiral for which the Professor at the London School of Economics was famous. He was capable of beginning a formal lecture on the British Constitution with the sentence: "As a member of a special committee of the London Council, it has been my function to count the attendance at the female lavatories in the British Museum."

Carl Brandt returned and I moved to the Park Lane Hotel. The opening night was January 24. Carl took me to the Garrick Club for dinner; then we went to the Playhouse. We stood at the railing in back of the orchestra. Carl kept rattling the change in his pocket. This was an irritation as it seemed to be in unfair competition with the dialogue. But things went well anyway and there was an enthusiastic reception at the end, especially for Noel. I had had a telegram from him earlier. It read: "Things transcendentally jake. All the best, Noel." They seemed sufficiently jake at curtain time. Carl and I went backstage to Noel's dressing room and witnessed a minor, controlled spat between him and Tallulah Bankhead. The notices next morning were satisfactory. My day book said: "1:00 P.M., lunch Sovrani's — Sir Roderick and Lady Jones." When I read this my heart sank. Why today? How Siegfried would disapprove. Why did I have to make a lunch appointment for today? It was characteristic of me, and having passed sentence, I appeared at Sovrani's at one. In the foyer I saw Jones and Enid with a group of about fourteen people. It was a dreadful moment for me when I realized that Enid had taken seriously my satiric suggestion to invite a roster of stars. I was presented to Arnold Bennett. It was a mercy to meet him. I was fascinated by his seignorial manner of dress. I was reassured by his expression of good humor and rapport and by his stutter. Siegfried had given me an instance of its effectiveness. He had been at a literary evening which included Aldous Huxley and Hilaire Belloc. They were discussing a female novelist whose success was stupendous. They left her not an inch of space to stand on. They comminated her on the grounds of psychology, structure, taste and pretentiousness. They all had their say, eloquently and minutely. When they were all through Bennett, who had not uttered a word, said: "I'll tell you the trouble with that woman. She c-c-c-can't WRITE!"

Bennett said: "I saw your play last night. The first act was all right but then we both know it isn't hard to write a good first act. The second I thought fell off a bit and I was q-q-q-quite p-p-p-pleased. But the third came back a bit and I was quite a-a-a-annoyed." I prayed that I would be sitting next to him and I was.

I knew that he had been on Otto Kahn's yachting trip in the Greek islands. I asked him how that was. He told me: "Well, you know, the minute the party got on board, Mr. Kahn and three others went below and started a bridge game. I don't play so I was left to my own devices, which I didn't mind much. The next morning it was beautiful. I went on deck. We approached an island. I asked the captain what it was. He said Ithaca. My heart missed a beat. There was nobody to look at it. I made my way below. There they were, playing bridge, 'Gentlemen,' I said, 'we are approaching Ithaca!' Mr. Kahn looked up at me for a moment — only a moment — then back to his hand. 'I double,' he said."

During lunch Bennett and I talked mainly about the theatre. Bennett had finished a play about Don Juan. He thought it the best play he had ever written; he couldn't understand the difficulty he had in placing it. He said he would like me to read it. "What people don't seem to understand," he went on, "is that my Don Juan isn't just a chippy chaser; he represents the search for the ideal woman, the perfect woman."

For the rest of the lunch we talked agreeably of this and that. About Siegfried: Bennett loved him. He spoke of his wonderful talent, his courage and his gentleness. Yes, he would rate Siegfried high among his favorites. It was a lifesaver to me to have Bennett beside me. I arranged to read his play. He invited me to Cadogan Square where he was living with Dorothy Cheston, whom he could not marry because his first wife would not give him a divorce. Miss Cheston, he told me, was a very fine actress.

I never was so taken by a man as I was by Arnold Bennett. There was great kindness there, enormous good will, enormous charm and common sense. There was also something very touching; a fatigue in his eyes, a sense that, successful though he was, he still was aware of not having the upper hand in life. I was to see a lot of Bennett for the rest of my stay. It was not till after he died, when I read the excellent biography of him by Reginald Pound, that I realized the stringencies he was under during this very period.

I soon went to Cadogan Square to lunch and met Miss Cheston. She was strikingly handsome but I got the sense from her, which I often get from actresses, that she felt herself the center of interest. She talked all the time; Bennett, whom I had come to see and hear, said very little. She talked mainly about a play in which she had appeared that spring (Bennett had financed it), about the difficulties of it, in rehearsal and in production, and how she had by will, determination and natural skill, brought it off. In summation she said: "I got the notices." In a tired echo, I heard Bennett repeat: "Yes, she got the notices." To this day when I think of Arnold Bennett I hear that tired echo: "Yes, she got the notices."

One thing that forcibly struck me on this visit was the difference between New York and London in what you might call the cultural and social position of the theatre. During the run of *The Second Man*, it seemed to me that the actors' dressing rooms were, after each performance, lively and entertaining social centers where you could meet the most brilliant figures in London society. The actors were casual and accustomed hosts. Of course Noel was rapidly becoming something of a social star himself. He rose on one occasion to the defense of Lady Sibyl Colefax, accused of being a lion-hunter. "I think it's quite marvelous that Sibyl fills her house with artists rather than stuffing it with dull dukes and duchesses." Nevertheless, there were more of the latter stuffing Noel's dressing room than of the former! The actors, themselves, "belonged." Zena Dare, who played Lynn's part in the play, was the daughter-in-law of Viscount-Esher. Harold

Laski had told me about him. Esher, he said, was a man of very great ability and probably closer than anyone, as friend and adviser, to King Edward VII. Raymond Massey was the younger brother of the Governor General of Canada. Ursula Jeans was very pretty and charming and didn't need relatives though she probably had some. I invited Harold Laski to the play one night and looked for him in the lobby in the intermission. He was talking to two tall and assured men in white ties; he presented me to one lord after the other. I didn't catch their names. They continued their conversation. Finally Laski, feeling probably that I was being unduly left out, said to his friends: "Mr. Behrman wrote the play you are watching." One of them looked down at me from his great height and said in the friendliest voice: "I don't believe it." I recovered from this blow sufficiently to go back to see Noel after the performance. In fact, I repeated the incident to Noel and his friends. Noel said: "Lord Whoever's skepticism is quite justified. I have a letter from a Miss Burroughs telling me that she knows perfectly well that I wrote the play mistakenly attributed to you. Quite ingenious." He picked up the letter and read from it. " 'I think you did well not to put your name on it. After the reception of your last two plays, you didn't want to risk another under your own name.' " He put the letter back. "I quite agree with her, don't you? It was clever of me." We all enjoyed this and went on talking. A very pleasant, ruddy-faced, middle-aged bald man came in, accompanied by three ladies. There was a tremor of deference — at least I thought so — but the newcomer put up a restraining hand — at least I thought so. Noel poured drinks for the new guests. The genial stranger plunged into a story about his grandmother: While he was at Eton he had written to his grandmother asking whether she could please send him five pounds for Christmas. He got a peppery letter telling him that he was developing rather expensive tastes. He wrote back and said: "Dear Granny, Please don't bother at all about the five pounds because I've sold your letter to another boy for seven pounds." This seemed to go well with everybody — I couldn't understand it. The gentleman went on; illustrious names cropped up in his conversation. Everybody seemed to hang on his every word. Finally he left and I, for one, was rather pleased. I said to Noel: "Who is that man? He seems to be well connected." At this I thought Noel would have a paroxysm. "Oh, my God," he cried. "Well connected! It's Prince Arthur of Connaught! Queen Victoria was his grandmother."

Thanks to John Balderston this gaffe of mine received international circulation.

As I was going home in a few days, Siegfried wanted me to meet his mother before I left. We drove down to Weirleigh the day before I sailed. We talked in the car about Arnold Bennett. Siegfried adored him; he said that Bennett, busy as he was, would hold up anything to help a friend. I told Siegfried I felt a deep malaise in him. Siegfried had felt it too. It made him sad. The yachts and the complicated, frilled evening shirts, he felt, had perhaps been too much for him. "Isn't it sad," he said, "that writers who, in their youth, break their backs to escape the bourgeoisie, end up by imitating them — at least the wealthy ones." I thought of examples of this at home. We brooded over it. Siegfried had been to see Edmund Gosse. Lady Gosse had died after a happy marriage of fifty years. Siegfried had been afraid to go, felt that he would find Gosse too depressed. Lady Gosse had been a great friend of Siegfried's mother; it was like a death in the family. To Siegfried's surprise he found Gosse in radiant spirits; when he came in, Gosse rose from the sofa where he was lying and greeted Siegfried with Longfellow's line: "The thoughts of youth are long, long thoughts." Siegfried said he was glad to find him in such good spirits. "At my age," Gosse said, "death becomes such a commonplace that you can't take it seriously." Siegfried recalled my visit to him and told him that I had a play at the Playhouse.

"Ah!" he said. "And who is in it?"

Siegfried said Noel Coward.

"Noel Coward! That young man."

Siegfried expressed surprise that Gosse knew him. He imitated very well Gosse's booming voice.

"Certainly I know him," said Gosse. "I met him at dinner at James Barrie's."

"Well," Siegfried asked, "was he nice to you?"

"Nice to me! Why he fluttered round me like a butterfly round an OAK."

"Very Gosse, that," Siegfried added.

Siegfried began to talk about his mother. She was a Thornycroft — a family famous in English history for achievement in the arts and in government. Her brother, Hamo Thornycroft, was an eminent sculptor. Siegfried visited him often and was devoted to him. Next time I came he would bring me to see him. I asked Siegfried about his father. Siegfried had known him, but not for long. The marriage to his mother had broken up early. His father was a vague, exotic figure to him. His grandfather, who came from Bombay, had been a great friend of Edward VII when he was Prince of Wales. On one of his grandfather's visits the Prince took him for a walk on the front at Brighton. Looking at all the bathers, the elder Sassoon said suddenly to the Prince: "Have these women undress." He was shocked at his host's limited prerogative when the Prince said that he couldn't do that. Things, evidently, were better ordered in Bombay.

Siegfried was very conscious of his dual heritage: the Thornycrofts and the Sassoons.

Weirleigh was an enchanting sixteenth-century village. "You should see it in the summertime," Siegfried said. Mrs. Sassoon was sympathetic and gracious. She was very quiet but one felt great reserves of strength in her. She had always wished me to come, she said, ever since Siegfried wrote to her about me from New York. We sat before the fire in the large, beautifully furnished living room. I wondered how a room could manage to be, at the same time, cozy and soberly distinguished. I took it in at leisure. Here was tranquillity. I wondered what it must be like to be born in a house like this and in a village like this and grow up in it. How could you fail to be a poet! I said this to Siegfried. "It's in my own room," he said, "where I did my poetry. Come — I want to show it to you." I followed him down a narrow curved passageway into his simply furnished bedroom. On the desk were neat piles of his poems, written out in his beautiful handwriting and dated. There were copies of all his published works, beginning with the little red *War Poems* — a copy of which he had given me in New York — with a list of all the places where he had read them. "It was a night in April," he said "that a strange thing happened to me. I didn't want to go to bed. I was too restless — but there was nothing else to do. I had done no work that day — just idled it away and that depressed me. Then the odd occurrence — I *heard* 'Everyone Sang.' I sat down at that desk and wrote it out — as if from dictation. It is the most widely anthologized of my poems."

I knew the poem — a jubilation for the end of the First World War. Siegfried, rapt, was reciting from memory:

> *"Everyone suddenly burst out singing;*
> *And I was filled with such delight*
> *As prisoned birds must find in freedom*
> *Winging wildly across the white*
> *Orchards and dark green fields; on; on; and out of sight.*

> *"Everyone's voice was suddenly lifted,*
> *And beauty came like the setting sun.*
> *My heart was shaken with tears and horror*
> *Drifted away . . . O but every one*
> *Was a bird; and the song was wordless; the singing will*
>   *never be done."*

When he'd finished, he said: "Just like that. I wrote it down like that and never changed a word of it."

We were called into the dining room. Dinner was rather a trial. Siegfried had become somewhat abstracted. I thought he was still hearing his poem — dictated by an unseen amanuensis — or was he listening to a new one? Mrs. Sassoon seemed to be interested in our New York days and I told her how narrowly, on several occasions, Siegfried had escaped getting arrested for stealing things out of hotels and his destructive effect on taxicabs. While I was talking, Siegfried's face grew darker and darker. I felt some sort of tension between him and his mother, the tension of great love but incomplete understanding. I asked Mrs. Sassoon whether she knew Burton. "Indeed I do," she said. "I dote on her. Such a refreshing personality, don't you think?"

Dinner ended finally; at ten o'clock we left. Mrs. Sassoon asked me please to come again when I returned. Actually I felt — I don't know

what gave me the feeling — that this particular visit was not successful. In the car on the way back to London, Siegfried's dark mood
intensified.

"Mother liked you very much," he said. "She made me promise to
bring you back."

"I don't feel it was a successful visit," I said. "It seems to have
depressed you."

"It's all those New York stories."

"Why?"

"They remind me of something that you don't know — that I never
told you."

"What?"

He didn't answer. He was driving. His eyes were intently on the
road though there was very little traffic.

His answer, when finally it came, startled me.

"Edna Millay," he said. "You remember my meeting with Edna
Millay?"

"Of course," I said, "at her play."

"Yes, but you know I saw her several times after that."

"I know you enjoyed seeing her."

"I did. I liked her very much."

My mind raced. What could have happened?

There was an immense interval before Siegfried said anything more.
We were approaching London. Siegfried went on.

"A friend of mine told me . . . someone was praising my war
poems — perhaps excessively. Miss Millay said . . . 'Yes, yes, I
agree. But I wonder whether he would have cared so much if it were a
thousand virgins who had been slaughtered.'"

"I don't believe she said it."

"She did." There was a pause. His cheek muscles were twitching.
He was suffering.

"What's the use?" He added, "What can one do?"

Did he mean against the concentrated malice and venom of the
world? — of even a fellow poet — a nice creature like Edna Millay?

"It couldn't have meant much to you," I got out finally, "or you'd
have told me."

"It meant so much to me that I didn't tell you. It all came back while you were telling those stories at dinner."

We drew up before the Park Lane.

"I'll call you in the morning," he said. "Good night."

"Good night, Siegfried," I said.

He shook my hand. My heart ached for him.

I went upstairs to my room. I sat on the bed thinking of him. Everyone sang, I thought, except the poet.

VIII

The Cloven Hoof

SERENA finally went into rehearsal, and in January 1929 we all embarked for Philadelphia where we were to open at the Broad Street Theatre. I don't think that ever again has the offstage scenario been so intense, so complicated and so unsolvable, as in this production. It was a never-ending vortex of misunderstandings which engendered lifelong enmities. The end result was a succès d'estime, a category that fits George Kaufman's famous definition of satire — something which closes on Saturday night. Though it was written about beautifully by Brooks Atkinson in the *Times, Serena* was not a success. The preliminaries before we left for Philadelphia were pleasant. Jed had engaged Richard Burton to direct and the cast was superlative. I enjoyed very much talking to Constance Collier. She was looked up to by most actresses as the high priestess of stage deportment and speech. She knew everybody in London and Hollywood and was fun to talk to. Had I known that she was once engaged to marry Max Beerbohm, I should have certainly pursued her more assiduously. But I didn't know. When, eventually, I came to write about Max, I asked Constance what had happened to their engagement. She said, "Oh, well, the manager sent me on tour with a very handsome leading man and you know how things are in Manchester."

It was then the custom of the *Times* to print one out-of-town review of incoming shows. For Philadelphia the *Times* used the *Inquirer* and George Kaufman, who was at that time drama editor, had no choice but to print the *Inquirer*'s review of *Serena*. It was less than favorable; the other reviews were good. That George should print the less favorable review made Jed furious, and in a frenzy of anger he wrote George a shaming letter attacking his domestic life. George, understandably, never forgave Jed for this. Many years later, embroiled with a pair of musical comedy producers who were famous and successful, he described them to me as "Jed Harris rolled into one."

The antagonist who handled Jed better than anybody was the English actor A. E. Matthews. He was well established in London as a high comedian; he had been playing assured English gentlemen for so many years that he had come to believe himself to be one — indeed he acted like one. For *Serena* he had been engaged to play an imperturbable English butler. Uncomfortable in the part, he wanted to give it up. Jed decided to take him in hand and began to coach him. "Just what Shakespeare did for Burbage," he told Matty.

Matty never contradicted Jed; he simply ignored him. I had the feeling that somewhere in the back of his mind Matty wondered why he, who had been so many top-drawer Englishmen, should pay much attention to Jed, manifestly non-U. Jed, exacerbated already by George Kaufman, finally let go at Matty. In front of the whole company, gathered on the stage, Jed began to denounce him. Matty looked at Jed in wonderment for a moment, trying to figure out whom he was denouncing and what he was so excited about. Then he took up his walking stick and began an elaborate and intense game of golf to pass the time. Matty took so much care with his shots that we began to share his anxiety about the outcome of the game. Jed lost his audience. The stage of the Broad Street Theatre was a very large one. Matty played himself off it and into the wings. We watched till his final putt, which was impeccable. When he came back on stage modestly satisfied, he got from us a spontaneous hand. Jed remembered then that he had engaged Richard Burton to direct the play. He motioned Burton back on the stage and left the theatre.

By the time we got to New York the mythology of grievance had proliferated in the company. Constance Collier said that Jed called her in her apartment just as she was leaving for the first performance at the Morosco Theatre to tell her she was playing the part all wrong and that she had no equipment for it in the first place. Whether Jed did or didn't, he had created an atmosphere in which Constance felt he might have said anything. L'affaire Collier took precedence over such trivial matters as whether the play had gotten over, which actually it never did. It was as if a rivalry had developed in the company — which was large — to see who had suffered the most scarifying wound; I feel that Constance's first-night story gave her the happy feeling that she was well ahead, with a margin. I have often thought that the rivalry kept Jed alive too. He was, obviously, intensely theatrical.

One agreeable memory prevails. We were lucky enough to get the ideal actor to play the part of Lord Ivor Cream. This was Henry Daniell. He had the most extraordinary good looks and a naturally melancholy temperament which suited him ideally to play this disillusioned character. Several times during the New York run I dropped in at the Morosco to catch the seduction scene between Ruth Gordon and Henry Daniell. On one of these occasions I ran into Noel Coward, who said that it was the most perfectly staged and acted scene he had ever seen. It was pleasurable to watch.

Serena Blandish was my second play. I began to dramatize it after *The Second Man* opened, while it was running, in fact. I was far too inexperienced to see the enormous, unsurpassable difficulties presented by it. The Guild, far shrewder, did see, and rejected it. Jed Harris, in the full tide of success, could not imagine that anything he would do would fail; this is a form of imagination that must be acquired early by anyone who consigns his life to the theatre. Jed was attracted by the strangeness of the play and the fact that the role of Serena seemed to him to offer an opportunity for Ruth Gordon. I was beguiled by the vivacity and humor with which the novel was written. Many years later Harold Freedman told me that he was sitting beside Gilbert Miller at the opening performance of my play *Biography* in Princeton. At one point Miller whispered to him: "I feel the cloven hoof of literature here." The cloven hoof was all over *Serena*. Maybe that is why it failed. When I went backstage to see Constance Collier the room was full of her friends, thick with an atmosphere of euphoria. Constance embraced me. "You realize, don't you, that you have a world success!" I didn't know about the world; what worried me was New York. I felt that at no point had the play seized the audience. I went home and to bed, depressed and unhappy.

IX
Wit's End

I T HAD never happened to me before and has not since, but the mere first stage direction of a play called *Brief Moment* brought me a spectacular nonactor. I wrote:

AT RISE: *We discover Roderick Dean and his friend, Harold Sigrift, familiarly known as Sig. Sigrift is very fat; about thirty years old, he lies down whenever possible, spouting acrid remarks. He somewhat resembles Alexander Woollcott, who conceivably might play him.*

I had discussed the play with Guthrie McClintic, who'd read it act by act and busied himself with casting it. Sig was a juicy part and Guthrie had some likely possibilities for it. One of them I particularly liked and Guthrie was what is known as "keeping in touch" with this actor, having exacted from him the promise not to sign up with anyone else without consulting him. He was a well-known comedian with the proper dimensions. A few days after our discussion, Guthrie called me.

"I've got our Sig," he said.

"Oh, good," I said. "You've signed him, have you? He'll be fine." I was referring, of course, to the actor he'd been tantalizing.

"Didn't give it to him. Woollcott's going to play it."

I was sure Guthrie had been drinking.

"You're not serious!"

"I certainly am. So is Woollcott."

Woollcott was then one of the busiest nonactors in the country. He was writing a column for the *New Yorker,* "Shouts and Murmurs," and was immensely popular as a radio prima donna, the Town Crier. He had made himself into a national figure. As an illustration: I had been, some time before, in a hospital in Baltimore for a checkup. Woollcott was in Baltimore. He telephoned the hospital to tell them that he would be up to see me at three in the afternoon. About an hour after this portentous announcement, a nurse came in with a basket full of magnificent apples. I asked who on earth had sent them. The nurse said: "Mrs. Kimberly." I said I knew no Mrs. Kimberly. The nurse said: "She told me she didn't know you, but she heard that Mr. Woollcott is coming up to see you and she says that any friend of Alexander Woollcott can have all the apples she's got."

I persisted in my disbelief in Guthrie's announcement.

"How could Aleck do it possibly? How's he going to give up . . . ?"

"He won't give up anything. But he'll do it. Don't you know he's a frustrated actor?"

Guthrie was laughing. He was triumphant. I was the more surprised because Aleck and Guthrie hadn't been talking to each other lately. When I told Aleck that Guthrie was going to produce my play, he scoffed: "You can have him. I wouldn't even go on a picnic with him!" I also knew that he was working on a profile of McClintic for the *New Yorker* to be called "The Tyranny of the Tantrum."

It was all rather startling. But when I came to think it over, it was less so. Aleck may have had his reservations about Guthrie but he had none about Guthrie's wife, Katharine Cornell, whom he adored. He would at any time, and joyously, have gone on a picnic with her.

The first rehearsal was fun. Aleck took it over. In his coveted milieu at last, he was in wonderful spirits. He congratulated Guthrie on his ability to keep up the appearance of "that vintage boyishness of yours." He made a dedicated effort to treat the star of the show, Francine Larrimore, as an equal. This gallantry did not endure for long. Miss Larrimore, in her program biography, gave her birthplace as Verdun. Aleck took to referring to her as "The Miracle of Verdun." Louis Calhern, also in the cast, Aleck loved. He loved him, he told me, from the moment he heard that Calhern had said after a failure: "Well, we got good notices, but word-of-mouth killed us!" They were inseparable companions, on the road and all through the run of the play. Indeed, Calhern, besides being a beautiful actor, was one of the most engaging men I have ever known. He, Woollcott and I, walking out of the stage door of the Cass in Detroit, were obstructed by a drunk, prone in the alley. Calhern, stepping over the poor man, smiled at us. He pointed to himself: *"Me,* fifteen years from now!"

Happily, in this prophecy, Lou was entirely mistaken. Fifteen years from then he was playing with marvelous élan the Colonel, in the play I did from an idea of Franz Werfel's, *Jacobowsky and the Colonel.*

Aleck used the first rehearsal, and subsequent ones, to exercise his private talent. At one point Miss Larrimore, who was his opponent in the play, had to say:

"Oh, Sig, Sig, if you were a woman what a bitch you would have made!"

Aleck said: "Opening night in New York, you'll get a big hand on that."

The antagonism to Woollcott Miss Larrimore was supposed to feel in the play soon came to be very easy for her to project. It was a stormy tour; Miss Larrimore was on the point of quitting every week. I had to cut lines on which Aleck got big laughs because Miss Larrimore said she couldn't, after them, recapture her mood. Aleck drove Miss Larrimore crazy, but he did me too. He had the maddening habit of saying "And" before every speech. I complained to Guthrie. He begged me to be patient. "He needs it," he said. "It gives him a handle."

On the road Aleck was cosseted by the director, by the press, by the audiences. He defied the billing by knowing himself to be the star. A reporter in Detroit asked him why he was submitting himself to this tour. "Because," Aleck said, "I am an exhibitionist."

I walked into the exhibitionist's room in Pittsburgh. He was in his orchidaceous dressing gown, sprawled in an armchair. On his lap was a pile of galley sheets which he had been correcting till the telephone stopped him. He was talking to the president of the University of Chicago, whom he was fervently exhorting to give up that provincial post and to assume the presidency of Hamilton, Woollcott's alma mater. He seemed to be making headway; it went on and on. I waved good-bye to Aleck and started out. I heard him say into the receiver: "My semiliterate author is here and he seems to have ants in his pants. Let me call you later. Fine." He hung up and addressed himself to me: "Well, my beamish boy, and what troubles you?"

I wanted to say: "Your eternal 'ands' trouble me," but I had been cautioned against it. I sought a moment of neutrality before broaching it.

"Well, Aleck," I said, "I've had very few actors in my plays who switch university presidents around with quite this casualness."

"You're damn right," he said. "And you've had mighty few actors in your plays who correct *Atlantic Monthly* proofs with an eyebrow pencil!"

Aleck took the job of acting very seriously. He knew that he wasn't really up to it. The extra "ands" at the beginning of each sentence came in for criticism. He promised to abandon them and meant to but he didn't. He couldn't. He sought the "secret" of acting as earlier fantasists sought for the Fountain of Youth. He found it finally and this led to the first rift between him and Calhern.

The revelation happened on a Sunday night when Aleck was able to go to see the Lunts at a benefit performance. He had, of course, seen them innumerable times; they were great friends of his; but now, a fellow technician, he observed them with a new eye. So, watching, he grasped the secret. He called me between the acts, alight with discovery. He shouted the miracle through the telephone. "I see it all," he cried, "I've been all wrong with my approach, been working too hard. Lynn and Alfred — they make no effort at all. *They throw it away.*" Aleck was as elated as Archimedes in the tub. He called Calhern when he got home and shouted eureka at him. Calhern was pleased and congratulated him, just as I had done. It was of course true that the Lunts could whisper and be perfectly audible in the last row of the second balcony. Aleck just couldn't wait to practice his new discovery.

The next night Guthrie and I got frantic calls after the first act from Calhern imploring us to come to the theatre at once. Lou was in a fury.

"Goddamn it," he shouted, "Aleck is throwing it away to such an extent that *I can't hear my cues!*"

Aleck, who had expected to wow everybody with his new technique, sulked. It was especially painful to him that Calhern sulked harder. But, with time, he was persuaded to return to the bourgeois virtue he did have, audibility. Life resumed its normal course. The play ran though it didn't succeed. Woollcott kept it going. It was pleasant to drop into Aleck's dressing room after the play to jabber with Aleck's friends. They were soirées, Aleck said modestly, comparable to Sir Henry Irving's after-the-play parties at the Lyceum in London. The atmosphere was so genial that one night I talked too much, without thinking ahead, something you are very likely to do when you talk too much.

I had, not long before, made a short visit to Hollywood. I had gone to Goldwyn's for a Sunday beach party. Chaplin was there and doing uncanny imitations of Miss Slade, Gandhi's companion, who had the extraordinary capacity when she greeted you of advancing and withdrawing simultaneously. Chaplin said he didn't know how she did it, but he did it. He did an imitation of Sir Philip Sassoon, very English, very rapid, a Roman candle of speech, but darting out from it, every few seconds, hooded, viperish — the word "succulent." You knew that Sassoon existed in order to find things succulent. If you'd dropped in that afternoon from Mars and didn't know who Chaplin was, you'd have known that he was a genius. But I am taking a long time to get to the disgraceful point of my story. Groucho Marx was there with his then wife, a very pretty Polish girl. After Chaplin left, the party, now without focus, became what such parties usually are, noisy, airless and gnawingly talkative. Everybody talked without stopping and without saying anything. Except Mrs. Groucho Marx. She never said a word, just listened and smiled. I sat beside her. It was a great relief. By the time the party ended, I really adored Ruth Marx. She said she was going to be in New York in a week or two to see some shows. I said if she would call me I would take her to any show she liked. I gave her my number.

The day came. Mrs. Marx called. I asked her what she would like to see, thinking it would certainly be some big musical. To my surprise she said *Mourning Becomes Electra.* I had of course meant to see it but had not yet gotten around to it. You had to give up your life to it — for that day anyway. It started at five, you were released for dinner at six-thirty, and had to be back by eight. I called the Guild and got the house seats. I met Ruth in front of the theatre. We saw the first part, went to dinner, and were in our seats in good time for the second part.

Ruth had not said much at Goldwyn's nor did she say much at O'Neill's, but she watched the stage, the unfolding crimes and perversions and deaths, with tremendous interest. I saw her pretty little profile, the little retroussé nose, watching, listening. I felt that the play totally absorbed her. Finally, the last great scene came, between the two surviving characters. Ruth spoke. Behind her hand she whispered to me:

"Tell me — do they have kitchenettes at the Beverly Wilshire?"

I took Ruth to her hotel. She was profuse in thanks; never had she had such an "experience." I kept the cab and made it to Woollcott's salon at the Belasco Theatre. I had on a dinner jacket and Woollcott inquired. I told him about Ruth and her extracurricular question at *Mourning Becomes Electra.* It was very stupid of me; I should have known, but it never occurred to me, that Aleck would use it. It appeared in his next *New Yorker* column. I didn't feel any better when I was told what Groucho said to Ruth when he read it:

"Now the whole world knows how dumb you are instead of just you and me!"

Woollcott's crowning achievement was to come. It was not in the realm of acting; it was in the realm of money. With summer the play moved to another theatre. Everybody, including myself, took a cut. But Woollcott got a raise. The glee he felt over this was unbounded. He reveled in it. But perhaps the more lasting effect of the production was that it gave two virtuoso craftsmen — Kaufman and Hart — the impulse to write a classic comedy, *The Man Who Came to Dinner,* which Aleck eventually played. At least they told me so and that is my permanent increment from this play.

* * *

Dorothy Parker suggested to Aleck the name "Wit's End" for his luxurious apartment on East Fifty-second Street. She was intuitive as well as witty. Aleck was delighted. He divined its appropriateness.

One afternoon I got a call from Woollcott. He asked me to come over to Wit's End. "Anything wrong, Aleck?" I asked. "I'll tell you when I see you," he said.

"Tell you what," he said when I got there. "I'm restless. I want to take a trip around the world. Will you come with me?"

"I can't," I said. "I've been asked to go to Hollywood."

"To do what?"

"The film script of *Liliom*."

"What on earth do you want to do that for?"

I wanted to say "money," a commodity for which I knew Aleck had considerable respect, but I didn't. His question and his tone irritated me. It was imperialist. He tried to argue me out of it. It would be much more profitable for me, he said, to take this trip with him and start another play; if he liked the idea, we could do it together. I became restive under this pressure.

"My problem," he said, "is to find a companion. I need a companion." I was unnerved by him. One would have said that he had everything in the world that he wanted. He was a national hero on radio. He had great power. He could make or break a book, or a film, or a play. He had a great circle of adoring friends. Did Aleck belong to the great constellation of the wretched? I had begun to think deeply about my relationship to him, what it came to. What did I really feel about him? Knowing him, being part of his entourage was, in a sense, a symbol of arrival. But what else did it symbolize? He was, indeed, as he told reporters on the road tour, an exhibitionist. I remembered a profound characterization of Aleck made by one of his closest friends, Harpo Marx: "Aleck is just a big dreamer," he said, "with a sense of double entry." Aleck lent his name to cigars he didn't smoke, whiskey and cars — to anyone who would pay for the use of his name and photograph. He had come to terms with his fat, with his somewhat grotesque appearance; he had decided to make an asset of both since he was in any case stuck with them. He was impounded in the character he had created for himself; he couldn't escape from it. Not long before I had been a fellow-guest with him at a Long Island weekend. Aleck came down at noon on Sunday, rubbing his hands in glee. He made an announcement to the assembled guests having cocktails before lunch. "Well," he said proudly, "I've had my orgasm for this season!" Everybody laughed. Aleck was living up to himself. I agreed with few of his literary choices; I thought that many of the books he went all out for were mediocre. Moreover, his literary style irritated me: overwrought, veering constantly on the ecstatic. Just at this time the town — the Broadway part of it — was shaken by an all-out attack on him by George Jean Nathan in the *Smart Set*. He called it "The Seidlitz Powder of Times Square." It was a sensation. Nowadays it's common enough for critics to bedevil other critics in public; at that time it was unheard of. Nathan stormed the peak citadel of power, the *New York Times,* and its proprietor, whom he referred to as Mr. de Ochs. (Even in a blast detonated on Forty-third Street Nathan could not forget the *Almanach de Gotha!*) He took the thesis that Mr. de Ochs was a comic spirit bent on outrivaling as a comedian George M. Cohan, whose *The Tavern* — "a lampoon of reason" — was playing across the street from the *Times.* Having already produced a comic masterpiece with the *Times Book Review,* Nathan went on to say, Mr. de Ochs was determined to outdo himself, and he accomplished this by employing Alexander Woollcott to be his drama critic. Nathan slates Woollcott especially for his dithyrambic style:

> I do not set myself bumptiously to say that the *Times'* Hazlitt's estimates are always wrong (it is not a question of their rightness or wrongness; they may often be fully right); the style in which they are expressed is the particular bouquet that I invite you to sniff. This style presents an interesting study. It never strikes a mean; it is either a gravy bomb, a bursting gladiolus, a palpitating missa cantata, an attack of psychic hydrophobia, or a Roman denunciation, unequivocal, oracular, flat and final. . . . Adulatory frenzy over a certain cabotin sweats itself out in such verbiage as "one swoons at" the splendor of this or that performance. A style, in brief, that is purely emotional, and without a trace of the cool reflectiveness and contagious common sense suited to critics.

The fact is that Nathan was as stagestruck as Woollcott was. But the backgrounds of the two men couldn't have been more antipodal. Nathan was urban, rich and traveled; Woollcott was a poor country boy, brought up, as Edmund Wilson pointed out in an article written after Woollcott's death, in a phalanstery in New Jersey and was strongly influenced by Fourierism. Aleck was indeed somewhat frenzied in style and sentimental in judgment but when his frenzy coincided with a madness that was divine — as when he headed his review after the first appearance of the Marx Brothers: "Dancing in the Streets" — the collusion was appropriate.

Many people didn't like Aleck; they said he snubbed them when he met them. Aleck could certainly be cavalier toward people he didn't know on the general assumption that, by his standards, if they were worth knowing, he would already know them. He was also capable of outright cruelty. I knew of an instance where he caused a distinguished woman and her teen-age daughter great travail. Aleck was having tea with this lady in her town house when her daughter came in, an awkward and unsure child with braces on her teeth. The mother introduced her child. Aleck took one look.

"Disaster," he said.

The poor child left the room in a depression which, her mother told me, lasted for some time and which she had difficulty in coping with. The daughter became a distinguished lady herself; her hatred of Woollcott lasted all her life. Woollcott's death was no grief to *her.* Samuel Hopkins Adams provides a brief sketch of Aleck as a boy in school at the phalanstery:

One effect upon his character was to engender venom. As he grew older, he developed a knack of mimicry. He became an inveterate tease. Any physical peculiarity, a club foot, a strabismic eye, a stammering tongue, aroused the evil genius of caricature. At sight of a specially homely girl he would fall off his chair, cover his eyes, and writhe in histrionic agony.

Adams, in his interesting and fair book, also makes the point that Aleck wasn't really interested in plays and playwrights; his real interest was in actors and in performances. As a result the actors flocked around him and venerated him. The Lunts, to prove their loyalty to Woollcott, cancelled their subscription to the *New Yorker* when Wolcott Gibbs's profile of Aleck appeared in it. This, much as I was devoted to the Lunts, got on my nerves. It got on the Lunts' nerves too when they visited Woollcott in Bomoseen some time after their great sacrifice in their hero's behalf, to find the hero reading the *New Yorker* and taking editorial notes on it.

Here I was confronted by Aleck's invitation. I could see that it emanated from loneliness. Although I had grown fond of him and was touched by him, I found myself facing a bleak fact: I didn't like him enough to want to go around the world with him. I felt a pang at having to refuse him. I felt concerned about him. Nevertheless I went to Hollywood. Some months later I had another proposal from Aleck, in a letter. Since he was still planning to go away for a considerable time, he suggested that I take over his apartment to reduce expenses for both of us. He wrote: "As soon as I heard you were coming, I would depart at once, a social experience to which you must be not unaccustomed." I was greatly entertained by Aleck's letter. The shared-apartment scheme didn't work out either.

Gradually our friendship cooled. I saw less and less of Aleck as the years went by. I couldn't live up to his expectations. I couldn't be a companion on order. He died thinking that I didn't appreciate him, that I didn't like him. He was wrong on both counts.

X

"Will We Give You Heaven!"

FROM THE MOMENT *The Second Man* was produced I began getting urgent offers to come to Hollywood. The Industry, as it was called, had been through the chrysalis of revolutionary change — from silence into sound. There were great billboards all over Hollywood blazoning an eccentricity of Greta Garbo's: "GARBO TALKS." It was as if an animal trainer had taught a poodle to converse. One wondered how Miss Garbo had managed before she discovered in herself this special skill. How had she done her marketing or given orders to her servants? On the bosses, like Winfield Sheehan, the revolution had the traditional effect: it panicked them. The Los Angeles suburb, hitherto wrapped in silence, was forced to join the articulate world. The actors were panicked too. They had, up to then, put all their confidence in "titles," flashed on the screen, to tell their audiences what they were feeling. Now they would have to utter these titles themselves, and many of them felt, only too often justifiably, insecure about their ability to project them. For a long time after I began to work in the Hollywood studios, I found that directors and producers, rocking in the warm cradle of atavism, kept referring to whatever dialogue I wrote as "titles." Daniel Blum, in his much-consulted *A Pictorial History of the Talkies*, reproduces a Warner Brothers Vitaphone ad which announces triumphantly: "At Last — Pictures that Talk like Living People!"

131

Sheehan had already tried to entice me out West with the offer to work on the popular novel *Rebecca of Sunnybrook Farm.* It is a charming book, but as for a good length the heroine is in love with a toad and as I did not see how I could make the toad articulate, I turned it down. Sheehan thought this was improvident of me because Rebecca was to be played by his big star, Janet Gaynor. Now he was after me to transfer to the screen Molnár's *Liliom,* a play of considerable quality, which had been a great success at the Theatre Guild. It later served Rodgers and Hammerstein as the libretto for their great success *Carousel.* Moreover, Winnie had told Harold Freedman that he wished me to sign a six-month contract, at $1,250 a week, then and there, or he would get someone else. I was in a strangulatory dilemma. I had, up to then, tried to follow Bernard Shaw's advice to young playwrights: "Build up your repertory." That meant: "Go on writing plays and don't be diverted by brummagem side offers. If you write one good play it will help support you in your old age." Several years ago, forty years after the play was first produced, I got a check for eight hundred dollars, for a tour of *The Second Man* in Finland. I have come to realize the soundness of Shaw's advice, but to adhere to it required two qualities, in both of which I was deficient: courage and self-belief. At that time all I knew was that I had written two plays since *The Second Man* and that neither of them had been successful. In a time of drought it is scarcely possible to imagine a time of efflorescence.

I consulted a friend of mine, the playwright Arthur Richman, who had much experience of Hollywood. He told me that a six-month offer was merely an introductory offer; that I could never possibly get through in six months; that I might consider that I was through but that no one else would agree with me. He told me to put a heavy price on overtime. I spoke to Freedman about it and he added to the contract a provision that I was to get $2,000 a week for time required beyond the six months. Richman said: "They'll be happier with you at $2,000 than at $1,250. They don't really believe that a writer they can get for $1,250 can be much good."

The night before my crucial lunch-date with Sheehan I couldn't sleep, racked by indecision. Should I make this change? There was the money. I hadn't made much out of *The Second Man*, the Lunts had stayed in it only seven weeks. The receipts for the rest of that summer were greatly reduced; the houses were full of cut-rate tickets. The few hours of an opening night could demolish years of work. It was quite possible — in fact it was quite likely — that I would never write another successful play. Here was Winnie Sheehan offering me a trip to the Coast. I loved trains. I loved travel. Frederick Jackson Turner's book, *The Frontier in American History*, had pointed out how focal the Frontier was in American history. I would cross these frontiers. I would cross the Mississippi. I was torn between the desire to see the Mississippi and the urge to go back to Woodstock, Vermont, sit myself down at the bridge table in Room 202, and get involved again in the tense, warm claustrophobia of a new play. The next day I went to lunch with Sheehan in his suite at the St. Regis.

I had picked up tidbits of information about Sheehan, some of them unsavory. He was shortish, fair, with glassy, somewhat protuberant blue eyes. The head of a great company, he was benign and assured. We talked about *Liliom*. He said that at the moment of buying it he thought of me to do the screenplay. When I spoke of the difficulty of transplanting Liliom to heaven, he laughed it off. "Will we give you Heaven!" he said, brushing it aside as a difficulty, welcoming it as a glorious opportunity to display the resources of the Fox Film Corporation. In those days, the film magnates all talked that way. They controlled the earth and all the firmaments. While listening to him expound about how he would provide and furnish Heaven, I was reminded of a story I had heard about him: how he had handled an obstacle during his last marriage which showed the resolution he could summon in a crisis. He and his wife lived in an apartment in the Savoy-Plaza, furnished by themselves. He had asked for a separation agreement from his wife, which she was reluctant to grant. He sent her off on a Saturday afternoon to see a movie. He set to work with a team of movers to whom he was paying double time to unfurnish his furnished apartment. When Mrs. Sheehan returned from the movie there wasn't a stick of anything left in the apartment. She couldn't help but admire the speed and thoroughness of the job. The separation agreement followed quickly and then the divorce — whereupon Winnie promptly married Maria Jeritza, the famous opera diva. As he was tone-deaf, this marriage showed signs of promise. There were less urbane anecdotes about Winnie; as private secretary to Police Commissioner Waldo he looked with a tolerant eye on violations of the fire laws by the Fox theatre chain. For this openness of mind he was rewarded, after the legal difficulties were resolved, with the artistic headship of Fox Film Corporation. Some people thought he had been overtipped.

Winnie had just returned from abroad and he was pleased to be able to tell me that in Vienna he had engaged Leo Fall to write the score for *Liliom.* This did entice me. I knew Leo Fall's music through Oscar Levant, who never tired of playing the score of *Madame Pompadour* for me. I never tired of it either; it was a most beguiling score. Well —there was Leo Fall. Winnie went on: Frank Borzage would direct. He had directed the great Fox success *Seventh Heaven.* Moreover, he would give me the stars of that very film, Janet Gaynor and Charles Farrell. He made everything sound like a cornucopia which he had gone to great pains to store especially for me. Of course he did not omit the clincher: that I would be writing for the world (he included the universe in a gesture) instead of for a few scattered provincials in New York. He shook from the cornucopia another tidbit: Sonya Levien, a skilled scenarist whom all writers loved. He would put Miss Levien to work with me on *Liliom.* Of course I'd heard most of these arguments before but I did like the idea of Leo Fall.

He gave the cornucopia an additional shake. "I've ordered our transportation man to reserve a compartment for you on Monday on the Century and the Chief." I knew that the luxury of transportation was a preliminary bait. There was even a status symbol in the offered transportation, whether you got a drawing room, a compartment, or just a berth. He had another piece of information which he regretted to have to tell me. He had hoped to produce *Liliom* himself, he was so crazy about it, to make it his personal production, but circumstances over which he had no control made that impossible. He had to remain in New York for conferences with bankers as there was a depression impending. But I was to rest assured; the picture would be taken over, as indeed all production at Fox Film Corporation, by his assistant, Mr. Sol Wurtzel, a man in whom he reposed the greatest confidence, very able, very sophisticated, very hep. I was sure that a man who had won Winnie's confidence to that extent must be an ideal producer to work for.

Winnie asked whether I could arrange for him to meet the Lunts; they were then appearing in my play *Meteor*. I said that of course I could, any time he liked. Winnie wished to propose to them to come out West to do a film. I arranged for him to come the following night.

I have always been a collector of enigmatic remarks and all I remember of the occasion is a remark which Winnie made. I met him in the intermission after the second act. He had a lovely young girl with him. He introduced me and then took me aside for a moment. He looked quite anxious. He whispered: "May I take my friend back to meet the Lunts?" "Of course," I said. "Why not?" Winnie was relieved. "You see," he said, "she's not a professional. She's from Texas."

For thirty-seven years I have been trying to align this dichotomy. No dice.

In the flurry of the next few days, before I started crossing frontiers, I thought, with a sinking of the heart, about Hilda. I had neglected her; the busy have less time for the unhappy. She had finally divorced Gaige and had married again — to the consternation of her friends — a man whom she had known for only a short time. This marriage seemed not to be going well either. I called and told her I was going to Hollywood for at least six months and asked her to dinner. She said, "Fine," that she had been wondering when she was going to hear from me. I asked whether things were any better with her. "They're worse," she replied promptly. I had hoped to hear better news. At dinner she told me that her marriage was a complete disaster. There was nothing to do about it — she had made a sorry mistake, that's all. She was faced by an economic problem. She was penniless. Had she seen Gaige? She'd spoken to him but hadn't seen him. He couldn't help her in any case. He was hard up himself. In fact, he was working for the chief steward at the Waldorf-Astoria, putting his knowledge of food and wines to good use. But what was frightening, she said, was that he had turned fascist and anti-Semitic. She was, at the moment, trying to put her own taste in furniture to good use. She had gone into partnership with an old friend, Ruth Saylor, to start a decorating business. Mrs. Saylor was trying to raise initial capital. She had many well-placed friends, but so far things were going slowly.

She looked at me with her great blue-green eyes.

"Hilda," I said, "do you remember how you always used to say to me — when I was living in a rathole, how you used to encourage me, how you used to prophesy that I would do well and that you would find me a pleasant place to live, that you would furnish it for me?"

"I suppose so," she said vaguely.

"Here is your chance," I said.

She stared at me. Was I joking? In earlier days she would have known, but Hilda was not herself tonight. Her gaiety, her laughter, had vanished. Life had become too painful a chore.

"Look, darling," I said, "when I get back from Hollywood, I want a place of my own where I can live and work. I want you to find it for me, furnish it so that I can just walk into it when I get back."

She said nothing for a moment.

"Can I tell Ruth?"

"Of course. I'll make you a down payment."

"Our first commission!"

"Exactly. And I'm sure there will be many more. Run along and call Ruth."

Reassured, she asked the waiter where the telephone was. She gave me a last look and ran off to the phone. I couldn't stand the anxiety in her eyes.

She was back in a minute, smiling for the first time that evening.

"Oh, darling, Ruth was so pleased. She says now we're in business!"

That evening is an illuminated panel in memory. Some of the objects in the room in which I am writing this — chair, desk, sofa — were bought for me by Hilda for the lovely apartment she found for me, long since given up.

XI

Cornucopia in Close-Up

I N MY COMPARTMENT on the Century I watched the Hudson for a while, thinking of Hilda. I decided to write her a letter. I rang for the train stenographer, an emolument of the Century, like the red carpet in the station. The young woman came in and I began to dictate. "Dearest Hilda," I said, "I sit here thinking of you, etc., etc., etc." I finished the letter.

The stenographer got up to go. I asked her to wait a minute. While I had been dictating this to Hilda, my mind was divided. I began to think of another woman, older than Hilda, who had been in and out of my mind as a possible subject for a play. She was a successful portrait painter who had gotten some of the most famous people in Europe to sit for her: statesmen, composers, archbishops. I began dictating some notes; then a rough outline of the first act. Dialogue for it began to emerge in freshets. The stenographer, irritated by so many quotation marks, became restive. I let her go. The letter to Hilda she assured me would be mailed from Albany; the play notes would be left in my compartment that evening. I sat thinking, not about Hilda, but about the portrait painter. She was easy to think about. I took my notebook out of my briefcase and went on taking notes. I had already mentioned this idea to Guthrie McClintic; he was interested. He thought Laurette Taylor would be fine for it. I hoped for Ina Claire, but I put down Laurette Taylor. I went in to dinner feeling somewhat elated because after the long drought I felt that here was something I could work on. Maybe in the shadow of the brummagem and the marginal I could continue still to build up my repertory. One up on Shaw!

On the Chief out of Chicago, to absolve myself of contractual guilt, since I had been working on the scenario of the play to be called *Biography,* I read *Liliom* again. I began to be bothered by the last half of it, after Liliom is killed and goes to heaven. I knew that Winnie Sheehan had promised that he would give me heaven, but it still bothered me because I have no natural taste or liking for fantasy. I worried about *Liliom* till we crossed the Mississippi. I saw no way, given Molnár's play, of avoiding heaven. I also saw no way to stop thinking about *Biography* no matter what the contract said about exclusive concentration. Perhaps Sonya Levien with all her experience would know what to do about heaven. I began to be grateful to her before I met her. I would concentrate on *Liliom* but think about *Biography.*

My first day at the studio was so crowded I could neither think nor concentrate. I met everybody in the cornucopia and some who were not. Sonya Levien came into my just-opened office to welcome me. She was very attractive with lustrous black hair and big blue eyes. Sinclair Lewis, in earlier days, had wished to marry her. You could see why. She was warm, overflowing with vitality, an instant darling. She spoke an engaging pidgin English; she was constantly saying: "That's exactly!" You never knew quite about what. I told her my *Liliom* worry. She brushed it aside. She was terribly excited at the idea of working on it with me. She was especially elated that Frank Borzage was to direct it. She loved Frank Borzage and so would I. Would I come with her, for just a few minutes, to the set of a film on which she had been working, just being concluded, starring the Irish tenor John Mc-Cormack? After that we would look in on Greta Garbo in *Anna Christie* — also in its last days — then we could drop by to say hello to Will Rogers, who was just starting a new film. I begged off. Too many high spots for one morning. "That's exactly," said Sonya.

Saying she would be back shortly, she went off to the McCormack set. The telephone rang. It was Myles Connally, the supervisor of the RKO studio. They had bought the film rights of *The Second Man* and were now shooting it. He would like me to come over and have a look.

I said I'd love to but that I had just arrived and felt I should meet Mr. Wurtzel first. He understood perfectly. I asked how things were going. "Come and see for yourself." I said I'd call him tomorrow.

I hung up. The phone rang again. A secretary's voice said: "Mr. Wurtzel for you." A torrential voice shouted in my ear: "I want you to lunch with me today with Will Rogers and your director, Frank Borzage." "Fine. I'd love to." "Executive dining room at one o'clock." I said I'd be there. The call was over.

I was quite astonished by my boss's voice. I had seen photographs of him. He looked young, grave and scholarly. His voice sounded splattered, like a discharge from an instrument for crushing pebbles.

Will Rogers' voice was also gravelly, but much lower in key than our host's. I had been told that when he wanted to, he could speak perfectly normal and correct, not lariat-throwing, English. Still, the dialect was amusing. Rogers was talking about a visit he'd made in London to Lady Astor. "She set there," he said, "gnawin' on a cocktail — she'd pressed one on me but I wanted to be ahead of her and turned her down." I thought that Rogers was a shrewd man, that he specialized in keeping ahead of people, and that he had made a very good thing of it. We became good friends. He always referred to me, I have never known why, as "Sad Sam."

Frank Borzage was a big, powerful and gentle man. I'd been told he'd once worked as a ditch digger. He was silent and lovable. Sol was all over the place. I looked for sophistication in him as Sheehan had promised it to me. I did not find it; instead, I found something preferable — an engaging candor. "I read your play in New York," he said to me, "nothing but a lot of goddamn phonies in a penthouse."

That afternoon Sonya invited me to her house for tea. She wanted me to meet her husband, Carl Hovey, and her two children, Serge and Tamara. Sonya's house was on Rexford Drive in Beverly Hills, a commodious, unostentatious house, such as might belong to a well-to-do legislator in Concord, New Hampshire. There was lawn in front of it, garden and trees in the back. In the ample, comfortably furnished living room I met Carl Hovey. Sonya turned us over to her maid, Bertha, and went upstairs to rest a bit after her strenuous day. Carl Hovey was a tall, good-looking man, with keen blue eyes, and very outgoing if encouraged. He had had a career in New York and had started to have one here. He was a vastly well-read man from a very old New England family. There is a statue to an ancestor in Boston. He had been editor of the *Metropolitan Magazine* in New York. When that folded he was sent for to be story editor of a big Hollywood company, a role for which he was eminently suited. It did not work out somehow; he couldn't get along with the executives at the top. He lost his job and found himself with nothing to do. Sonya succeeded brilliantly as a scriptwriter and the somber aspect of Carl, the emanation of defeat, must have been due to the ambiguous position in which he found himself.

I was curious about the *Metropolitan Magazine,* which had enjoyed a vaunted reputation. Carl said that from the beginning he had engaged the best writers available: H. G. Wells, Scott Fitzgerald, John Reed. Theodore Roosevelt, after he retired from the Presidency, became an associate editor of the magazine. Carl had sent John Reed to Mexico to write up Pancho Villa. He described a meeting in his office between Reed and Roosevelt. "Why," T.R. demanded of Reed, "did you spend so much time with Villa? He's a bandit and a rapist."

Reed stood up to Roosevelt. "You see, sir, I believe in rape."

Teddy laughed. He clapped Reed on the shoulder. "I'm glad," he said, "to find a young man who believes in *something!*"

Sonya came down. I told her that Carl's stories about the magazine were fascinating.

"That's exactly," said Sonya.

Her husband looked at me, smiling. "That's exactly," he repeated. Carl made a habit of teasing Sonya about her English. Sonya was sensitive about it. Carl and I used to pick up some of her quaint expressions and mimic her. I think there were times when we overdid it.

Sonya invited me to stay to dinner. After dinner we went into the living room and played records, Mozart and Ravel. It was a mellow evening. It began a pattern for the ensuing Hollywood years. Rexford Drive became a second home to me. The children, Serge and Tamara, were both delightful. The Hoveys became family. They took in my friends, especially Oscar Levant.

Sonya and I settled down to work on the *Liliom* script. We worked

Sonya Levien

Carl Hovey

either in her house, in my office at the studio, or in hers. Sonya's office proved impossible; she was immensely popular, her social involvements were incessant; every writer she had ever worked with came to her to get her help. At dinner in her house or wherever, I began to feel sorry for Carl. He took a deep interest in what we were doing and we aired our difficulties before him, but ultimately he remained an outsider. He was so knowledgeable and so resourceful that I asked Sonya one day how it was that no studio had grabbed him to be its story editor.

"He missed his chance," she said dolefully. "You know he came here before I did. Story editor for Paramount."

"What happened?"

"I don't really know; somehow he couldn't get along with the people. Too reserved, I think. I think they got the feeling he was upstaging them."

"But Carl isn't like that at all," I said.

"I know it, I don't understand it."

"Can't you get Sol to take him on?"

"Sol likes Carl very much, but he said to me one day: 'He's too educated.' I think that's the trouble."

"What does he do all day?" I asked. "How does he kill time?"

"He reads."

"It's lucky," I said, "that he's a reader."

"I'm not sure," she said. "He reads too much. It's an opiate."

That shocked me a bit. Sonya went on:

"There's such a thing as too much reading; it can ruin you. It's ruined Carl." We left it there. I could see that to some degree Sonya agreed with the executives. Carl was overeducated. As time passed I often heard writers say that they'd much much rather work for hardheaded, run-of-the-mill executives than for those who, like Walter Wanger, had been to college.

When John McCormack finally left for Ireland, Sonya, greatly relieved, was able to devote her vast energies to the *Liliom* script. We met daily to work on it. The more I got involved in it, the more bothered I became about Liliom's death and transfiguration. I kept pestering Sonya about this but she wanted to postpone all worries till we got to the embankment scene. The embankment scene is the last scene in which Liliom remains alive. Up to the embankment scene *Liliom* is a beautiful play; it has in it all of Molnár's best qualities: his imagination; his humor; above all, his compassion for poor and ignorant people. I felt, when I got into the embankment scene, in which Liliom commits suicide, exactly in the same position in which Molnár must have found himself when he got to it: what to do next, how to finish it? The rest of the play, the scenes in heaven with the kindly, magisterial, celestial police commissioner are fantasies. They are fantasies which I, a confirmed agnostic, could not swallow. It seemed to me that in the heaven and return-to-earth scenes Molnár's imagination slipped into a facile groove. After thirteen years in heaven, Liliom is sent back to earth to do a good deed for his daughter. It is obvious that Molnár had fallen in love with an idea — he makes it obvious in a scene between Liliom and Julie — that if you are beaten by someone you are in love with, you don't feel it. He contrives for this to happen between Liliom and his daughter. He is provoked by her and hits her. The child is amazed that she doesn't feel it. Her mother repeats the anesthetic truism she has expressed earlier when Liliom beat her. I couldn't help reflecting: it is an encouragement of flagellation. I expressed these doubts and fears to Sonya; she postponed consideration of them till we'd gotten to the embankment scene. That was still several months away.

Sonya took on everyone who came her way and she took on the Falls, Mr. and Mrs. and two children, a boy and a girl. She told me what a dear and lovable family they were. One day she said to me: "We're having the Richard Falls to dinner. You must come. After all, he's writing our score and you should get Richard's ideas."

"His name is Leo Fall," I said. "He's a marvelous composer. He wrote the score of *Madame Pompadour*. I'll get Oscar to play it for you."

"Oh, wonderful," she said. "Shall I invite Oscar?"

"I think better not," I said, "not for the first time. You can't always count on Oscar."

I thought later what a mercy it was that I had decided against Oscar. The Falls were everything Sonya had said: very endearing people. Carl and Sonya kept calling Mr. Fall, Richard. "Haven't they got your name wrong?" I interposed at one point. I addressed Mr. Fall directly: "Isn't your name Leo?" Mr. Fall said: "Leo is my brother." "Really?" I said. I was quite shattered; I saw that Winfield Sheehan, in the intoxication of Viennese life, had made a clerical error. Richard Fall went on to tell me that his brother Leo was a marvelous composer, far more successful than he, Richard, was, and rattled off a list of Leo's operettas, including *Madame Pompadour.* I asked whether Leo had met Mr. Sheehan in Vienna. "We asked Leo," said Richard, "but he refused to come. My wife and I were sure that he refused deliberately. We were convinced, weren't we, Tina," he addressed his wife, who was smiling at the joke, "that Leo was afraid Mr. Sheehan would engage him instead of me and he didn't want to cost me a job."

We discussed the script. Fall asked how the transition to heaven was to be accomplished. "That will be wonderful," said Sonya on general principles. Carl Hovey said the music should be a great help there — that it should be sublime. He mentioned Strauss's *Death and Transfiguration.*

"I have my own ideas," said Richard Fall.

Back in my room at the Beverly Wilshire I couldn't fall asleep. I thought of that little family under the Damoclean sword of studio options. Would they survive? Would their first option be taken up? The six months of the first would soon be over. Would Sheehan discover that he had made a mistake, that he had signed up the wrong brother? It was not bearable to think about.

The months went by. We passed the embankment scene and found ourselves squirming in heaven. I had achieved with Sol a kind of critical intimacy. We seemed to be in a kind of contest in which he tried to discredit me on points of knowledge, as if I were a savant traveling under false pretenses. He made me go with him to surrounding towns — Riverside and Fresno — to previews of Fox Film Corporation pictures. You couldn't really have a conversation with Sol. Remarks erupted from him without preamble or contextual balance; they were islands in a stertorous silence. Driving to Riverside, passing a huge clock advertisement, set as they all were at three o'clock, he suddenly barked out at me: "Do you know why all these clocks are set for three o'clock?"

I said I had no idea. I could tell this confession of ignorance pleased him.

"There's a hell of a lot of things you don't know — I suppose you know that."

"Yes, I do," I said. "Why are they set for three o'clock?"

"It's the hour Lincoln died," he said, and that ended that field of inquiry.

I had been to Sol's house several times for dinner with Sonya and Carl. He lived in a small Renaissance palace in Bel Air, "the kind of a house," Carl said afterwards, "that a Grand Duke would build for his mistress." Sol's wife, Marian, I greatly liked, very good-looking, warm and humorous. She painted. She had commissioned a young artist protégé of hers to do a series of murals, in the living room and dining room, of her family in medieval costume; she herself was made to look like Isabella d'Este; Sol, deprived of his glasses and cigar, was powerfully recognizable in parti-colored doublet and hose.

I made other friends during this period, Samuel Hoffenstein, the poet, and Ernst Lubitsch. These I cherished; they were never in a quest to expose me. They were just delightful friends. I have never had better times with anyone than I had with them. The friendship with these two lasted as long as they did.

Finally the great day arrived. We sent the finished script to Sol and waited to be summoned. In a few days we were — to a full-dress meeting in Sol's paneled office: myself, Sonya, Frank Borzage, Mr. Oliver, the scenic man, and a casting director whose name I have forgotten. Sol sat behind the big desk — the script open before him.

"I don't like a picture," he growled, "where the hero dies in the middle! Especially if he's Charlie Farrell."

Borzage, a gentle man, came to my aid.

"In *Seventh Heaven*," he reminded Sol, "the hero goes blind."

"Yeh," Sol shot back, "but a blind man can still go to bed!"

It was up to me to answer the unanswerable. I said that I couldn't keep the hero alive, that *Liliom* was a minor classic, and that while I would be willing to make any incidental adjustments that might be suggested, I couldn't change that. Borzage deflected the conversation to casting; Mr. Oliver said he intended to build — in miniature — a train in which to take Liliom to heaven, I imagined in a drawing room. Sol's part in all this was listless; I could see that he was unhappy; he saw himself giving his okay to a film in which the hero dies in the middle. It violated all his instincts.

"All that heaven stuff," he said, "don't mean a thing to me. I don't know what it's all about."

Again Borzage came to the rescue.

"I'm a churchgoer," he said, "and I can tell you this. Lots of people still believe in heaven and will take comfort from it. And, Sol, isn't it marvelous, that moment when Liliom, with the best intentions in the world, slaps his own daughter — and she doesn't feel it? He does what we've seen him do on earth to his wife — to Julie!"

"What's wonderful about it? It shows — he was a punk on earth and he's a punk in heaven. What benefit did he get from dying?"

Borzage was exhausted by the length of his own speech and gave up. The odd thing is that Wurtzel was right. The film was done beautifully in France, after our version was released, and it failed as ours did. The conference ended on a dying fall.

Sol had invited me to Riverside for a preview of a new Fox film. It was part of his program to indoctrinate me into the business. I sat beside him while he drove. He was grim. I saw his cheek muscles working. We drove in silence for a time, a silence which was broken into suddenly by a volcanic remark:

"You know, Sam, out here you ain't writin' for a lot of goddamn Hindoos!"

I inquired. I tried to bring the Hindoos into focus. I found that Sol had recently experimented with a book on Indian philosophy and the notion of Nirvana had loomed up on him.

"You know," he barked, "those bastards love death. Out here we don't care for it!"

After the film Sol drove me back to the Beverly Wilshire. He didn't discuss the film. There was nothing to say about it since it was already earmarked for all the Fox theatres. Sol was thinking of the future. Just as we were approaching the hotel, he said: "I'd like you to do two pictures for me next year: *Life Begins at Forty* and Dante's *Inferno.*"

"That's formidable," I said. "I don't know Dante."

"You don't have to read it. I'll show you the silent picture. Anyway, I want you to come to my office tomorrow. We have to have a talk."

"What about?"

"A long-term contract. You'll find it in your room."

We had arrived at the hotel. I was alone on the sidewalk. Sol had driven off. He hadn't said good-night. I imagined his cherished Charlie Farrell's dying in the middle still bothered him. Nevertheless, in my room I found the document, a three-year contract, which at the start gave me a raise to $2,000 a week. From there the salary kept ascending. I sat at the desk and made a rough estimate of what it would come to if I signed and fulfilled its terms. I stared at the result. It came to about half a million dollars.

The next day I went to Sol's office and turned it down. Sol made no fuss.

"We'll talk about it in New York," he said. "I have to go there. I think I'll go with you."

We went together on the Super Chief. Sonya and Carl saw us off. She was elated. She thought it was a great compliment to me that Sol had chosen me as a traveling companion.

On my return I went to Woodstock, Vermont, where I finished the first draft of *Biography*. By doing this I avoided the blandishments of Winfield Sheehan and Sol. I was in constant correspondence with Sonya, who kept me informed about all the current gossip in the studio. She was working on a screen treatment of the immensely popular play *Lightnin'*, for Will Rogers. She wrote me that he came upon a story outline I had drafted with a long word in it. The minute he spotted that, he said: "That's a Behrman. Wrap it up and send it to the Theatre Guild. Also my best to Sad Sam." In a year I had finished the final draft of *Biography*. The Gershwins were by this time in Hollywood and invited me to stay with them. Harold Freedman thought it might be a good idea for me to go, that I might be able to cast several difficult parts in *Biography*. I wired the Gershwins I would come. I picked up where I left off with Sonya and also with Sol.

Sol had not been idle. He had yielded to the craze to get Dante's *Inferno* on the screen and had made it himself. On a June night he invited Irving Berlin and me to his château to see it.

The major premise of the film was that, if you spent all your time reading Dante's *Inferno,* no harm could come to you, that the future would be swathed in felicity. The scene is Coney Island. It is a father-and-son story. The son runs the carousel concession; the father sits home and reads Dante. The sorrow of his life is that he cannot get his son to share his preoccupation. He pleads and pleads but the son just won't read it. He prefers to hang around his carousel. The father's worst fears are confirmed. At the climactic point the carousel goes up in flames. It is a holocaust. It is a major Inferno done with great realism. But it has a salutary effect. When the disaster is over, the son, chastened, begins reading Dante.

As the sultry story unfolded, Berlin, sitting next to me, whispered in my ear: "What are you going to say to Sol?"

I whispered back that I would trust to the moment.

When it was over, for want of anything better, I said to our host: "Are you going to release this picture right away, Sol?"

"You can't release Dante's *Inferno* in the summertime!" said Sol.

XII

Scott Fitzgerald: Available

A FTER MY FIRST IMMERSION, with *Liliom*, at Fox Film Corporation, I began to be sent out on loan for quick jobs to other companies, chiefly to Metro-Goldwyn-Mayer. The first of these was to rewrite the script of *Queen Christina* for Greta Garbo. It was to be directed by Rouben Mamoulian, who was unhappy with the script he had and wanted it completely rewritten. He had already begun the filming; the set, the queen's palace in Stockholm, was up; the snow had been piled up around it. I was to keep a day ahead of the shooting. There had been great to-do about the casting of the leading man. Laurence Olivier, who would have been ideal for it, was tapped and rejected. He still does a hilarious imitation of the executive who peered at him, put his finger to Larry's face and said: "What am I going to do about this actor's uuuuug . . . ly face?" It was decided finally to take a chance on John Gilbert. Miss Garbo had had a romantic attachment to him when she first came to Hollywood. This, from the executives' point of view, was all to the good. Gilbert was signed up. The film was rolling when Gilbert would disappear for a day or two — he drank. This stopped everything. The delays were tremendously costly.

In those days Garbo and Salka Viertel, her friend and adviser, used to drop in for a cup of tea in my rented house in Beverly Hills. One day when Garbo couldn't work because the leading man had not shown up, my guests were in a state. I complained to Garbo: "How

Greta Garbo as "Queen Christina"

could you have ever got mixed up with a fellow like that?" It was a rhetorical question; I expected no answer. But I got one. Garbo meditated; it was a considered reply, as if she were making an effort to explain it to herself. Very slowly, in her cello voice, she said: "I was lonely — and I couldn't speak English."

The *Christina* film was a success all over the world. Stalin's daughter, Svetlana Alliluyeva, in her book of memoirs, *Twenty Letters to a Friend,* remembers seeing the film in Russia and being "tremendously impressed." No one could have been less like the actual Queen Christina than Garbo. But she was thrilling as a symbol: a queen, and beautiful, and she spoke up for peace. She was a modest queen; the aristocracy which Garbo brought to all her performances was lambent in this one. You wouldn't know from this film that the French philosopher Descartes, who came to educate Christina, died in her court of the cold and the awful hours.

It took a corps of secretaries to handle Miss Garbo's fan mail, which flooded in daily from all over the world. I was handed one as a curiosity. It was written on the creamiest gold-crested stationery from a maharani in India. She congratulated Miss Garbo and the studio for having abandoned the decadent films she had been making under Semitic influence and welcomed finally a truly Nordic heroine who was a refreshment and an inspiration. She hoped that Miss Garbo would continue in this vein and that I would continue to write for her such healthy and untainted films. I thought of writing Her Highness that I was neither Nordic nor untainted but I forbore.

I became, in some sort, a Garbo specialist, as I had the reputation of being, in some sort, a Lunt specialist, since I had written five plays for them. I came out again to work for David Selznick on the script of *Anna Karenina.* I worked again with Salka Viertel, who collaborated on all of Garbo's films. Getting this film ready to preview took an unconscionable time, far beyond my contract time. But finally the happy day arrived. I drove out with Mr. and Mrs. Selznick, Mrs. Viertel and Miss Garbo to Riverside for the preview. The delicacy and distinction of Garbo's performance affected me as it did the audience; I felt as I always did watching her, that she is the most patrician artist in the world. Mr. and Mrs. Selznick were pleased. But on the way home, in the car, Garbo sat silent. She spoke once, in reply to a query from Selznick as to how she felt. "Oh," she said, "if once, if only once, I could see a preview and come home feeling satisfied!" None of us could get anything more from her than that. The next day the retakes began. I had long outstayed my time. I was dying to get back to New York; Hilda was furnishing a charming apartment for me at 815 Park Avenue and I had just received a telegram saying that it was ready and that she had found a French couple to look after me. A day was finally set when Mr. Selznick said I could go. Sonya Levien gave a farewell party for me at her house. Many people came, including George S. Kaufman. It was Saturday night. I was to leave on Sunday. In the morning Mr. Selznick called me early. He said he had been talking to Miss Garbo; she was unhappy about several points in the film; she insisted that I remain to fix them. He was sorry but he could not let me go for at least another week. It was like being told, after weeks in a hospital, that you could leave on a certain day and then at the last minute having the promise revoked.

I met Selznick at the studio at nine on Monday morning. We were walking to the commissary for a cup of coffee. George Kaufman was walking in the opposite direction. He had said farewell to me on Saturday night. His face showed no surprise.

"Oh?" he said, "forgotten but not gone."

Some years later I repeated this story to Arthur Schlesinger, Jr. Eras went by. I was in Detroit for the road tour of a play of mine when I got a call from him inviting me to a small dinner party at the White House which the John F. Kennedys were giving for Isaiah Berlin. After dinner Schlesinger asked me to tell the Kaufman story. The President was greatly amused. When he came up to say good-night to me, he said:

"Thank you very much for that line of yours."

"It's not mine — it's George Kaufman's."

He said: "Whoever said it, it will come in very handy to me in the corridors of the White House!"

I came out presently on another Garbo project, the film which became *Ninotchka*. On this I worked with Gottfried Reinhardt. It was a first-rate satiric idea but Gottfried and I made slow headway on it. The producer had an inspiration: he took the story away from Gottfried and me and gave it to Ernst Lubitsch, who began to work on it with his celebrated writing team: Charlie Brackett and Billy Wilder. I had a talk about it with Ernst; he said he would switch the whole thing on a device which he knew would seem to me a cliché: jewels. "The nice thing about jewels," he said with a happy grin, "is that they are photogenic."

I returned to New York. When I saw *Ninotchka* announced I went the first day to see it. I was astonished and delighted; I saw Garbo doing what she had never done before — giving a first-rate high-comedy performance. I wired to Ernst to tell him my pleasure in it and when I came to Hollywood again telephoned him on arrival. I went at once to see him. I told him that he had opened a new vista for Garbo. She could play comedy; she must. He said he had several ideas for her along this line but that the difficulty was that he couldn't get her on the telephone. I spoke to Salka Viertel about this. She told me that Garbo had really not been happy on the set with Ernst. There was no *"Stimmung"* there, she said. It was never patched up. I cite this as an example of how often great artists simply do not know what is good for them. It is sad when this ignorance destroys the careers of lesser artists; in the case of major ones, it is tragic.

There followed a halcyon period. There were few places in America where you could go out to dinner with Harpo or Groucho Marx, the Franz Werfels, Leopold Stokowski, Aldous Huxley, Somerset Maugham, George and Ira Gershwin.

In Harpo Marx's drawing room you encountered high art: four full-length oil paintings by the great masters of the Renaissance, museum-lit, magniloquently framed, with gold plates accommodatingly supplying the names of the painters and their dates: Tintoretto, Botticelli, Leonardo da Vinci and Michelangelo. The painters outdid themselves in rivalry; they were ahead of their times; they concentrated on the Marx brothers, painting them all in magnificent Renaissance costumes as doges of Venice. Groucho was a rather sinister doge; you didn't feel you would go to him to help you out of a jam. Harpo, on the other hand, had the quality of wild serenity that he had in life, the quality that endeared him to so many people in varied walks of life. A guest once complimented Harpo on these paintings. He said they were wonderful. Harpo said: "They'd better be. They cost me five thousand dollars."

The last time I saw the sinister doge, Groucho, he told me a Goldwyn story. Harpo, after his retirement from films, moved to Palm Springs with his wife and children. He seldom came to Hollywood. Every time Groucho met Sam Goldwyn at a party, Goldwyn singled him out and impaled him with a stock question: "Tell me, how is Harpo?" Groucho imitated perfectly Goldwyn's high-pitched, somewhat strangulated voice. These confrontations had been going on for twenty-five years. Groucho knew that Harpo had always been Goldwyn's favorite as he was everyone's favorite. The last time Goldwyn had subjected him to the standard query Groucho rebelled. "Look here, Sam, every time you meet me you ask me how Harpo is. This has been going on for twenty-five years. For God's sake why don't you, for once, ask me how *I* am?" "Someday I will," said Goldwyn patiently, "but just now — tell me — how is Harpo?"

I once shared a house with Harpo in Beverly Hills. He always took guests up to show them his library. His library consisted of two books, affectionately inscribed to him by their authors: *Saint Joan* by Bernard Shaw and *Of Human Bondage* by W. S. Maugham. Every once in a while Harpo would dreamily express his intention, someday, when things were quieter, to read his library.

At another time I shared a house with Edgar Selwyn. His wife was the sister of Mrs. Nicholas Schenck. Schenck was the head of Metro-Goldwyn-Mayer in New York; he was called the General. Every year on his annual official visit, the Selwyns gave a party for him and this party enlisted the Social Register of Hollywood. Orchestra. White tie. The crème de la crème. It was midnight; the party was in full swing. The massive security officer in charge of the front door was accosted by a not entirely sober character in a business suit and no tie, and with a two days' growth of beard. It was David Selznick's brother, Myron, a nonconformist fixture in Hollywood life.

The custodian blocked Myron's path as he lurched up.

"I beg your pardon, sir, but were you invited?"

"Not only was I invited," said Myron grandly as he swept in, "but I declined!"

An elite corps existed in Hollywood about which outsiders were unlikely to know. This was a select professional group known as "the trainers"; they upheld the "Cult of the Body," a necessary religion for the stars of course, but the executives, producers and Name Writers were acolytes too, as impassioned as the stars. There were gymnasia and sauna baths in all the studios but the chosen had them in their homes. Lubitsch had a gymnasium in his house and a personal trainer who came at eight o'clock each morning to exercise him. I had a trainer. His name was Bolt. Sidney Howard had Bolt too. Sidney was very funny about him. "Well," he would say when we met for dinner, "what flatteries did Bolt hang around your neck today?" On arrival, you signed up one of these trainers for the length of your stay, to come so many times a week. Once you signed him up, you felt you had done enough for hygiene. You were then faced with the excruciating problem of avoiding him. How many unwanted engagements we made in order not to be home when the trainers arrived with their hideous gear, a folded massage table and a black bag full of rubbing unguents. They would put you through painful gymnastic exercises in grotesque positions and make you run around the garden. It was horrible. But they were also purveyors of intimate studio gossip, since they tended the executives when they were, presumably, off guard. They knew the dissolving ratings of each writer. Sidney Howard said that our Bolt was a liar, a flatterer and a sycophant. He enjoyed drawing him out to test his perfidies. Bolt always gave him a good report on my studio standing; he knew that Sidney and I were close friends. I was able to tell Sidney once that Bolt had told me that Sam Goldwyn was so pleased with Sidney that he had ordered a Cord roadster to give him as a present. The following week the Cord was delivered at Sidney's door. Bolt rose in our estimation. "If only the s.o.b. didn't exercise us!" groaned Sidney.

A memorable, an unprecedented event took place one day which thrilled and excited us: Ernst Lubitsch was made the head of Paramount! Nothing like that had ever happened before; we all felt

Ernst Lubitsch and his daughter

exalted by proxy. Lubitsch had great camaraderie with writers. He was one himself, as those who worked with him knew. I was so excited that day and so busy calling up Lubitsch to congratulate him and others to celebrate the news, that I forgot that it was my day with Bolt. There he was with his massage table, which he promptly began to set up. Bolt was stirred up too; Lubitsch's trainer, Kip, was his closest friend. "Kip must be happy," I said. "Very happy," said Bolt, "Kip loves Mr. Lubitsch."

Months passed. I had gone back to New York and returned to Hollywood to do some rewrites. A few weeks after, my phone rang, early in the morning. It was Lubitsch. He was in a state.

"Vot you think?"

"What's the matter?"

"I am no longer head of Paramount!"

"So early in the morning? What are you talking about?"

"But is true. And how do you think I find out? Hour ago — from my trainer. He comes in usual this morning. He is something sad. He say: 'Good morning, Mr. Lubitsch.' I say 'Good morning, Keep. Something is not good with you?' He reaches out his hand to me to shake. I shake. 'I am verry sorry to have to tell you bad news,' he say. 'For God's sake, Keep,' I say, 'vot are you talking?' He say, 'I hate to be the first to tell you — you are no longer the head of Paramount.' I say he is crazy. He say, 'No, is true.' I ask him how it is true and he say last night he massages front office and they are all saying it. So I call front office and yes it is true. They are vaiting for me to come in to tell me. From my trainer I have to find it out. Verry funny. You do not think it is verry funny? Don't tell yet. It is so funny I vant to tell. From my trainer I find it out. Is not funny?"

He hung up.

Metro-Goldwyn-Mayer was run in those days by a triumvirate: Bernie Hyman, who was a producer; Bennie Thau, who was an executive without portfolio; and of course Louis B. Mayer. When it was asked exactly what Thau did, Herman Mankiewicz said that his assignment was to watch at the window of the third floor of the Thalberg Building and to report at once to his colleagues the approach of the North Wind, which they all felt somehow was in the offing. Bernie Hyman was a very amiable fellow with a streak of stubbornness. He would read a scene and say it lacked "zip." He was affected by the opinions of the last person he talked to. Sam Hoffenstein said of him that he was like a glass of water without the glass. He also said that he was like Dr. Jekyll, in the uncapturable moment before he merged into Mr. Hyde. I knew Bernie's secretaries and had the run of his splendiferous office. When he was late for a lunch-date, I used to wander into his office, sit at his desk, and look over his memoranda. Once I saw: "Miss Harlow called. She was very anxious to talk to you." I wrote on the memo: "Why is she no longer anxious?" Another memorandum interested me more: a sheet of yellow paper, headed "Writers Available." It was a macabre list: playwrights who had written one success twenty years ago and had not been heard from since; novelists whose novels you could not remember. But then I saw a name that gave me a turn — Scott Fitzgerald. It made me angry. To be on a list of the available in Hollywood was to be on a death-list. When Bernie came in I let him have it on Scott. "He's easily one of our greatest writers," I said. "Maybe he is," said Bernie, unruffled, "but he's slow." I expressed myself on Scott to other producers; I got the same reaction from all of them, that he was slow.

Louis B. Mayer, the chief of the triumvirate, was a man of extraordinary shrewdness and even, as far as the Industry was concerned, of vision. He was incorrigibly histrionic and put on a great show. Sometimes it slipped his mind what role he was playing: whether the benevolent autocrat, the humanitarian concerned for the well-being of everyone except his enemies, the emotional sentimentalist, the religious leader. His relationship with God was intimate and confidential; he spoke for Him as well as for himself; they thought along the same lines. He sat behind his circular desk in his presidential office, surrounded by the large, silver-framed photographs of another triumvirate, which bounded his spiritual and political horizon: Cardinal Spellman, Herbert Hoover and Douglas MacArthur. He called me up one morning and asked me to write a speech for him to be delivered at a St. Patrick's Day celebration in San Francisco. I did what I could. I tried to make it entertaining. L.B. was not pleased; he promptly rejected it. "It is not," he said, "what they expect of me." I gathered that from him they expected the solemn and the lofty. To show that he had no hard feelings, he invited me to lunch in the executive dining room, an accolade that had never been extended to me before.

Every producer on the lot was there. L.B. sat at the head of the table. The seat beside him, reserved for Eddie Mannix, the studio manager, was empty — Eddie was late. It caused concern and speculation: where was Mannix? "It's not like Eddie," said L.B. But he ordered lunch to be served. Suddenly Eddie appeared. His face was flushed; he was very angry. He had just heard the music for a trailer and had had a fight with the arrangers. The music was so complicated, so full of "fil-fals," he called them, that he couldn't hear the melody. He begged to be allowed to hear the melody. But the arrangers would not remove a single fil-fal. He bared his heart to L.B. He couldn't have asked for a more compassionate sympathizer. Mannix was very loud; L.B. very quiet.

"Listen, Eddie," he said, "do you think *I* run the studio? Do you think *you* run the studio? Oh no, Eddie! The arrangers — they run the studio." L.B. spread his hands in a votive gesture; his voice was prayerful. "I go down on my knees to 'em, I beg 'em, I pray to 'em, 'Please let me hear the melody.' But they won't — they stick to the fil-fals. Counterpoint, they call it."

But the effect of this on Mannix was not sedative. He threw his napkin on the table.

"Well, goddamn it," he shouted, "either counterpoint leaves the studio or I leave the studio!"

If the advent of sound panicked the producers, they were, before they had fully recovered from the first shock, confronted by a second — another variety of sound — music. It was even more esoteric than speech. It threw them. They couldn't put Schubert and Schumann, Chopin and Brahms into drawing rooms on the Chief, but they could get them on celluloid and they did. They raked Europe for singers who could sing like living people and for composers who could write for them. The list of their importations is impressive. Gian-

Carlo Menotti, as an incitement, was shown a film just made about the Schumanns and Brahms. In one scene Brahms is sitting with his girl, listening to the first performance of his first symphony. In the middle of the first movement he leans over to the girl and whispers to her to come out and have a beer. I was present at the showing and I saw Menotti's pain. In the gentlest way he protested. "Not," he said, "at a first performance. No composer would walk out on his own symphony being performed for the first time." It was explained to him that it established firmly Brahms's interest in the girl. Menotti grasped the basic axiom but his pain was not diminished. A famous coloratura, Miliza Korjus, was imported to sing in a film about Johann Strauss, the composer of the *Blue Danube* waltz. The director, Gottfried Reinhardt, brought in one of the prima donna's records to play for the producer, Bernie Hyman. Madame Korjus sang a Mozart aria with trills that ascended to heaven. Mr. Hyman was transported. "That's great," he exclaimed. "We'll put it in our picture." Reinhardt told him that this would be impractical since the aria was by Mozart and the film was to be about Johann Strauss.

Hyman, usually a mild man, exploded.

"Who the hell is going to stop me?"

If I had a projection room of my own there are a few little classics of that era that I would give anything to show for those who haven't seen them. I would start probably with the film *A Song to Remember,* a great success in its time. It is about Chopin. The virtuoso is introduced to George Sand by Franz Liszt. Chopin is a little slow on the uptake but Mme Sand isn't; she sizes him up at once as likely material. She gives him an appraising look and says meaningfully: "What are your plans, Mr. Chopin?" Chopin stares at her, planless. Later, when they are cozier, he is playing nocturnes for her. "This one, George," he says as he begins a new one, "is for you." It was Sainte-Beuve, I think, who said of Mme Sand that she had a magnanimous spirit and a perfectly enormous behind. Merle Oberon didn't quite live up to that. She was just magnanimous.

In all the films about music the famous composers and instrumentalists are treated uniformly as being great humanitarians, altruists, congenital do-gooders. They are scarcely human: self-effacing, without vanity and immersed in schemes for helping each other out. I suppose it's because to the producers music was a celestial exercise; it belonged, for them, in a nonhuman realm. For the last night of my hypothetical series in my nonexistent projection room, I would show a film called *Carnegie Hall,* because I don't think that any of the other masterpieces of unconscious humor could possibly top it.

The major premise on which this film rests is that if you are a mother who loves music and you have a little boy whom you passionately wish to follow a musical career, the best thing you can do for him is to take an apartment in the residential part of the Carnegie Hall building. That way he will grow up in close contact with the virtuosi and the conductors who appear in the Hall. So it comes about. The boy stands in the wings and it would appear that all the virtuosi who give recitals there are concerned with the ambitious boy's future. Practically every famous musician in America appeared in this picture. Artur Rubinstein, as he exits at the end of a concert, ignoring his own ovation, gives the waiting boy sound advice. "Bach," he quacks at him, "play nothing but Bach, Bach, Bach, Bach." The years pass; the mother sits and waits. Her patience is rewarded but not in the way she had hoped. The day comes when her son is booked to play a concert in Carnegie Hall. She has a box for the concert and doesn't have far to go to reach it. Walter Damrosch and other celebrities are her guests in the box. But she is in for a terrrible shock. Her son has not followed Rubinstein's advice. He is the leader of a jazz combo! Damrosch and the others try to console her but it is a hard blow to bear.

After the showing I asked the producer how it was that the mother, whose life was spent in following the careers of musicians, did not know that her son had become a jazz celebrity. He winked at me:

"I'll tell you," he said. "She was taking a long vacation at Grossinger's."

I am aware that I have indulged a personal idiosyncrasy to the point that my description of Hollywood in its Grand Epoque is partial and even distorted. It wasn't all that funny; it was flecked with tragedy. The endearing Richard Fall family, for example: their second option was not taken up; they had to go back to Austria, where they were murdered by the Nazis. Had it not been for a clerical error on the part of Winnie Sheehan they might have remained at home, seen for themselves how things were going, and contrived an escape in time. There was the cataclysmic death of George Gershwin. There was the suicide of Marilyn Monroe, which shattered the community — briefly. The sophisticates developed a theory about Miss Monroe's death: that some theatrical intellectuals had persuaded her that she was not living up to her potential as an actress. She tried to develop this potential in private study. When it failed her she did away with herself. Actually, she was doing what she was meant to do; it exercised her potential fully. It was a merciless time and Hollywood did not escape the penalties of living in it.

The historical films made in this era were mainly ludicrous. When I came to work on *Conquest* for Garbo, who played Mme Walewska, with whom Napoleon fell in love, I wished to convey my personal feeling that the existence of Napoleon, "the archaic little man," as H. G. Wells calls him, was a disaster for the human race. But it was not easy to get sympathy for this point of view from a group of men who had busts of Napoleon in their offices, since he represented their secret wish-dreams of conquest. And yet it was an extraordinary world. There were the Chaplin films. There were the Marx Brothers films. There was *All Quiet on the Western Front,* directed by Lewis Milestone. There were the Harold Lloyd and the Douglas Fairbanks films. There were the Lubitsch films. Ernst Lubitsch was the only director in Hollywood who had his own signature. You knew it was a Lubitsch film before it started. Under the credit titles of *The Merry Widow* you saw a dedicated geographer, with a hand-glass, peering at a map of southeastern Europe, trying vainly to locate the country which Prince Danilo deserts for the blandishments of Paris. He gives up in despair. Lubitsch himself was a remarkable man as well as a unique director. He was gay, full of fun, impassioned, serious. I shall never forget one night at a Hollywood gathering when some cynic pooh-poohed the idea of the Warner Brothers inviting Max Reinhardt to make *A Midsummer Night's Dream.* Lubitsch poured vitriol over the skeptic. He said it was too bad if Hollywood, swimming in riches, could not afford to take a chance on the most imaginative and daring director in the world, to invite him to film a masterpiece which he had already produced, with fabulous effect, on the stage. (In the course of making that film, incidentally, Reinhardt discovered Mickey Rooney, whom he engaged to play Puck.) It was a terrible day for very many people when Ernst Lubitsch died.

With the influx of the refugees in the thirties, Hollywood became a kind of Athens. It was as crowded with artists as Renaissance Florence. It was a Golden Era. It had never happened before. It will never happen again.

XIII

Chacun à Son Goût

I N THE EARLY FORTIES, three escapees from the Nazi death-trap changed the color and tone of my life and, after agonizing tribulations, gave me a successful play. The three were Franz Werfel, the novelist, poet and playwright; Oskar Karlweis, the Viennese actor; and one, Samuel S. Jacobowsky, whom I was never to meet, but whose destiny and foibles engrossed me, on and off, for three years.

For some time Ernst Lubitsch had been campaigning the executives in Hollywood to bring Max Reinhardt to the United States. He had been a member of his company during Reinhardt's great days in Berlin, where he was the reigning lord and owned four theatres. Another refugee, Bruno Frank, the novelist and playwright, in an access of nostalgia, told me what it was like to see a Reinhardt production in Berlin. He remembered a performance of Galsworthy's *Loyalties* in Reinhardt's theatre, the Kammerspiel. "It was like chamber music," he said. "The theatre was small and exquisite. You sat in armchairs. The performance was flawless. You sat there, in thrall to the world Reinhardt had created."

Max arrived, took a palatial house, and reigned like a king in exile. He invited me to dinner to meet the Franz Werfels. Max was unchanged after all he had been through, the charm and the humor undiluted. It is no more possible to convey in writing the constituents of a man's charm than it is to convey in writing the effect of music; in Max it was the resonance and timbre of his speaking voice, his laugh, his easy manner, his presence, his looks. Max's charm was proverbial, a trademark. His wife was gracious and withdrawn.

I told Max how much I was looking forward to meeting the Werfels. I was a friend of Ben Huebsch, Werfel's publisher, and Ben had been in great distress about Werfel. There had been an item in the *Times* that Werfel had been captured and killed by the Nazis. Efforts to reach him, even through the Red Cross, had been unavailing. Max said it was nice to find out that the *Times* was fallible.

The dinner guests began streaming in; there were ten altogether, among them Lubitsch and the Werfels.

Alma Mahler Werfel was a large blonde woman with violet eyes; she could be safely described as statuesque. Her husband was little; she towered over him. She was stately, her expression grave, immobile, calmly observant. Werfel was mercurial, chubby, round-faced, hair brushed straight back and beginning to recede. His eyes, behind thick glasses, were on the alert for humor; he made fun of almost everything, including himself. On his escape through France he found himself in Lourdes; he made a vow there that if he ever came out of it alive, he would write a novel dedicated to the saint of Lourdes. He did: *The Song of Bernadette.* It became a best seller. It was being filmed in Hollywood while he was there. I sat next to Frau Alma Mahler Werfel at dinner. She made no bones about it; she could take an interest only in what she called "productive" men. Her first husband, Gustav Mahler, had been so spectacularly productive that she would have thought it sacrilege, on his death, to extinguish his name, so she kept it and attached Werfel's to it when she married the latter. It exalted Werfel to be the successor of so great a man as Gustav Mahler. He was intensely musical. He worshipped Mahler. He carried his scores around. He knew them by heart.

Sitting across from Frau Alma was one of Hollywood's most successful writers, Charlie Brackett, looking very tidy in his dinner jacket. Alma was staring at him. She asked me who he was. I said: "Charles Brackett."

"He is Aryan?"

"No doubt about it."

"Write me down his name."

I did, on my place card. I saw her lips move as she learned Charlie's name. She picked up her handbag from the floor, opened it, and shoved the Aryan's name inside it for future reference. I teased Charlie about this for a long time; I prophesied a union between himself and Alma.

"Do you think I am productive enough?" said Charlie wistfully.

"Leave that to Alma. Of course you realize you will just be a number in a series?"

"Oh, that'll be fine with me. I'll be Charlie Mahler-Werfel-Brackett — all three of us productive!"

It was a jolly dinner party. Werfel dominated it. He kept the table in a roar of laughter, oddly enough, by describing details of his escape through France, a time during which he was in danger of losing his life at any moment, day or night. Here, at Max Reinhardt's, talking an ersatz English, was Werfel, being funny about it. I had met many refugees, great and small, and from all of them I had heard accounts of their experiences. But Werfel's was something new in horror stories. Talking with a gusto unhalted by the idiosyncrasies of English syntax, his blue eyes alight with enjoyment, Werfel kept the table spellbound for well over an hour. He conveyed what it meant to be in France in that summer after her fall, a step ahead of the Nazis: the frantic crowds in front of the consulates, the pulverization of consciousness into one acrid grain of desire — to get a stamp on a piece of paper. Werfel told with the greatest zest the story of an overworked consulate official besieged by the frantic crowd outside, lost, himself, in a mountain of visas waiting to be stamped, who suddenly went mad, lunged at the mass of visas as though they were his jailors and destroyed them, ripped them to pieces and hurled them into the fireplace.

An incident of his escape from Paris had amused Werfel. It was about one Samuel S. Jacobowsky, a Polish-Jewish businessman, who, in his prosperous days, had found time for literature and chamber music. He buys a car from a rascally chauffeur. He can't drive but he trusts to luck to find somebody who can. An anti-Semitic Polish colonel, a cavalry officer, happens along; he has a military mission to the south of France. The idea of traveling with Jacobowsky revolts him, but he has

Oskar Karlweis

to get away and here is a car. His aide beside him, he takes the wheel. Jacobowsky is allowed to take the back seat. To Jacobowsky's horror, instead of heading south, the Colonel heads north where the Germans are, to pick up his sweetheart, a French girl.

I was seized by this anecdote; it had some peculiarity of compactness — I felt there was a play in it. Werfel went on weaving his farcical extravaganza — for when the conventions of property, justice, the divisions of life and death are all held in abeyance by an arbitrary God, the habits based on these conventions evidently jumble into farce, like a macabre *Alice in Wonderland.* I kept thinking: "Two men in an ambivalent relationship, two men from the opposite ends of the earth though they are countrymen — opposites physically, spiritually, mentally, held together during flight by a common enemy and a vehicle — they hate each other — they part — they find they miss each other."

After dinner, in the living room, I took Werfel aside. I told him that I had been fascinated by his story of the Polish refugee and the reactionary cavalry officer. I thought there might be a play in it, a beautiful comedy. It seemed simple and natural.

Werfel was delighted. "Do you think so?" he said.

"Yes," I said, "you must write it."

"No, you must write it. It could be a play for Reinhardt."

"Ideal for him," I said.

I began to work on the Jacobowsky play with enthusiasm. I wrote the At Rise: "In the subterranean laundry of the Hotel Mon Repos et de la Rose. It is evening on the thirtieth of June, 1940. There has been an air-raid alert and the laundry of MADAME BOUFFIER'S fourth-class establishment is doing service as an air-raid shelter." I got an idea — that Jacobowsky entertains the Colonel's girl, Marianne, by making her laugh. Whenever the Colonel comes upon them she is laughing. It drives him crazy. I devised a scene in which the Colonel tries to emulate Jacobowsky, to make Marianne laugh. The Colonel's attempt is pitiful since he hasn't a grain of humor. I enjoyed developing this idea. I felt it might serve.

Chaim Weizmann came to town. I gave a lunch party for him at the Beverly Wilshire. Of course, I invited the Werfels. Franz was delighted to accept, but Alma refused. When I asked her why, she said, "I've been in Palestine. I didn't like it. Too many Jews there." Alma Mahler Werfel endlessly fascinated me. I knew something of her amatory history — you couldn't not know because she talked about nothing else — and it was studded with Jewish names. I mentioned this. "That's the trouble," Alma said. "The minute I get involved with a Jew, they begin talking about Jesus Christ to me." I mentioned Gropius — not a Jew. "Oh," she said, "he was just a bore."

My brother-in-law, the late Samuel Chotzinoff, told me that he had worshipped Mahler and never missed one of his concerts when he conducted the Philharmonic here in Carnegie Hall. In the Green Room once, he beheld Alma. He said she was the most ravishingly beautiful creature he had ever seen. I repeated this to Alma. She nodded emphatically: "I *was!*"

A scene in the Werfel's tiny living room returns after twenty-five years to solace me. Arnold Schoenberg was present. He had the most intense eyes and gaze I have ever seen in anyone. You felt that there were immensities behind the tightly drawn skin on his yellowish skull-like head. Alma sat beside me on the sofa, Werfel facing her, Schoenberg, withdrawn, on the other side of Alma. Alma had chosen to narrate her life story. Werfel and Schoenberg listened as if it were all new to them. I was a new audience for Alma. She was sorry that I had never seen their new house in Vienna — "black and white marble" — she wished to give me an insight into the life she led in Vienna when she was married to Mahler. She called to her maid, who was clearing the table in the dining room. "Marie. Bring in Beethoven's hair." The maid left off her task and disappeared, returning a moment later with a little gold box. Alma opened it to show me: there was a wisp of brownish hair in it. Alma explained: "Given to Mahler by the Vienna Philharmonic when he left to conduct the New York Philharmonic." Schoenberg asked if he might take the box for a moment; he sat staring at his predecessor's hair, lost in reverie. Alma went on with the spangled narrative of her conquests. There was, for example, the case of the painter Kokoschka. He was so in love with her that he had a life-sized mannequin made of her to take with him on his travels. When something in one of her letters displeased him he would stick a

Alma Mahler Werfel as a debutante

Alma Mahler Werfel, later in life

pin in the mannequin. "Childish, no?" But Alma didn't wait for my opinion. "Alban Berg . . . *Wozzeck* — dedicated to me. Gropius . . ." She went on and on till she came to Werfel; she included him in her list as if he weren't there. Finally, looking straight at her husband, she made a grand summation: "But," she said, "the most interesting personality I have known — *was Mahler*."

Werfel nodded fervently. He would be the last person in the world to contradict an authority so eminent or to pretend to rival a genius whose memory he held in awed reverence.

I was seeing the Werfels constantly and working happily on Jacobowsky. Suddenly I got a call from Harold Freedman telling me that Werfel was evidently working on a version of his own and that he had asked Clifford Odets (another of Harold's clients) to collaborate with him. To ameliorate the blow, Harold hazarded the opinion that Werfel might have preferred a collaborator who was a fixture in Hollywood, whom he could keep under his eye, instead of an ambulatory character like me.

I hated to say good-bye to Samuel S. Jacobowsky, but in those days I had the habit of writing plays and I had, before I met Werfel, been fascinated by the idea of writing a play about Montaigne. I returned to that. But what was disturbing was the deterioration of my personal relationship with Werfel. I loved that man. To this day I don't know what was the cause of his grievance against me but it was there and embittered for me the eventual production of this play and even its success.

I saw Werfel only once more and this was by accident. I'd gone to see Noel Coward's *Blithe Spirit,* not for the first time, as it is a favorite comedy of mine. Going up the aisle after the curtain fell there was Werfel, trailing after Alma. I asked him how he liked the play.

"Welt ohne Frauen," he said. *"Wunderbar."*

It was not then all honey and roses between him and Alma. Alma, in her turn, after her husband's death, demoted Werfel. The preface to one of her books is signed: ALMA MARIA WERFEL-MAHLER.

One day, a year later, my telephone rang. It was Theresa Helburn at the Theatre Guild, asking me to come to her office. Elia Kazan was there. I was astonished to learn that the Guild was going to put on *Jacobowsky and the Colonel* and that Kazan was to direct it. They wanted me to rewrite the play and very fast as they had already booked time for it on the road. I asked about Odets. He had finished his draft but neither Kazan nor Miss Helburn thought it playable. They did not want me to see his version. I went home, found the notebook in which I had kept the notes I had taken after my first meeting with Werfel. I sat at my bridge table — Paul Valéry's definition of inspiration: "the act of drawing the chair up to the work table" — and went to work. In their casting of the play the Guild was inspired: Louis Calhern for the Colonel, Annabella for Marianne, and for Jacobowsky the Viennese comedian Oskar Karlweis.

I had seen Karlweis once, some time before. An Austrian friend had invited me uptown, to the East Side, to see a performance of *Fledermaus*. "You will see an enchanting actor," she promised me. Karlweis played Prince Orlofsky. I was entranced by him from the moment he appeared on the stage. He was stylish, he was crisp and elegant, he was an aristocrat who saw through aristocracy's pretensions. Through everything he said and did there was the sportive, javelin thrust of humor. The refrain *"Chacun à son goût"* he sang with a *je m'en fiche* nonchalance, an air of "I can take it, but I can leave it," that was irresistible. He had the audience in the palm of his hand. That's where I was. Without thinking, I thought: "Here is my Montaigne." I no longer had an excuse; I must write this play, and for him. He even looked like Montaigne as I knew his looks from the engravings in the various editions of the *Essays* I had at home.

And now here was Prince Orlofsky-Montaigne sitting with me, Kazan and Miss Helburn in the Oak Room at the Plaza. He had made the same journey through France that Werfel had made. He had been singing in a Paris nightclub. A high-placed friend, whom he later married, knew the way things were going and facilitated his escape. He was a brother-in-law of the German novelist Jacob Wassermann. He was, himself, half Jewish. "So was Montaigne," I said to myself. But Karlweis said: "The way things are, half is more than enough."

Jacobowsky and the Colonel

Jacobowsky and the Colonel

He captivated all of us; he was so light in touch, witty and self-deprecatory. I determined as soon as we'd opened in New York to sew him up for Montaigne.

All through rehearsals, which went swimmingly, the Guild and Kazan were after me to find a title for the play as it was manifestly impossible to call a play *Jacobowsky and the Colonel*. For one thing it was unpronounceable. "Can you imagine people coming to the box office and asking to buy seats for a title like *that?*" I couldn't imagine it myself and promised to find a title. I wrote down scores but didn't like any of them. Neither did anyone else. We decided, finally, to open with the one we had and, with false confidence, were sure we'd get a workable title on the road.

We opened in New Haven.

When Karlweis walked on, after he'd spoken a few sentences, we knew we were all right. The audience took him to its heart. In the first intermission Terry Helburn came up to Langner and me, beaming. "We're in," she said. "I've just talked to Lee Shubert. He says it's Potash and Perlmutter with class!" In the inevitable conference that night at the Taft, attended by Stewart Chaney, who did the sets, and by Paul Bowles, who had written a modest but evocative score, the atmosphere was optimistic, even though we all knew that we could do with a stronger last act.

From New Haven we went to Boston. I had spent the weekend in New York doing rewrites. I watched from an aisle seat in the fifth row, taking notes. In front of me sat two elderly gentlemen of the type more frequently encountered in London than in this country: tall, slim, elegant, with narrow faces, keen eyes and beautifully brushed silver hair. The first act had gone well and Karlweis had captivated the audience as he had done in New Haven. I wanted, if possible, to get a comment on the play from these two gentlemen. I walked up the aisle just behind them in the intermission.

"You know," said one, "I think that fellow Karlweis — is Jewish."

There was a long pause. The other man took time to assimilate this bizarre fact. "Well," he said, ". . . I don't mind!"

We sold out in Boston and in Philadelphia, which was our last stop before New York. Audiences seemed able to pronounce the title so we all forgot that we were going to find another one. After we opened in New York at the Martin Beck, Louis Calhern told us that walking in for the first Saturday matinee, he saw two bearded East Side Jews staring up at the marquee. He overheard one say to the other: "Jacobowsky and the *what?*"

But there are few undiluted pleasures and this one was darkened for me by acrid difficulties with Werfel. Harold Freedman came to Boston to report that Werfel, through his lawyer, had demanded that my name be taken off the play. As I had written every spoken line of it, the demand seemed unreasonable. The Guild fought it out with Werfel's lawyer, but it was a bleak fact and I had to face it: Werfel and I were now enemies. I had given him a hit; the play was sold for a considerable sum to the movies; I never heard a word from him although he was not averse to collecting the major part of the royalties. The only one who later tried to shed light on it was a friend of Werfel's. He explained to me that German writers consider that no writing is any good unless it is symbolic and tragically serious. They love symbolic characters which represent profoundly somber abstractions. Werfel had by this time written his own version of the play and it was full of them. It became the libretto for a tragic German opera.

I studied Karlweis during the run of *Jacobowsky and the Colonel.* We became friends. More and more I identified him with Montaigne; he was aristocratic, as Montaigne was; he was skeptical, as Montaigne was. I told him I was writing a play for him. He was very excited. I didn't tell him what it was about but I told him I would soon have something to show him.

After *Jacobowsky* closed in New York, the Guild sent it on tour. In Chicago Karlweis had a heart attack. He was sent to the hospital. The tour ended.

Karlweis recovered and, one bright September day, he came to see me in my apartment. He looked wonderful and was in wonderful spirits and very excited about a new project for which he wanted to get my help. There was to be a drama festival in Berlin, the first postwar free one, and he had been invited to appear in it. He wanted to do *Jacobowsky and the Colonel.* Wouldn't it be marvelous, wasn't it a wonderful, a poignant choice? Wouldn't it really prove that the Nazi horror was over? He wanted me to try to get Kazan to direct it. I said I would do my best and that I'd call him the minute I'd spoken to Kazan. He was radiantly happy.

Two days later I got the news. Oskar was dead.

I went that afternoon to see Madame Karlweis. She asked me if I would speak at Oskar's funeral. I said that I was no speaker, but that I would.

The next morning I stood beside Oskar's coffin in the Catholic church and said farewell to him. I said that as a man and as an artist Oskar had had a green thumb.

XIV

Siegfried's Bower, Osbert's Nook

ONE MORNING during one of my Hollywood stints in the early thirties, Sonya Levien burst into my office with excitement.

"It's all settled," she said. "On the *Aquitania.*"

"Has there been a dispute on the *Aquitania?*"

"Sol just told me. He asked me to tell you."

"In that case why don't you?"

"We're going to England," she said. She sat down on the sofa and began fanning herself with a huge silk handkerchief. I gave her a minute to get control of herself.

"The studio bought *Cavalcade.* Noel Coward's. They want us to go to London to see it. They want us to write the screenplay."

This excited me as much as it did Sonya. It seemed too good to be true.

"The studio has made all the reservations, the Savoy."

"Well," I said, "that *is* news. When do we leave?"

"Friday, on the Chief. Gets us in just in time for the *Aquitania.* She sails Tuesday."

"Just the two of us?"

"Oh, no. Frank Borzage and Lou." Lou was Borzage's brother and on Frank's staff.

"What about Carl?" I said.

"Oh, he's coming. I'm paying his transportation."

"I'm glad," I said. "It'll be fun to have him."

"Carl loves England. He used to go all the time when he was running the *Metropolitan* — to see authors."

I was aware of a poignant feeling about Carl. I knew that he had run pieces in the *Metropolitan* by H. G. Wells, by Arnold Bennett. He had gone to London to see them. Now Sonya was paying his expenses to accompany a project with which he had nothing to do. It seemed awful to me. But then it had grown on me before that Carl's position, generally, was awful. In a community where everyone was employed in one consuming occupation, to be a nonparticipant seemed to me a sad life. I had wondered before how Carl stood it. He was always humorous, always charming. How did he manage it?

I went to the studio post office and cabled Siegfried.

We had a pleasant journey on the *Aquitania*. Carl had suggested that we postpone discussion of the film version of *Cavalcade* till we had seen the play. Sonya concurred; she said that was exactly. Perhaps it occurred to her that Carl deserved a rest from the perpetual story conference in which his life was spent, during meals at home, in the family car — Sonya was always traveling with one or another of her collaborators — everywhere and all the time. We were free as birds. We dined together every night, Frank Borzage, his brother Lou (I called him "Soothin' Lou" because he always agreed heartily with everybody), Sonya, Carl and myself. On the wall above our table in the dining room hung a tremendous oil painting of Colleoni. Carl was the only one who knew who Colleoni was; he enjoyed teasing Frank about the resemblance between himself and Colleoni.

"But isn't it extraordinary," he said. "Don't you *see* it? Same chest, same arms, same shoulders."

Lou was the first to see the resemblance.

"Spittin' image," he said.

"Oh, no," said Sonya. "He looks so fierce and our dear Frank is so gentle."

"That's true too," said Soothin'.

Frank, a true innocent, was embarrassed. He didn't like being the subject of conversation. He blushed. To spare him, Sonya changed the subject.

"Isn't that a wonderful little scene in *Cavalcade* when he calls up and makes a reservation for his family on the *Titanic?*"

That did it. The story conference was on. Everybody except Carl, who hadn't read the play, became articulate and combative: little quarrels about casting; ideas on where to stay with the script and where to depart from it; where to place Queen Victoria's funeral which the Cavalcade family watches from a window with its final, blackout line: "She must have been a very little lady." It went on full tilt. I watched Carl nursing a liqueur. He smiled wanly. I suggested we all go to the smoking room. When we had settled ourselves there, the change of environment encouraged Carl to try a new tack. He spoke to me:

"Have I ever told you how I met Sonya?"

"No. How was it?"

"Through a rejection slip I ungraciously sent her while I was editor of the *Metropolitan*."

Sonya protested.

"Oh, Carl! Nobody wants to hear about that."

"I do," I said.

"So do I," said Lou Borzage.

"It was over a short story Sonya sent me. I'd never seen her name before. There was something about the story I liked but I thought it was too long. I sent a note to Sonya asking her to cut it and send it in again. She wrote back — rather peppery — to say that *Ainslee's* had accepted the story — length and all. That is why I'm here on the *Aquitania* sailing with you as a guest."

When you traveled for a film company in those days you traveled in the height of luxury, and in London I found myself in a river suite looking out at the twilit Thames. It was thrilling. I felt at home at the Savoy though I had never stayed in it before. Arnold Bennett had devoted his last novel to describing it and the intricate mechanism that manipulated it. It was amusing to keep testing Bennett's accuracy. He held up pretty well. I found a message from Siegfried; he was still at Campden Hill Square. I called him. He was having dinner with Glen Byam-Shaw at the Reform Club. I had become fond of Glen on the several visits he had made to New York, where he had come to direct English plays. He was sensitive, modest and all kindness. I insisted that he and Glen come to the Savoy. "I don't want to leave the river," I said. "I have become very attached to it." Siegfried laughed and said he was sure it would be all right with Glen. "What about Angela?" I asked. Glen had recently married Angela Baddeley, a well-known English actress. "Angela is playing," said Siegfried. It was set.

We had a happy time in the Savoy dining room. Glen wanted the Grill because theatre people were addicted to it but I insisted on getting a table in the dining room with a river view. Siegfried looked older. He was very quiet; it pleased him greatly that Glen and I had become friends. In a satirical voice he expressed a criticism of me for making this journey to see someone else's play when I should be retiring to the country — to the Spread Eagle at Thame, for example — to write one of my own. I made a weak defense. I said in that case I shouldn't be entertaining him and Glen in the style to which they were accustomed.

"I don't think I've been in the Savoy in twenty years," said Siegfried mildly.

I asked Siegfried whether he had succeeded in finding a country house for himself.

"He hasn't succeeded for himself," said Glen, "but he's succeeded for Burton." Half Moon Street proved no longer possible for Burton, and Siegfried had found a pleasant house for her in Woodside with a large garden.

"Angela and I went up to see her," Glen said. "Her new house is lovely but somehow everything about it is huge; the tomatoes are huge, the sunflowers are huge, the sofa in the drawing room is huge, and the lunch was huge. I don't know how we ever got through it. But she's always wonderful. You must go and see her, Sam."

"Of course," I said. "I can't wait."

"I always kiss her when I see her," said Glen. "It's like kissing a large, wet gooseberry."

Back in my river suite I telephoned Burton. She invited me for lunch on Saturday. I said I'd prefer tea. She yielded to my preference. Neither the Hoveys nor the Borzages were back yet. The Borzages had gone to see *Cavalcade* and the Hoveys to spend the evening with their London friends, F. Tennyson Jesse and her husband, H. M. Harwood. I sat at my window to see what was doing — so late in the evening — on the Thames.

The following night we all went to *Cavalcade*. We arrived at the historic theatre and were ushered into a stage box reserved for us. The vast house was crowded; one felt a palpitant expectancy among the audience. As the play unfolded one could feel increasingly a deep wash of sympathy, of recognition, of national identification, of pride. The things that were happening to this family had happened to all of them. Those who had not seen Queen Victoria's funeral had deeply felt it: the symbol of the great Empire laid low. Borzage, though not English, had tears in his eyes.

In the intermission after the first act we were greeted by C. B. Cochran, the producer. "You've made Borzage cry," I said to him, "and he is a very hard man." Cochran laughed; it was only too obvious that Borzage was not a hard man. We asked for Noel. Cochran said that he had gone to South America. Having directed and opened *Cavalcade,* and having received the thanks of the King, he'd treated himself to a holiday. Cochran asked if we didn't think it would be a good idea to photograph the play so we'd have a record of the London production. We all thought it would. Cochran said he would see to it. He also told Sonya and me that Noel would be in Hollywood before we really got working on the script.

I had invited Mr. and Mrs. Harold Laski to lunch the next day. Harold asked if he might bring a friend whom he greatly admired, prominent in the Labour party, Mr. Frank Wise. I said fine but that I would retaliate by inviting Siegfried. "That will be perfect," said Laski. We met next day at the Grill at one o'clock. I liked Mr. Wise at once — good-looking, very frank and open. Laski was in great form; he had a great deal to say, very edged, about Ramsay Mac — "The ribbon is in his coat and he will never know the verdict of history"; about Walter Lippmann and his "open mind" — "Open at both ends"; about Arthur Henderson, whom he loved. He had spent Justice Holmes's ninetieth birthday with him and the recollection of this made him happy. He quoted the Justice on Coolidge's writing: "He makes even his platitudes seem vulgar." Mrs. Laski was very quiet; she had learned, evidently, that this was the destiny of the wives of great talkers. I asked the Laskis whether they had seen *Cavalcade*. They had. Laski took a poor view of it: "Sentimental nationalism, in which the whole play was drenched." The treatment of Queen Victoria particularly irritated him. The Queen, he said, was a hard woman who would not abolish whipping in the navy. Frank Wise took issue with him on this. "I don't agree with you, Harold," he said. "The Queen is, by this time, a symbolic figure. She is part of the mystery which made this little island a great power in the world. Don't forget — while she lived, they lived. They shared, more or less, the same fragment of time. They share, with her, the national memory. I don't at all agree with you." Laski then said that of course she was a symbol universally accepted, a symbol of the nationalism that was the greatest breeder of wars. He attacked Cecil Rhodes and Standard Oil as conquistadors who enticed their governments to protect their investments. He touched on the conflict over Morocco, the scramble for Africa, the fight for the spoils of Manchuria, the Middle East. Siegfried and I exchanged glances. Laski was way beyond our depths. To show that I was not without international outlook, I quoted from Maurice Hindus's just-published book on Russia, in which he tells of an official who told him that they couldn't have gypsy music because it didn't help the Five Year Plan. Frank Wise laughed but said he was sure this was an improvisation of Hindus's. I found out later that Wise was unofficial representative of the Soviets in England. He was a most charming and likable man. He had just returned from America; he had seen all our labor leaders. He was struck by our heterogeneity; whereas in England, he said, labor is so homogeneous that "I can mobilize all of British labor in one morning."

I rode back with Siegfried in a taxi to drop him at Campden Hill Square. I asked him whether he didn't feel himself lost in a conversation like that, with Laski's dizzying spirals all over the world.

"But my dear Sam," he said, "that is my habitual feeling wherever I go. I am totally uneducated and the people I see know everything. I often think I should call my book, instead of *Sherston's Progress*, *Simpleton's Progress*."

Siegfried asked me to meet him in Salisbury so I could see the cottage he'd taken for the summer at Teffont. I had to go to see *Cavalcade* again and had an engagement to meet a new friend of mine, Rudolph Kommer, who had invited me to have dinner with him and Randolph Churchill the next night. I asked Siegfried to join us but he said he simply had to get some quiet in the country. He told me a good train to Salisbury on Friday morning. I said I'd be on it; he said he would meet me.

I was very glad to see Kommer again though he looked tired and depressed. "I wish," he said, "I could be a plant." Young Randolph Churchill, who came in just then, had no such wish. He was full of life and energy and very amusing about a trip he'd made to Hollywood. He'd gotten a job as an extra — a plain MP in a film being shot at Metro on Parnell. He got paid better than the MPs who played at the real thing in Westminster. I was pleased to hear that he'd made friends in Hollywood with Oscar Levant. He was very funny about Oscar as, later, Oscar was about him. Randolph said that *Cavalcade* was the "Home Sweet Home" of the galleries; I said that I'd been twice and that the orchestra seats were full too.

Siegfried met me at the train in Salisbury on Friday morning and drove me the fourteen miles or so to his cottage in Teffont. I was enchanted by the beauty of the country and the villages through which we drove. To get into his cottage we had to cross a little bridge over a brook that ran right beside his front door. I have never forgotten that day; Siegfried and I talked about it many times in Heytesbury, Wiltshire, where he finally settled. He showed me the poems he had written — enough for another book. He also had been rereading George Meredith and was about to gather himself to write a biography of him. He hoped to revive interest in this unjustly neglected author and especially to reanimate interest in him as a poet. We talked until late in the evening. I said what I felt: that I could spend the rest of my life in Teffont, and there have been times when I wished I had. I had to get back to London to keep my date with Burton. We were sailing the following Monday on the *Berengaria*. Siegfried suggested that I come back on Sunday. He would drive me to Southampton — an easy drive — to make the sailing. I accepted his offer.

Sitting and brooding, with large silences, Siegfried's face would crease into a smile. It was always some memory of Burton. "I came back from Bayreuth one summer," he said, "full of excitement about the performances I had seen there. I could get no adequate response from Burton. I did my best over *Tristan*. She cut me short. Her favorite opera was *Carmen*. She had seen it in Berlin with Mrs. Ross and, she said with a great suspensive silence before to set it off, there had been nine horses on the stage! Could Bayreuth match that? I had to confess it couldn't. Burton loves animals."

On Saturday, after lunch, I hired a car at the Savoy, gave the address to the chauffeur, and started out for Woodside Park. It took about an hour. The car stopped finally before Burton's new home: a square verandahed house on a leafy street. Burton opened the door. I hugged and kissed her. Never having tasted a gooseberry, I couldn't test the accuracy of Glen's comparison. We were certainly glad to see each other. She was a bit older, a bit grayer, but otherwise unchanged, the same look of irrepressible beneficence and gaiety. She was tidy; everything about her was tidy.

"Come in — come in," she said. I followed her down the front hall and into the living room. It was large and pleasant. It was a rare afternoon for England — full of sunshine. On the piano I saw a photograph of Burton happily cuddling a lion cub on her lap. I asked her how she had acquired this pet. "I got 'im in the Berlin zoo when I was there with Mrs. Ross. They lent 'im to me. 'E was 'appy with me. I was 'appy with 'im. 'Is nyme is Siegfried."

"I saw Siegfried," I said. "He sends his love. So does Glen Byam-Shaw."

" 'Ave you been to Teffont?"

"Yes. I spent the night there."

"It's good for Sieg. It quiets 'im."

"I think so."

"Come into the garden. Then we'll 'ave tea."

I followed.

"You look wonderful, Burton."

"You can see I don't use pynt or powder. I'm a natural woman."

"Where's Mr. Fleming?" I asked. "When I see you, I miss Mr. Fleming."

" 'E went to America. 'E's naughty. 'E 'asn't written yet."

"Did he go to consult Evangeline Adams?"

"Very likely. 'E'll 'ave no trouble. 'E 'as very 'igh connections."

The garden was lush. Sunflowers as tall as I was, birch trees, maples and elms. Burton took me by the hand and led me to the bottom of the garden, on the side farthest from the road. It debouched into a small clump of trees. There was a circlet of enormous sunflowers and, in their center, a bamboo reclining chair, like a chaise longue. Burton had a great air of showing it off.

"Siegfried's bower," she said. " 'E loves to sit 'ere an' muse."

"I don't wonder," I said.

She took my hand again. "An' over 'ere I'll show you — Osbert's nook."

The nook was less relaxed and less protected than the bower. It had a swing between two trees in the clump behind the bower with an ordinary wicker chair and a huge ashtray on a tabouret beside it.

"Cigars, 'e smokes," said Burton.

"I should think they'd spend all their time here."

"Osbert 'as a 'ouse in Italy," said Burton, to account for his non-presence at the moment.

We walked back to the house. Burton rang and a maid entered who served tea in a bay window overlooking the garden — a Half Moon Street tea. Burton produced a bottle of champagne. We sat drinking it. Suddenly she said:

"Do you think 'e's 'appy, Siegfried?"

The question startled me. Actually, I'd had the feeling that all was not entirely well with Siegfried.

"Tolerably," I said. "Not specially."

She shook her head.

"It's no good," she said. "That's why 'e's in Teffont. No use 'is styin' there. No use. The longer 'e styes, the worse 'e'll be."

I did not inquire. I knew she would not tell me.

"I'm going back there," I said. "My last night in England. He's driving me to the boat."

"Good," she said. "I'm glad you'll be there. I wish — just now — you'd take him back to America."

"I'll ask him," I said.

There was a long silence. I saw that it was time to go. Burton walked me to the door.

"Well," she said, "they're a genius, I suppose, meant to leave some wonderful book or poem — and that's all?"

There was a query but I could not answer it. Did she wish me to say: "That's enough?" It would not be good enough for Burton. Instead I said:

"I'm happy to see you so nicely settled here. I loved Half Moon Street, but this is ampler."

" 'E did it — Siegfried — 'e took the trouble to find it. 'E bought it. 'E pyed for it. You couldn't 'ave a more loyal friend in the world than Siegfried."

"I have found that to be true."

Burton was moved. She held my hand.

"I can sy this," she said. "Between Siegfried and me — it's a pure love."

She stood outside the front door and waved to me as the car moved down the street. It was the last time I ever saw her.

On Sunday afternoon Siegfried met me in Salisbury and the externals were as usual, but I knew Siegfried well enough to know that these might be deceptive. I felt that all was not well. Also, I had been troubled by Burton's odd remarks. Why had she said that he should not stay in Teffont, that I should take him to America? I was troubled by this but also cherishing the appealing beauties of the countryside. Siegfried said:

"Would you mind if I made a detour here? I feel I should pay a call on the Hunter girls. They have been extraordinarily kind to me during a difficult period — they are taking care of a friend of mine. Also, they are theatre crazy and eager to meet you."

I said I'd be delighted.

We drove along in silence for a while. Siegfried told me that the estate we were about to visit belonged to a famous British public figure. The Hunter girls, who were in charge of the house, were at present looking after the famous man's nephew, who was there alone and ill.

The next hour or so still has a quality of phantasmagoria, and when I consult my diary I find it there, too. The quiet, ordered beauty of the estate we entered — the gardens, the lawns, trees — was warm as an embrace. The house with its tower and its solitary invalid exercised a spell that was disquieting, necromantic. I met the Hunter girls: two ladies, one past forty, her sister a little younger, who were manifestly darlings. They adored Siegfried and were eager to do anything in the world to make him happy. Siegfried asked a few questions about the invalid: did he know that he was coming? Yes, they had told him, but he was not well enough to see anyone.

"He's perfectly well, as we know," said Siegfried.

This seemed to embarrass the Hunter girls, but one of them quickly covered it up by asking me questions about the theatre. They were especially keen about the Lunts, whom they had seen. Were they coming again? When and in what? I answered these as well as I could. All the time I was in a daze at the beauty with which I was surrounded, the dappled lawns, the vista of the far hills, the church steeple in the village that belonged to the estate.

Siegfried and I walked a little way down the lawn to the great flower beds, streaming color.

I followed his glance. He was looking up intently at a window in the square tower.

"Yes," he said, "it *is* beautiful. It's like *The Turn of the Screw.*"

Siegfried turned to go back to his car. We stood for a moment chatting with the Hunter girls. And then suddenly we were not alone — a young man had joined us, a flamboyantly dressed and arrogant young man. The women knew him, evidently. He treated them with condescension.

" 'Ow is 'is Lordship today?" he asked, with a jocular wink at them.

The elder Hunter girl introduced us.

" 'Ow do you do?" He nodded up toward the tower room.

" 'E expects me an' I 'ave to make the six-thirty to London. Apologies."

He turned abruptly and walked into the house.

The Hunter girls suffered. Having told Siegfried the invalid was too ill to see him, they were embarrassed and unhappy. Siegfried had gone white. He turned and walked toward his car. I followed.

We rode in silence. Siegfried's face was set; he kept his eyes on the road. I wondered. Had the invalid contrived this visit from the dis-agreeable young man in order to humiliate Siegfried? The ride back to Teffont passed in painful silence. The incident was ugly, grotesque. We crossed the rivulet in front of Siegfried's house and entered his cottage. I said I thought the Hunter girls perfect. He said it would be nice if I sent them something from America. I said I certainly would. Conversation at supper lagged. The visit had left an impression of evil, intensified somehow by the surrounding beauty. It remained with me that Siegfried had mentioned *The Turn of the Screw*. It was like that, a poisoned beauty. After supper I gave Siegfried my new play to read. He gave me his new poems. Next morning, before we left for Southampton, he gave me a lovely little book of woodcuts of churches and village street scenes in the Salisbury environment. It is before me now. I read Siegfried's inscription:

> *Fitz House — 23/4/32*
> *On Shakespeare's Birthday —*
> *Off to the boat.*

I had a good deal to think about on the boat. I remembered Burton. I thought I saw why she had suggested to me that I should take Siegfried back with me to America. About a year later, in New York, I had lunch with a famous English stage star. He said that there was no more pernicious young man in England than the occupant of that tower room.

I sat in my cabin thinking about Siegfried with a heavy heart. He was one of the few people I had known with a true quality of nobility;

he was a poet of exquisite sensibility; he was a genius. I had been a witness to his humiliation — a humiliation due to a vulnerability that had nothing to do with his character. Because of the loftiness and sensitivity of his nature he could not defend himself. It was tragic. I sat thinking of him with a deepening sense of the inescapable tragedy of life.

XV

Ina Claire

I N 1915 I WAS A JUNIOR AT HARVARD. I blew myself to a second
balcony seat at the Colonial Theatre to see the Ziegfeld Follies,
which featured Ina Claire. She was then under twenty and a star of
musical comedy. She came before the footlights in an organdy dress
and in a spotlight sang a satiric song called "Marie Odile." The big
musical reviews then used, for material, scenes from plays which had
recently been successful. *Marie-Odile* had been a tremendous Belasco
success starring Frances Starr. She played a young peasant girl whose
knowledge of biology was rudimentary; she did not know how babies
were generated and was shocked when she had one. Ina sang:

> *How sorry I feel*
> *For Marie Odile, that she should be disgraced*
> *She thought that babies*
> *Grew on trees, at least that's what she said*
> *(And got away with it)* . . .*

There was malice in that parenthesis, even envy. I craned forward
in my faraway seat to take in this personality because she saliently was
one. There was a comedic edge to "and got away with it" that made
the audience laugh warmly at the envy of such pervasive innocence in
a young girl. By the end of that song Ina had the audience at her feet.

* Marie Odile (Hirsch-Pollack-Wolf) © 1915 by M. Witmark & Sons. Copyright renewed. All rights reserved. Used by permission of Warner Bros. Music.

Ina Claire

The next time I heard her sing that song was in Paris some forty-five years later. I was staying briefly with my friend and erstwhile producer, Joseph Verner Reed. Reed was doing a stint as cultural attaché to Eisenhower's Ambassador to France. In the Place Vendôme I ran into Ina. She had, by then, done three plays of mine. I hadn't seen her in a long time. We fell on each other's necks. She was free for dinner. I asked her to come to the Reeds'. I was sure they would be delighted to have her. They were. As we sat having cocktails before dinner, I said: "Ina, do you remember the song you sang in the Ziegfeld show in Boston in 1915, the Marie Odile one?" She said: "Of course I do." "Won't you sing it for us?" Joe Reed asked. She sang it, two verses and the choruses. She wowed the Reeds as she had wowed the audience in Boston more than forty-five years before.

I first tried to get Ina for my play *Rain from Heaven,* but that didn't work out. Ina was busy; Jane Cowl played it. I had given *Biography* to Guthrie McClintic, who wanted Laurette Taylor for it. I had an unhappy correspondence with Miss Taylor about it; things swerved the way they irrationally do in the theatre and in life too. Ina was in Philadelphia, trying out a European play for the Theatre Guild. Terry Helburn called and asked me to come to see Ina in this play which, she said, had almost gotten over. She felt that if I were to do a rewrite on it the play might work. I went. I would go anywhere to see Ina in a play. We made a date in Terry's suite at the Ritz-Carlton to discuss a possible rewrite. We met after the performance: Ina, Lawrence Langner, Terry and myself.

Ina is the most candid, most unsecretive person in the world. She is like some British aristocrats I have known who tell you everything about themselves and their families at first meeting. This candor has often astonished me. I think it comes from a feeling of independence, ultimate security. Ina likes to talk about her love affairs, especially if they haven't gone well for her. Soon after I met her she told me of her romance with Vincent Astor. He was in love with her and wished to marry her. The great obstacle was his father, John Jacob Astor. One day the obstacle disappeared in the *Titanic* disaster. When the obstacle disappeared, so did Vincent. She simply stopped hearing from him. Years passed; she had written him off long ago. One day she arrived in

New York, feeling low, and went to the Pierre, where she always stayed in a single room. She felt she must find a place for herself, a home. "I thought, goddamn it, Vincent. *One* thing he could do, with all the real estate he owns, is find me an apartment. I'll call the swine." Before she could follow up on this plan, the phone rang. It was Vincent. He was awfully glad to hear her voice. She was the one person in the world he wished to see at this moment. Ina kept listening. He finally came to the point. "The fact is, darling, I've written a play. I'd love to have your opinion of it. Frank, you know — utterly frank — will you read it for me?"

"I never got an apartment from him — I never got a chance to mention it. I just found myself reading his goddamn play. It was lousy, I'm happy to say."

In Terry's suite Ina began to talk about a more recent love affair of hers with a European princeling. Ina had begun to wonder about him and she went on to clarify her feelings in front of all of us. She went on and on. Meantime, I was getting very sleepy. I hated midnight conferences anyway. Terry jumped up. "We're all tired," she said. "Let's postpone this till tomorrow — the noon train to New York. I've got a drawing room for Ina. We'll have our conference there."

This suited everybody. I went thankfully to my room. I was glad to be alone, because that afternoon in New York I had received a most surprising letter from Siegfried, announcing his marriage. I had brought the letter along with me and I now reread it for the third time. Siegfried had been to a fête champètre given by some friends of his. It was a costume party on the lawn of their country place. He had danced with a masked girl in a Renaissance costume. He had been so entranced with her that by the time the evening was over he had asked her to marry him. She had accepted; they were married a week later and were at this moment of writing about to leave on their honeymoon. His mother was a friend of the bride's parents and liked her greatly. His mother was very happy. So was he. He longed for me to meet her. He would write presently when they were settled. I had cabled at once, saying how happy I was.

Another correspondent wrote me from London about Siegfried's marriage. He had been told about it by D. H. Lawrence, who had made the peevish remark that he hoped the marriage would fail so that Siegfried wouldn't stop writing.

The next day Ina appeared at the train: tall, sparkling, beautifully dressed. The members of the company were gathered in a knot at the Pullman entrance. When Terry, Langner and I arrived, we found Ina in a graphic conversation with her leading man. The company distributed itself on Pullman chairs. Ina's conversation was going full-tilt when the train started. Terry told Ina we'd wait for her in her drawing room at the end of the car. We marched into the drawing room and sat, leaving the door open. We watched. Ina and the actor showed no sign of having reached a conclusion.

"What on earth are they talking about?" Terry asked.

"She's talking to him about the play," said Langner.

"That's what we'd like to do," said Terry. "We certainly couldn't get to it last night."

Langner placed himself so that he could look down the length of the car.

"Take it easy, Terry," he said. "I'll report."

In about half an hour he did. "I think they're through," he said. We looked. Ina and the actor were lengthily saying good-bye to each other. Ina started to her drawing room but she stopped to say good-bye to the ingenue, the character woman, the second lead. She sat in an empty chair to accomplish these farewells in depth. Trenton passed, and Princeton, but Ina did not pass. She had something personal and interesting to say to every member of the company. By the time we got to Newark, Ina had not yet reached the drawing room. Terry appealed to Langner.

"For God's sake, Lawrence," she implored, "do something."

"Stop Ina talking?" said Langner hopelessly. "It can't be done."

We arrived in the Pennsylvania station. Langner, Terry, Ina and I started the long trek up the platform.

"I've never been in a company I liked better," said Ina. "They're charming — absolutely charming. When are we going to talk about the play?"

"That's what we're beginning to wonder," said Terry.

"Well," said Ina, "I'll be at the Pierre and available."

"What about five o'clock this afternoon?" said Terry. "Okay with you boys?"

Langner and I said it was all right with us boys.

"I just remembered," said Ina. "Five o'clock is no good for me. There's a feller coming up to talk to me at five o'clock."

"He will not," I said with some bitterness, "realize his intention."

Ina laughed. "These wisecracks of yours! Why don't you get them into your dialogue?"

I knew in my bones that the play I had seen in Philadelphia was a dead duck, but I was glad to have seen it. Ina's timing and diction were miraculous. I wanted more than ever to have her do *Biography*. I knew that she had read it — Harold Freedman had given it to her — and that she was tepid about it. I'd identified her so passionately with the heroine of *Biography* that I felt I didn't want to do the play without her. Her readings were translucent, her stage presence encompassing. The flick of an intonation deflated pomposity. She never missed a nuance. She was under contract to the Guild; I told Terry and Langner that I must have her. But she was reluctant; in fact she asked the Guild if she might not try out another play which she fancied. I was furious that they allowed her to do it. The all-wise Miss Helburn advised me to allow her to burn her own bridges. I went to see that tryout too without making my presence known to Ina. My obsessive feeling about her was only deepened. That play closed on the road also. I then heard a story, told me by one of Ina's offstage friends, which quickened my heart. I have never asked Ina whether it was true or not and I cannot vouch for it. According to the story, Ina told how she had outwitted the Theatre Guild, "They gave me a lousy play of Behrman's," she said, "sure that I would reject it. But I was hard up and needed the money. If I'd rejected it, it would have broken my contract. So I fooled them — I accepted it!" We opened in Princeton. Ina, who had trouble remembering her lines, was prompted all evening by her pet stage manager. When the final curtain fell, Ina rushed to him, embraced him, and said: "Darling, it's the best performance we ever gave!"

Between its New York run and the road tour, Ina appeared in *Biography* for two seasons. When she played it in summer stock after the tour closed, the stage manager at Marblehead, Massachusetts, made a record of a performance there. After all these years, it projects Ina's special qualities: her timing, the edge and clarity of her readings, her acute gift for comedy. Some people think of Ina as a brittle actress. The truth is that in addition to being a superb comedienne, she had great warmth with profound emotional control. Somerset Maugham said of *Biography* that it was a tragic play. It was Ina's performance that made it so.

Ina was immensely voluble and graphic on the subjects close to her heart: posture, dress, proper breathing, the function of the diaphragm in voice control and diction. You could achieve poise only by frantic discipline. She would think nothing, in the middle of a party, of lying down flat on the floor to illustrate one of her five points. Her diaphragm stayed perfectly flat but still cooperated subtly in voice control, which she illustrated by reading Shakespeare lines at different volumes of speed and sound. Her diaphragm never let her down. She had made a deep study of clothes in different epochs and in different regimes; she had a library on the subject.

When I told her my idea for *End of Summer*, the next play I was writing, hopefully for her, she was delighted and accepted it at once, though she was no longer hard up. She cautioned me. "Don't put it all in the stage direction," she said. "You fool yourself doing that but you don't fool me. Get it in the *dialogue*." I promised to try. It ran successfully in America for two seasons.

There is a moment in the third act of *End of Summer* where the heroine, preparing for her wedding which doesn't come off, comes downstairs in her grandmother's wedding dress. As played by Ina, it was a moment of rare loveliness. Someone said what a pity that Réjane had died; it would have been an ideal part for her in France. My friend Arthur Richman, who had had Ina in a play of his, when he heard about this, scoffed: "People talk about Réjane, what a great actress she was. I saw her many times in Paris. She couldn't touch Ina, especially in serious parts, because Ina is a great comedienne, and you have to be a great comedienne to dig everything possible out of a serious play."

It was tremendous fun having Ina in a play. Before we came to New York we played Boston. One day Ina said that she'd never seen Harvard. Would I take her to see it? On a sunny afternoon I took Ina for a walk through Harvard Yard, passing Weld Hall, where I had lived, and other landmarks. We must have made a rather bizarre couple as we walked along: Ina, taller than I, golden, dressed with great chic in expensive simplicity; I in an unpressed suit which I'd been wearing for weeks. We hadn't walked very far when dormitory windows started popping up and wolf calls began to fill the Yard. As we continued our walk we were serenaded by whistling undergraduates.

"You see, Ina," I said, "they are awfully happy to have me back on campus."

Ina smiled.

XVI

Profitable Failure

S IEGFRIED WAS AWAY when I came to London for the English
production of *Biography,* which was just as well, since getting a
play going is at best time-consuming. Noel Coward was directing the
play; Hugh Beaumont, the rising star in the London theatre who was
soon to dominate it as Jed Harris did the New York one, was the im-
presario in charge. Beaumont — called Binkie — got Laurence Olivier
to play opposite Ina. It seemed a perfect setup, and yet it turned out
to be, as Binkie referred to it ever after, a *"dis-ah-ster"* — he
lengthened the vowel into a moan of despair. The opening night,
which according to custom, I did not attend, was, Binkie reported to
me that night on the telephone, "damp." The notices were unfriendly.
The next day I went with a friend to the Ivy restaurant, analogous to
our Sardi's, for lunch. Binkie, looking extraordinarily handsome and
youthful, came up to my table carrying the evening paper open at the
notice. He threw it on the table before me. There ensued a conversation you would be unlikely to overhear, after a similar dis-ah-ster, at
Sardi's.

"This," he said, "makes me faintly livid."

"I've seen it," I said. "Not so good, is it?"

"Good! It's definitely dire!"

My telephone rang very early a few mornings later — at seven-
thirty. In a half dream I had been listening to Binkie Beaumont
enunciating doom. "Definitely dire." It was Harold Laski, whom I'd

seen a few days before. He apologized for calling me so early but he had two things he wished to tell me. One: he wanted me to come that afternoon to his office in the London School of Economics to meet Felix Frankfurter, who was to deliver a lecture on the American Constitution. Two: he wanted to deliver a message from Frankfurter, whom I had never met. Frankfurter had seen John Maynard Keynes, who told him that his wife had fallen in love with *Biography,* and insisted that everyone must see it. Did not that neutralize for me the effect of the notices? I said it greatly did and thanked him. "Mrs. Keynes is going to call you," Laski said. "I gave her your number — do you mind?" I did not. I thought how kind it was of Laski. I determined to call Ina, who had been quite depressed since the opening and was wondering what she could do to keep the play running. The New York producer, Max Gordon, was in London and he had told Ina in his blunt manner: "There's nothing in the world wrong with *Biography.* They just don't want it." Well, that darling and ineffable Mrs. Keynes wanted it! It did make a difference. I remembered Mrs. Keynes from my early days in New York. Lydia Lopokova! The Russian Ballet! I had never met her but had been in love with her. She was utterly lovely. I had my breakfast, got dressed, and at a seemly hour called Ina. I told her about Mrs. Keynes. She was at her most realistic: "Even if her husband comes to see it, it won't give us a run," she said, and hung up. Presently Mrs. Keynes called. She had a lovely voice and a tantalizing accent. She wanted me to meet her husband and said Professor Frankfurter would arrange something. I said I'd been reading her husband's book on the boat and was especially eager to meet him. It was the first rift in the lute:

"You *read* him?"

I said that I had read his book and that the description of Woodrow Wilson vis-à-vis Lloyd George and Clemenceau . . .

She did not let me finish.

"I can't read him," she said. *"Slumps* and *Booms* — that's all it is — *slumps* and *booms."*

But we patched it up quickly and vowed to meet.

I sat thinking. I didn't see how anyone — even a wife, even a Russian, could fail to be carried away by the most merciless description of Woodrow Wilson being slowly pulverized by the grinding pincers of the sophisticated brains of his ravenous colleagues, Clemenceau and Lloyd George. "A non-conformist minister," Keynes made out Wilson to be, expounding the Pentateuch to two agnostics.

At four-thirty I arrived at the London School of Economics: cold, bare walls plastered with typewritten lecture announcements. There were many Indian students and male and female English, plainly dressed. The ground floor contained a bookshop. I stepped in and bought a life of Lenin. Professor Laski's office was quite full. He greeted me and introduced me to a professor of jurisprudence at Oxford and to the editor of the *New Statesman*. "Felix," he said, "is talking to a countryman of yours, Mr. Kennedy." He brought me up to Frankfurter who was talking to a very good-looking, engaging young man. "Tell me," Frankfurter was saying, "why is your father so bent on being Ambassador? Doesn't he know that he'll be besieged by Americans imploring him to get them reservations on the Orient Express, after the train is sold out?" The young man smiled. Frankfurter turned to me. He was a small man, but I got an instant impression of great power and great accessibility. "Well," he said, "I have unearthed a fan for you — Lydia Keynes — a fan I am in love with." Laski reminded him that he had a lecture to deliver. We all, including the professor of jurisprudence, the editor, the young Kennedy and the others in the room, walked into a small lecture hall down the corridor. Frankfurter, who was then on the faculty of the Harvard Law School, was on an exchange professorship at Oxford. I sat with Laski and Professor Born, who had written a book on America I'd read the year before. Frankfurter spoke with great strength and simplicity; the lecture was thrilling: the Constitution far transcended a legal document. He quoted Justice Marshall: "It is a Constitution we are expounding." He expounded it. I sat breathless; I forgot I had a flop at the Globe Theatre.

That afternoon, Laski told me that he had been invited to visit Russia the coming June and would I go with him? I returned to the Carlton Hotel in a whirl of excitement. Should I go? There were, after all, other things than the theatre, possibilities more expansive. When I got to the hotel there was a message to call Harold Freedman, who had arrived in London a few days before. He had arranged a lunch appointment for me to meet Alexander Korda. I was disinclined to accept. My head was full of the American Constitution and the heady atmosphere of the London School of Economics. There was the possibility of Russia in June. Freedman, in his calm voice, told me that Korda wanted me for a quick job now but whether I did it or not, it would be valuable for me to meet him. "You like London so much," he said, "and Korda would ask you to come over once a year to do a job for him." I said okay.

The next day, I met Freedman, Korda and an assistant of his, another Hungarian named Biro. Biro was a tiny old man with a keen wit and a pleasantly cynical outlook. I found out later that he had been Prime Minister in a Karolyi cabinet. Korda was immensely likable, tall, somewhat stooped, and apologizing for the slowness of his brain, not because he was deficient but because he was tired. He was always tired. He wanted me to do a quick job on a film on his immediate schedule, *The Scarlet Pimpernel,* by Baroness Orczy. "It's for Leslie Howard and Merle Oberon," he said. He would leave the script for me at my hotel. "It will not pain you to read it," said Biro. "The Baroness has a simple mind which enables her to write best sellers." Korda was engaging and Biro most amusing. Harold and I walked back to the hotel. I told him that I would like to try it. "Three weeks," I cautioned him. It was early May; it would still leave me time to go to Russia with Laski.

Professor Frankfurter invited me to dinner to meet the Maynard Keyneses in the Carlton grill. We were both staying at the Carlton. We waited a few moments for Harold Laski in the lobby. Frankfurter told me with boyish excitement, clutching my arm as we walked down the lobby, of going to dinner in Oxford with five Nobel Prize winners. "As I walked in with Lord Rutherford, he said to me: 'You'll meet Eddington — you know the trash *he* turns out!' " He squeezed my arm for emphasis to make sure that I shared his delight over Eddington's trash. Laski and Mrs. Laski came; we went into the grill. Mr. and Mrs. Keynes had already been seated. They rose to greet us. Mrs. Keynes scarcely resembled the silvered coryphée whom I had seen on the stage twenty years before. She was a middle-aged lady, warm and lively, with her hair done up in a topknot. I was struck by the appearance of her husband. He seemed to me the most impressive-looking man I had ever met: tall, slim, rather gray-faced, tremendous power and incalculable reserve. They began talking about Frankfurter's speech to the Institute of International Affairs a few nights before. "I hear," said Keynes, "that you were badgered by Shaw." "Yes," said Frankfurter, "he chose to heckle me. And you know about what? The American Constitution, to the study of which I have devoted all my life and which I know as a surgeon knows anatomy. I wished for his sake that he had chosen another subject. He'd have come out better and I'd have been more entertained." "We'd all have been more entertained," said Laski. "I was there and I must say Shaw cut a poor figure for a great man."

Mr. Keynes had just returned from America. He had seen the President and the leading industrialists. He found our capitalists bewildered and without successors. "The young men," he said, "are all in Washington." He described a lunch with Mr. Morgan and his insignificant junior partners. The big businessman, he said, had a sense of insecurity because for the first time in history money was no longer believed in. He spoke of the telephonic shifting of fortunes during the boom.

Mrs. Keynes shot me a mischievous glance and turned the conversation to the theatre and to films. It was easy for me to tell some Hollywood stories which seemed to amuse them. Keynes told us that Radio City had made a great impression on him. He said he had a theatrical problem of his own, would I be so good as to discuss it with him. I said I would be happy to. He invited me to his house for lunch. Frankfurter asked Laski to bring me to lunch with him in Oxford. The evening ended in a bloom of invitations.

I spent the whole of the next day in my room assimilating *The Scarlet Pimpernel* material to be ready for a conference with Korda that night in his house in St. John's Wood. Leslie Howard was my favorite light comedian. I enjoyed writing a scene for him: the born dandy, trying on a new suit, lightly and fancifully giving instructions to his tailor. Oddly enough, this scene, which I wrote on that first day, is all that remains in the film of my three weeks' work on the script. The rest was ultimately written by Robert Sherwood. Dinner that night at Korda's was very pleasant; there were Korda, his brother Vincent, the artist, Biro and myself. Vincent was quite different from his older brother; he was small, dark and intense, passionate for primitive African art and sculpture and his own work. "When he's not painting," Korda said, "he's thinking about it. He is never away from his easel." Nevertheless, he was to do the sets for *The Scarlet Pimpernel,* and was already looking for locations.

I read the treatment aloud after supper, explaining that I had allowed myself to burst into dialogue when I felt like it. I read the scene I had written for Leslie Howard. They liked it. For the rest, Korda pointed out that if I were to follow the dramatized version of the book at all, several of the scenes I had outlined at the end would be structurally impossible. But it was all very relaxed, none of the life-and-death tension of the Hollywood conferences.

The next morning I went back to my outline and tried to amend it structurally, though I didn't see why we had to follow the script so closely. I left in time to keep my lunch appointment with Keynes. I had received that morning a triumphant and amusing letter from Abraham Flexner, telling me that he had raised enough money to start his Institute for Advanced Study at Princeton. He had cabled an invitation to Einstein to join the faculty and Einstein had accepted. I brought the letter along; I thought it might interest Keynes. I was again impressed by the extraordinary effect of Keynes's personality: prodigious authority, prodigious reserve. When we sat down to lunch I poured out at him the contents of Flexner's letter, how excited he was at the prospect of a fully endowed institute to be devoted entirely to research. Keynes did not share Flexner's enthusiasm. "Out of the marsh gas," he said, "into a vacuum." It was the wrong way to go about getting pupils. It was like advertising for a wife. You must get pupils as you do a wife — out of the ordinary contacts of life. These must be kept up. "When I first saw Lydia in New York, she was sitting on Heywood Broun's lap. I did not feel this was her proper destiny and I diverted her." He insisted on what he called normal contacts. Flexner's Institute did not appeal to him at all — the sterility of having no drudgery, no administrative routine, no stupid pupils. There is always enough time, enough leisure, for creative work.

He said suddenly: "You're a great friend of Siegfried Sassoon's, aren't you?" I said I hoped so. He said he was too, that he admired him greatly. He had been very surprised, even incredulous, at hearing of his marriage. He recalled his first meeting with Siegfried in the war — Welsh Fusiliers. He said that Dr. Rivers' prescription for Siegfried ran counter to his, Keynes's, personal fetish, about interfering with one's normal contacts. I told him that Siegfried thought that Rivers had saved his life. "I wonder," said Keynes, "how long he will think so."

"I have been wanting," he said, "to build a theatre in London. I wanted to ask your advice about it. But I've decided to build one in Cambridge." He spoke of his wish to keep Cambridge small. "I see," he said, smiling, "you've been looking at Cézanne."

I had been — a self-portrait. We got up and looked at it more closely. "I bought it," he told me, "for a few francs when I was young and didn't know I was buying a Cézanne — just a portrait of a man with an interesting face."

We sat talking for a while. He was glad, he said, that he was not a playwright, especially at this moment, which he argued was a time for the epic novel. He spoke of the Chekhov trilogy which was at this moment running in Moscow. Noel Coward he tossed off as a "tenth-rate genius." The trouble with the Shakespearian season at the Old Vic was that it was run by a man who had no ear for the music of Shakespeare's speech. He admired C. B. Cochran as a producer, said that he had considerable talent for it.

I had another look at the man with the interesting face.

I told Keynes that I had to go back to my hotel to work for Korda on *The Scarlet Pimpernel*. I didn't know how I could concentrate on it. "Can I console myself," I asked, "on the score that it is, at least, a normal contact?"

"Certainly," he said, laughing.

When the two bulky volumes of the Holmes-Laski correspondence (1916–1935) were published by the Harvard University Press, the editor, M. A. de Wolfe Howe, asked Mr. Justice Frankfurter (as he had become) to write a foreword. Frankfurter did — a brief one. He enlarged on the almost total impossibility of the two volumes existing at all:

"Neither David Belasco nor Max Reinhardt could have contrived a more dramatic contrast than Laski and Holmes when their friendship began. Facing one of the most impressive personalities of his day was a frail stripling of twenty-three. More than half a century separated them. Until he spoke, Laski was not particularly noticeable. But it was not the first time that Laski struck fire in an old man who was the leader of his profession. When Francis Galton, the famous geneticist, discovered that the author of an article which had attracted his attention was a 'schoolboy at Manchester, aged seventeen!' he wrote: 'It is long since I have been so much astonished. The lad probably has a great future before him and he will make a mark if he sticks to Eugenics. . . .' "

Frankfurter goes on to tell that Laski did not stick to eugenics but went into teaching: a few years as a tutor in McGill and then "an obscure junior instructorship in the Department of Government at Harvard" and filled out his "academic pittance" by writing for Herbert Croly's *New Republic* during the summers. When I met the frail stripling — a little stockier now but not much — the next morning to catch the train to Oxford to visit Frankfurter, I had no idea of the tremendous effect of Laski's teaching at Harvard. "For," Frankfurter goes on, "he taught his colleagues as well as his pupils as do all great teachers." Professor Charles H. McIlwain, one of the glories of Harvard both as scholar and teacher, said of him: "His influence on students was greater than that of any other instructor I have ever known. His influence on me was profound." I was as ignorant of all this as I was of most things when I sat chatting with Laski on the Oxford train. All I knew was that he seemed willing to take a great deal of trouble over me, like taking me to Oxford just now, for instance. He was always like that. I never came to London again without calling him the first day. He was never too busy; he always had time for me.

I told Laski that I had met a former pupil of his, the son of a great

Harold Laski

American industrialist, at a dinner party. After dinner this young man announced that he was being psychoanalyzed. When he was asked why, he said, "Well, last year I went over to London to study with Harold Laski. He's pretty magnetic, you know, and under his influence I found myself getting over pretty far to the left. Now I'm being analyzed to get back where I belong!" This story put Laski into a rapture. His wife told me that he kept telling it for years afterward.

We arrived presently at Frankfurter's in Norham Gardens. Mrs. Frankfurter received us, a tall, beautiful woman with gray hair parted in the middle. The other guest was Ellery Sedgwick, the editor of the *Atlantic Monthly*. Sedgwick asked Mrs. Frankfurter how she enjoyed Oxford after Harvard.

"Well, it is a man's world here. Women have really no place in it. There is nothing for us to do except wait around and get dowdy."

At lunch the conversation lunged: Frankfurter on the hectic American electorate, Sedgwick on a recovery program for the United States; he adverted to two essays by Matthew Arnold. Laski agreed that these two essays contained the essence of the answer to our problems now. I hadn't read either of them; I felt like running out to the library to get them. How awful it was to be ignorant! I remembered how Siegfried felt about this; the same sense of inadequacy: *Simpleton's Progress*. I asked Sedgwick — perhaps to get him to talk about something I did know — how he came to print Frankfurter's two pieces on Sacco and Vanzetti in the *Atlantic*. Sedgwick answered at some length: "I kept hearing about Sacco and Vanzetti. I didn't really want to hear about them. I was very tired. I needed a holiday badly. I finally left for one. I got off the boat at Montevideo. I went to the hotel to sleep. The first morning I went for a walk. I found the great public square crowded with thousands of people. They were shouting and staring up at an immense poster — great letters: 'Sacco and Vanzetti Murdered by the United States.' The feeling in the crowd was so passionate, so hostile to the United States, that it shocked me. I thought, well, if in Montevideo thousands of people get up early in the morning to denounce the United States over Sacco and Vanzetti, I ought to go back home and do something about it. I took the next boat home. I called up Felix and

Felix Frankfurter

asked him to show me what he'd written. I'd refused to read it before. And I warned you, didn't I, Felix?"

"You did," said Frankfurter. He explained to me: "Ellery warned me that I'd become an untouchable. So I became. Old friends would cut me in the street. I could hardly go into the Harvard Club."

I asked Sedgwick what Frankfurter had said when he warned him.

"He said, 'It will be interesting to see if I can survive it.' He did."

When I left to go back to London with Laski, I felt that it had been a radiant occasion.

I don't know whether Mrs. Keynes ever persuaded her husband to see my play, but even if she did, it did not, as Ina predicted, give the play a run. It closed after a few weeks, an utter failure. What I see now is that this failure provided me with the most rewarding few weeks of my life. I have been living on them ever since. I met Felix Frankfurter, Alexander Korda, Maynard Keynes, deepened my friendship with Harold Laski. I did not go to Russia with Laski; I don't remember why I chose to do something else; all I remember is the missed opportunity. At Christmas I got a present from Keynes, a pamphlet illustrated by Low. H. G. Wells had gone to Russia to record an interview with Stalin; the recording is commented on by Shaw and Keynes. Keynes is marvelously funny about it: "My picture of that interview is of a man struggling with a gramophone." I read the pamphlet when it arrived and several times since then. Now with the advantage of hindsight, it is remarkable that of the three Keynes is the only one who is mature and immensely readable. He has Shaw's number — that he loves dictators — and Stalin's — that he loves to murder people. Low's caricatures of Wells, Shaw and Keynes enhance this pamphlet; Shaw and Wells, in the caricatures as well as in the text, are naïve beside Keynes. Korda, Laski and Frankfurter remained lifelong friends — not for my life because I appear to have the somewhat vulgar gift of survival — but for their lives.

I was abroad when I read of Felix's elevation to the Supreme Court; I cabled congratulations. Some time after, I was in Washington and I telephoned him at the Court. Within an hour I had a message at my hotel to come there at four-thirty. When I arrived his secretary ushered me into his private office, telling me that the Justice was still in the Court but would be in at any minute. I sat beside the great desk and waited, awed by the augustness of the building, of my surroundings. I heard a rustle, as of a skirt. Felix, in his robes, swept by, sat at his desk, swiveled his chair around, and faced me.

"*Nu?*" he said.

I had not heard this monosyllabic Yiddish greeting in a long time. When I was a boy, my uncles, who were peddlers, used to greet each other so after a separation. It means loosely: "Well, how are things? What's doing?" It was startling to hear it in this august room, from the black-robed figure behind the great desk. It was the essence of Felix to greet me in this homely way — of his gallantry, his warmth, his gift for the common touch. I went to see him in his hospital bedroom a few months before he died. The head nurse told me I would have to wait for a few moments as Justice Harlan was with him. When the Justice came out he wiped his forehead and smiled at me. "He wore me out!" he said. When I went in I found Felix full of excitement — he was getting a new education, submitting to a new discipline, learning to use new muscles. He said to me once — a parenthetical remark — while I was lunching with him, "We are all poor creatures." I am surrounded still by the reverberations of his personality; I remember that *"Nu?"*

XVII

Playwrights' Company

O NE SPRING DAY IN 1939, Sidney Howard called and asked me to have lunch with him at the Plaza. I had known Sidney for a long time; he had been a comember with me in one of Professor George Pierce Baker's playwriting classes, English 47, at Harvard in 1916. I had seen him only sporadically in the intervening years, but I had a healthy regard for him as a writer and as a person. I had been impressed by him early in English 47. Professor Baker's first assignment to us was to dramatize a short story of our own choosing in any of the current magazines. Sidney chose an unusual one — a short story by Galsworthy. The scene is a mangy nightclub on Christmas Eve. The comedian, a raffish and illiterate scavenger, tries to pick up laughs by denigrating Christmas. In the middle of this unholy doggerel, Jesus Christ appears, a figure of compassionate dignity. He does not reproach the comedian who has been making fun of him; he takes him into his confidence. The Christ figure vanishes; the comedian and the audience remain to bless the gracious apparition, vanquished by the display of good manners. I chose a story from the *Smart Set* about a bounder who makes love to the nurse of his dying wife; the rest of the class was similarly addicted to sensation. Professor Baker praised Sidney for having chosen an impossible theme from a practical point of view, but one which had spiritual significance. I had watched Sidney's work since then — his magazine articles and his plays. He had written *They Knew What They Wanted* and *Yellow Jack,* the first play that ventured to dramatize a heroic episode in medical science. In one season he had had two plays produced by the Theatre Guild — *The Silver Cord,* the first exposure, as far as I know, of virulent momism, and *Ned McCobb's Daughter,* a study in bootlegging with a wonderful performance by Alfred Lunt.

What Sidney wished to propose to me was that I join the Playwrights' Company, an organization about to be created at the urgency of Robert Emmet Sherwood. Bob was then surely the most popular playwright in the English-speaking world. The Theatre Guild had been producing his plays *Idiot's Delight* and *Reunion in Vienna* with tremendous success, all with the Lunts, who were members of the Guild acting company. The other members of the new company were to be Maxwell Anderson and Elmer Rice. Max Anderson had also been produced successfully by the Guild. So had I. I asked what we could do for ourselves that the Guild couldn't do. This was a sore point. Sidney told me finally that Bob was not happy with the Guild for all sorts of reasons, too minute to go into now. "Bob wants to talk to you," Sidney said. Bob had a new play, *Abe Lincoln in Illinois,* with which he wanted to start the company's season. What had I? I said that I was just finishing a play called *No Time for Comedy.* "I have one too," said Sidney, *"Madame, Will You Walk?* That will give us a start — three plays!"

The truth is that Sidney's proposal bowled me over. This would mean breaking with the Guild. They had produced my first play and several since. The members of their board were friends of mine; I was fond of Terry Helburn, Lawrence Langner and Phil Moeller, who, as a director, suited me perfectly. Maurice Wertheim had been extraordinarily kind to me. I was flabbergasted; I just didn't know what to say. "It bowled me over too," said Sidney, "but Bob cleared any doubts." Sidney added that Bob had persuaded John Wharton, a highly regarded theatrical lawyer and a member of a distinguished firm, to be president of our company. There it was, already in existence, seemingly, a company of five playwrights, with a president. Sidney had a paper for me to sign stating that I would join the company. I put off signing it. Sidney agreed that it would be better to wait till I had seen Bob. I filled in the rather awkward interval by telling Sidney a story of another playwrights' company that had been told me by James Forbes.

The Playwright's Company: S. N. Behrman, Maxwell Anderson, Robert E. Sherwood, Elmer Rice. Behrman sits in the presidential chair

James Forbes was a receding, successful playwright who had written many plays which I had seen at the Worcester Theatre when I was a boy. *The Chorus Lady* was one of them. I used to meet Forbes at parties; he was tired, disillusioned, slightly cynical. He was no longer in demand as a playwright and didn't mind it. He told marvelous stories about Clyde Fitch, who had been a friend of his. His playwrights' story was as follows: he and some colleagues decided to form a producing company of their own with the highest motives — to lift the tone of the American theatre by producing masterpieces. Their first production was to be *Macbeth.* They went into this with high-minded passion. They put their own money in. They worked very hard. They opened in Stamford. From the first minute, Forbes said, his heart sank. Nothing worked; the casting was awful. By the end of the first act he knew that he had never seen anything so terrible in his life. In the intermission, in conference with his colleagues, Forbes made no effort to conceal his despair. It was rending. Finally, Augustus Thomas made an effort to cheer him up. He tapped Forbes on the shoulder:

"Come on, Jimmie, don't take it so hard. After all — you didn't write it!"

Of course I discussed the idea at once with Harold Freedman. He took a very poor view of it. He did not believe in playwrights producing their own plays. Four of us were his clients. He believed in deciding on a manager in each individual case. He believed in the Open Market — even if it meant that most of us, in any case, ended up with the Theatre Guild.

I had met Bob Sherwood, but I never got to know him intimately till I became his partner in the Playwrights' Company. He was a tremendously impressive personality: six feet seven inches tall, straight and thin, almost cadaverous. He had dark, expressive eyes, which deepened, when he was seriously involved, into a tragic look. He was self-conscious about his abnormal height; I had been told that when he was young he felt sure that girls didn't want to dance with him. He was at the top of his profession, at home in the London theatre as he was in New York. He was powerful. He could get the Lunts whenever he wanted to; when it came to casting a new play for which he wanted

Spencer Tracy, he got Spencer Tracy away from Metro-Goldwyn-Mayer. This was a thing that could not be done, but he did it.

He had an overflowing sense of humor; he was known throughout the city as a party-turn. I had seen him, just a few weeks before, at a party given by Kaufman and Hart, get up on an improvised stage and do the number for which he was famous: "When the Red, Red Robin Comes Bob, Bob, Bobbin' Along." He wore a dinner jacket, an opera hat and wielded a vaudeville comedian's ebony stick. With all this his face was set in troubled seriousness. His eyes were somber with tragedy. The walking stick cavorted, circling and pointing irrelevantly, following some sinister choreography of its own. The total effect was incredibly and strangely funny. The applause was vociferous, but Bob refused to sing another verse and chorus.

In my first talk with Sherwood about the company I was overwhelmed by the intensity of his feeling about it. It was as if it mattered to him more than anything else in the world. "Why don't we simply do our plays ourselves?" It seemed like a plausible question to which there was no ready answer. About the Guild Bob was voluble and bitter. They had offended him as an author. I asked for specifics. He produced some — the kind of trivialities that tear people apart for a few hours during rehearsals and are forgotten the next day. I could not believe that a man of Bob's stature could be so riven by such differences. It was clear that his passion to start his own company came from some deeper, fundamental impulse for self-assertion. But I felt from that first talk, from the very beginning, a reservation about the venture. My first response was emotional; I hated the idea of breaking with the Guild. I had no interest whatever in profits made from play production; I was interested only in author's royalties made from plays I had written. If I needed money — and I often did — I could go to Hollywood. Sometimes I didn't even have to go. A few weeks before, Nicholas Schenck, the grand panjandrum of Metro-Goldwyn-Mayer, had called me from Hollywood to ask me to come out to work on the screenplay of Sherwood's *Waterloo Bridge.* I said flatly I couldn't come; I was finishing a play of my own. Presently I got a wire from Eddie Mannix, the studio manager, saying that they were sending Gottfried Reinhardt, the son of Max, to work with me on it in New

York. In those days being allowed to work away from Hollywood's direct supervision was practically unheard of. Gottfried was an immensely entertaining companion and I welcomed his arrival. The first thing he told me was that I had acquired a new reputation in Hollywood: the first writer who had frontally turned down Nicholas Schenck.

It was very hard for me to hold out about the company. Who was I to resist a man so eminent and lovable as Bob Sherwood? I didn't. I signed. Neither Bob nor I divined the problems that would beset us: the underlying one — the assumption that any play any of us wrote would be produced. The sieve of play-peddling which Bob resented so did not operate with us. We did not foresee having to produce the output of writers who mask sterility with incessant productivity. One day, early on, Bob grumbled to me: "Max [Anderson], who hasn't even paid his initial investment, has got us involved in a musical comedy he wrote with Kurt Weill, *Knickerbocker Holiday.*" Sidney and I sat through a rehearsal. We were entranced by Walter Huston, who sang the to-become-famous "September Song." Sidney exclaimed: "I love that man."

Sidney had married Polly Damrosch, the daughter of the conductor. They had bought an old house and a farm in Tyringham, Massachusetts, a village nestling in the foothills of the Berkshires. Sidney was an outdoor type; he was descended from a long line of California shipbuilders. He meant to farm it in Tyringham. He bought tractors and manned them himself on his acres. I had married Elza, the younger Heifetz girl. The Howards invited us to Tyringham for the weekend. It gave Sidney and me a chance to go over his play, *Madame, Will You Walk?* The play presented problems. Bob had tried to get the Lunts for it but he found them intractable when he approached them for a play that was not by himself. It was a very pleasant weekend. Polly was the most unobtrusively considerate of hostesses. Sidney and I didn't get very far on his play. It lacked the clarity and drive of his best plays; you could discuss endlessly without hitting on an expedient that would pull it together. Sidney and I made a lunch date for Wednesday in New York to go on discussing.

Sidney Howard

Elza and I returned to New York on Sunday night. On Monday morning I got a telephone call from Victor Samrock, our publicity man. He told me that Sidney was dead. He had been killed by one of his tractors. He had stood between it and the back wall of the barn. He cranked the motor, not knowing the tractor was in gear. It leaped forward, pinned him against the wall of the barn, and killed him.

The following Saturday we were all at the little church in Tyringham for his funeral. At the graveside Polly threw a rose on Sidney's coffin as it was being lowered. I have never forgotten the expression on her face — anger and defiance, as if what she had left could not be taken away from her.

Tom Finletter, Polly's brother-in-law, called me to tell me that Sidney had not left much in the way of worldly goods (everything had gone into the tractors) and that he hoped that I and the others would do everything we could for Sidney's play. We were left with a tragic chore. Bob, with the best will in the world, refused to rewrite Sidney's play; he wished it to be Sidney's play, not his. He felt terrible about Polly; he had been best man at their wedding.

We did the best we could. We engaged George M. Cohan for Sidney's play. It was an expensive contract. Cohan explained that it was his habit, when he went on the road, to travel with an entourage and that previous managements had not hesitated to pay for it.

We opened Sidney's play in Baltimore. I don't think that four playwrights could have worked harder than we did to make a play acceptable. The company had instantly acquired great prestige and publicity. We made formal entry into the various cities of the tour. We saw the critics and did our best to condition them. In Baltimore the publisher of the Sunpapers gave us a lunch, to which he brought his drama critic, Louis Azrael, who was to review the play. We dwarfed the poor critic with our pooled greatness. We listed Sidney's earlier plays and told him that in our considered judgment, his latest, which he was to see that night, was his maturest, his best. While we were flooding him with encomia, a note was handed to Bob Sherwood. It was from George M. Cohan, giving notice that he was quitting his part after the opening. Actually, the play was kindly received, but it was no go. The audience was disappointed that Cohan did not sing or dance. Feeling the frustration from the audience, he finally did a little dance on his last exit with a salvo of applause from the audience. In the discharge of this tragic chore the company failed. Coming back one day on the train with Bob and Madeleine Sherwood from Baltimore, Bob said: "I like the plays of Robert Emmett Sherwood. He hasn't got much to say but at least he doesn't try to say anything else." This was a semiconscious reflection on Sidney's play. He had tried to say something else but had not dramatically integrated it. We were conscious of our failure and were desperate to make it up to him. One day, at a full dress meeting, Bob suggested that we revive *Yellow Jack*. It seemed to us a good idea. We applauded it, but by the time the applause had died out, the worthy idea had vanished. The envoi to the history of *Madame, Will You Walk?* was supplied on his deathbed by George M. Cohan. He had a twinge of conscience for having made us pay so heavily when he signed his contract with us for himself and his entourage. He sent us an explanatory note and a check for fifteen hundred dollars.

The company had started out auspiciously. *Abe Lincoln in Illinois* was an impressive success. It was the first Lincoln play which made salient the melancholy side of Lincoln's character. It opened at a singularly tense moment. Hitler had taken over Czechoslovakia; no one knew what was going to happen next. It was reassuring and moving for Americans to see a play which revealed that in a great national crisis of our own, we produced a sad man of great moral force who steered us safely through a fearsome crisis. My own play, *No Time for Comedy,* was a success also. Max Anderson's *Knickerbocker Holiday* was not a success when we produced it, but it had a fragrance about it which appealed to many people. Walter Huston, singing the "September Song," enraptured people, as he had done Sidney Howard, at the rehearsal we saw together. A great many years later Max Anderson told me that for the lyrics of this song he received, year after year, a royalty of eight thousand dollars. He deserved it. Serious musical comedy lyricists said that Max was potentially a unique writer of musical comedy lyrics. But he preferred to write verse plays in which he hovered imaginatively in "interstellar space."

I became very fond of Max. His personality radiated universal benignity. He had a great shock of brown hair, wore glasses, and was on the qui vive for injustice, especially that committed against the American Indians. You could hardly read a play of Max's, Sherwood said once, without stubbing your toe on an American Indian! Max's father had been an itinerant preacher in the Middle West. They were always traveling in impecunious piety. Max couldn't remember at any time in his youth having a home. Once, when traveling on his own, he met Lawrence Stallings. They collaborated on a play, *What Price Glory,* and this made a confirmed playwright of Max. Max didn't think it was good for creative artists to have money; he thought its possession devitalized them. Whenever he earned any, he promptly gave it away — to members of his own family.

One day Harold Freedman startled me by calling to say he'd had an offer from a reputable publisher to pay me an advance of thirty thousand dollars to write a book on Maxwell Anderson. I said the publisher must be crazy. Harold said not at all, that I didn't realize what a vogue Max had among the universities in this country. He was a campus hero; the undergraduates thought that Max, single-handed, was converting the shoddy American drama to poetry. I turned the offer down.

Things became very tense in this country, especially within the Playwrights' Company. Bob Sherwood got himself passionately involved in the war crisis on the side of England. He was fearless and courageous. He attacked Lindbergh and what he called his "mechanical heart." He got the idea of taking a full-page ad in the *Times* under the heading: "Stop Hitler Now!" It was a plea for us to send fifty antiquated destroyers to England right away. This proposal had been discussed. The Communists, better financed than Bob, had already propagandized the White House against it. I spent the whole of one night in Bob's apartment on Sutton Place helping him to edit the text of his ad. I asked him how he intended to pay for it when he finally had it finished. He said, without worry: "I don't know." I knew that he would manage it and he promptly did. The ad appeared and caused a stir. Harold Ross of the *New Yorker* asked me to do a two-part profile of Bob. I called it "Old Monotonous," a description applied by a member of his own family, to Bob. At one point my profile worried Bob. He had been asked to be commencement speaker at Milton Academy, which he had attended as a boy. He had accepted the Academy's invitation. The date was set. What worried Bob was that in recalling his history as an undergraduate, I recalled perhaps too much: that Bob hadn't done too well in his studies and didn't get very good marks. He didn't want his parents to see those marks. The solution he evolved was simplistic. With some other boys he set fire to the building containing the poor marks. Bob said that this arson might undermine his authority as an inspirational preacher at the commencement. I pointed out that the profile recorded also how hard he had worked to put out the fire. Bob still felt his new role would be vitiated. There was nothing to be done about it; the *New Yorker* inexorably came out. Bob delivered the commencement address. There were no cries of arson against him; the students evidently approved of his simplistic solution.

Presently the Playwrights' office in Radio City came to have a semi-official nimbus; Bob was made head of OWI. He became also a member of the President's official staff of speech writers. Bob told of bringing the typescript of a speech he had written for the President to his office. F.D.R. sat in his wheelchair going over the speech. Wendell Willkie was announced. "Ah, Willkie!" said F.D.R. "I sent for him. I am sending him abroad." While he was saying this he began mussing up the typed pages of Bob's speech and scattering them all over the desk. Bob looked on uncomprehending; he had thought F.D.R. liked the speech. The President, with an explanatory nod at the dispersed papers, simply said: "I want Willkie to think I'm a busy man!"

Elmer Rice I hardly knew at all till I met him through the Playwrights' Company. He was socially charming and humorous but apt to be strident when arguing for his plays at company meetings. When I first came to New York, in 1917, Elmer was already famous. The theatrical columns and the magazines were full of him. He was a phenomenon; he had been a lawyer and had written a tremendous success, a melodrama called *On Trial*. It had had a long run in New York and was touring the United States in various companies. He was then in his early twenties; he gave up the law and made playwriting a full-time job. By the time he came to us he had also written *Street Scene* (which Kurt Weill presently converted into an opera) and *Counsellor-at-Law*, which Paul Muni played with great success. There were innumerable others, none of them successful; his own productivity lowered his average. Elmer was public-spirited; he took an active part in the crusades of the Civil Liberties Union. There were those who said that the Playwrights' Company was a lifesaver for him because the regular managers had become leery of his product. I thought that he must be aware of this and that it made him unduly sensitive to criticism offered by his colleagues, not that we offered much. At one time, after reading Elmer's latest, I had asked Sidney how he liked it. He said: "Terrible, but I am not going to tell him." Nobody told him. We just produced the plays.

Elmer lived in the Hotel Ansonia at Seventy-third and Broadway and after one of his openings — *American Landscape* or *Two on an Island*, I have forgotten which — he gave a party. It was sad because we all knew that the play didn't have a chance. The walls of Elmer's suite were plastered thick with modern abstract paintings; they contributed to the sense of claustrophobia. Elmer, obeying some impulse to dig up one artifact of former glory, came upon what he wanted while rifling through a desk drawer. He displayed it to us. It was a yellowed box-office statement of the tour of the third company of *On Trial* from Erie, Pennsylvania. Elmer made it thematic: how the American theatre had, in the interval, become constricted and provincial. He said that throughout most of America now no one had seen live theatre.

I have on my shelves three published plays of Elmer's with the following dedications in his own handwriting. One: *American Landscape*, February 1939: "For Sam, with apologies, from Elmer. Two: *Two on an Island*, March 1940: "Dear Sam, I hope you'll forgive this invasion of your privacy — Elmer." Three: *Flight to the West*, February 1941: "Dear Sam, here is little Flopsy to keep Mopsy and Cottontail company. Affectionately, Elmer."

Generally, our company meetings were great fun. One day Max Anderson said he was on tenterhooks about something. Elmer asked: "What are tenterhooks, anyway?" Sherwood explained: "Tenterhooks," he said, "are the up-hol-ster-ry of the anxious seat." After he became head of OWI, Bob spent most of his time in Washington and came to very few meetings. He was flown to England on a bomber. He was full of inside stories of Washington, of the President, of Winston Churchill, of the war. After the death of Harry Hopkins, he undertook to finish Hopkins's half-done book. It appeared and was universally acclaimed under the title of *Roosevelt and Hopkins.*

One fateful day, John Wharton, our president, summoned us to a serious meeting. Bob was not present — just Max Anderson, Elmer Rice and myself. Mr. Wharton had some accountants' statements before him. He confronted us with the bleak fact that the company had lost twenty-five thousand dollars in the last year. At this announcement Max Anderson grinned widely and said: "That's good." He meant it; it was a major theme of his that financial stringency was a stimulus to creative effort. Without contradicting Max, Mr. Wharton went on to say that he thought it would be expedient for us to give up these expensive offices and move into cheaper ones. It was put as a motion and we accepted it. Victor Samrock was designated to find the cheaper offices. Mr. Wharton undertook to notify Bob of our decision. Bob demanded another meeting at which he would be present. That meeting proved more tense than our earlier one. Bob confronted all of us with a plea. "Do not," he said, "do not take away from a man who has already lost everything, do not also take away from him this office." We at once revoked our earlier decision. Victor Samrock was ordered to stop looking.

I did not know that Bob's statement was literally true, that he had indeed lost everything. I had lunch with him next day and he explained it. On a train several years before, Bob had asked me what I did with my money. I said that I kept it in savings banks. Bob said that that was very foolish; he had found a wonderful man, a well-known broker, to whom he had entrusted his entire capital — even his daughter, Mary's — and that the man was doing wonderful things for him. He would for me too. He gave me the broker's number and strongly urged me to call him, using Sherwood's name as reference. I devoutly meant to call him, but I am badly organized and never did. Now, at lunch, Bob told me what had happened; he had arranged for the broker to get his entire income directly; he lived on an allowance allotted him by the man. The allowance stopped coming. Sherwood demanded an explanation and discovered that the broker, through stupid investment and embezzlement, had lost everything Bob had in the world.

The story made me angry. How could Bob have let it run on so long without looking into things, without making inquiries?

Bob answered with simplicity. He spoke very slowly, islanding each syllable:

"He was so bo-ring," he said, "that I a-voi-ded him."

It was characteristic of Bob that he refused to testify at the broker's trial. Tom Dewey was then the District Attorney. Bob would not aggrandize the reputation of a political enemy of Franklin Roosevelt's.

There was nothing Bob wouldn't do for a friend. I asked him once whether he would deliver a speech to a gathering of New York editors and publishers, for a charity drive, that was to take place at the Harmonie Club. I had had a request for him. Bob was terribly busy, getting his play *The Rugged Path* ready, and rushing back and forth to Washington. Nevertheless he said at once that of course he would. I reported to the people who had asked me. They were delighted. Bob's presence, they said, would ensure a capacity audience. I have to explain that Bob suffered from tic douloureux, a facial disease which doctors say is the most acutely painful ailment that affects mankind. I had talked about this often with Madeleine Sherwood. She had told me that when this illness hit Bob, she didn't know what to do. He would walk endlessly around the room. She would sit up watching him for fear he might, when it got too bad, jump out of the window. The only thing he could take for it was codeine; sometimes it relieved the pain, sometimes it didn't. I had talked to many doctors about it, hoping to find some trick remedy, but I was not successful. Doctors threw up their hands over tic douloureux.

Bob asked me to come with him to the meeting which he was to address at the Harmonie Club. The room was terribly crowded and terribly hot. I found myself sitting between two doctors, Dr. Emmanuel Libman, considered the greatest diagnostician in the world, and Dr. Milton Charles Winternitz, dean of the Yale Medical School. Beside us sat Judge Proskauer, the chairman; on the other side of him sat Bob. Judge Proskauer launched into his introductory remarks. Bob was to be the first speaker. The chairman's remarks were lengthy; the room became really unbearably hot. I looked at Bob: he was looking at me and gesturing toward the door. I saw that he had to go out. I thought: "My God — not the tic!" But it was. I confided this to Dr. Libman; he and Dr. Winternitz followed us out. In the lobby Bob began to pace, trying to while away his agony. I urged him to let me take him home. He shook his head. He asked me to get permission for him to speak later. He asked for codeine. I got the permission and asked Dr. Libman to call a drugstore and get some codeine. I came upon a difficulty; neither Dr. Libman nor Dr. Winternitz were in practice. You can't get codeine without a prescription and neither of them could write one. I reported this to Bob, still pacing, his face twisted. I implored him to let me take him home. He shook his head. He had promised to speak and he would speak. Meantime, the two doctors were in conference. Dr. Libman went to the telephone and called up a young doctor who could write a prescription. The codeine finally arrived. Bob took it and went on pacing till eleven o'clock. Everyone had spoken. Bob paced inside and delivered the last speech of the evening.

I was told by the grateful publishers who had asked for Bob that his presence and his speech had added one hundred thousand dollars to the charity. When I called the next day, Madeleine reported to me that Bob had spent the whole night pacing.

I went to the dress rehearsal of Bob's play *The Rugged Path,* for which he had secured Spencer Tracy. Spencer was superb, a marvelously sustained performance, very quiet, intensively felt. By that time Bob's reputation had reached a pitch approaching infallibility. In the intermission a well-known lady expressed her disappointment: "Sherwood builds up a crisis for the hero which he solves by giving him a job on a destroyer where he fries eggs." I left the theatre with Arthur Hopkins, a meditative man. He said: "No playwright should be given as much power as Bob has been given. It distracts him from his true vocation — writing plays." The play was Bob's first failure.

The years went on. It was becoming increasingly clear that the company had become an entity with a life-force of its own which sapped my own life-force. I was constantly having to read, criticize, and watch rehearsals of four plays simultaneously. I had not Bob's facility; he could sit down in an office, preferably our office, with telephones ringing and people walking in and out, and write a play. I couldn't. I required privacy. Little differences arose between me and the company; they were trivial but they led, finally, to my resignation. The basic issue was that I felt that my original reservations about the company were valid; that playwrights should not produce plays, especially their own. The function of the manager, who had no axe to grind, was not dispensable. I came to this decision gradually and painfully, in great agony of spirit. I loved Bob and I knew that my resignation would be a blow to him. He was one of the most remarkable and admirable men I have ever known. His integrity was inviolable; on any question of principle he would be burned at the stake rather than abdicate an inch. I have often heard him say that he hoped to live to see the day when a Negro could be elected President of the United States. He meant it.

I began to see less and less of Bob, meeting him only occasionally in restaurants. I wanted to have a talk with him and I invited him and Madeleine out for dinner. I especially wanted to give him a message from Felix Frankfurter, whom I'd seen the week before, about his book *Roosevelt and Hopkins*. His play with Spencer Tracy had just closed. He was looking haggard. I told him what Felix had said; that he included *Roosevelt and Hopkins* among the two most memorable war books, the other being *The Memoirs of Stimson*. It was high praise from a distinguished source, but I could see that it meant nothing to Bob. His eyes did not light up; they were as somber as when he was singing the "Red, Red Robin." Among the writing arts, playwriting is the keenest killer. We talked. I asked him if he had written anything. He said yes, he had written a new play which he had sent to

227

Laurence Olivier. Larry had written him that the last act was un-ti-dy. I said that Larry was the most beautiful actor in the world but that actors could not read plays; they just read parts. Larry had once told me, I said, that Christopher Fry was as good as Shakespeare. Bob listened. There was a silence. Then he looked at me. I see still the look in his eyes.

"But you see, Sam," he said finally, "the thing is — it *is* un-ti-dy."

XVIII

Katharine Cornell

N O TIME FOR COMEDY was the third production of the Playwrights' Company. I sent the final draft to Bob Sherwood before I had even become a member. He was keen about it. He said
Katharine Cornell would be great for it, and undertook to get her for
me as well as her husband, Guthrie McClintic, to direct. Harold Freedman had wished to give it to Ina Claire, who was in a betwixt and between position professionally. Harold wanted passionately to keep Ina
in New York — "to save her for the theatre," as he put it. Certainly,
Bob had a lot on his side. Miss Cornell was the most popular star in
the country; an emanation of her rich and generous personality, as well
as her luminous beauty, had gotten across to the American audience. In
the course of the two-year run of my play I got to know her well. Ex-
hibitionism is taken for granted as the sine qua non ingredient in any
acting career; Miss Cornell had less of it than any actress or actor I
have ever known. Her position in the theatre transcended technique;
she was not, like Ina Claire and Lynn Fontanne, a great comedienne.
It was something essential in herself, as a person, that the audiences
sensed and reached out to. Had she not been an actress, she might have
been the effective head of a great humanitarian enterprise. Once, in
Boston, at the Wilbur Theatre, I peeped at the stage through the closed
auditorium doors. I could hear nothing but I saw Miss Cornell. I became instantly aware that the whole stage and the other actors took
light from the radiance of her personality.

Who to get to play opposite her? Harold Freedman, who knew all

Katharine Cornell

the great actors as well as those who were to become great, called up young Laurence Olivier, who was then in Hollywood. He sent him the script; Larry consented to play the part. Once we had Cornell and Olivier, Guthrie was able to complete the casting most felicitously. We had, besides Larry, two other Englishmen, Robert Flemyng and John Williams. Flemyng played the tiny part of Pym. Lynn Fontanne once told me that Pym was the best small part she had ever read. No member of the audience knew at the end of the play what a tiny part it was; Flemyng had made it salient. We had Margalo Gillmore, who had been in my first play, and whose satiric humor had cheered me up often during the intervening years; and Gee Gee James, who played the maid. We embarked by train for Indianapolis, where we were to open. I went to the station with Larry; I was surprised that he carried only one light suitcase. "What about your stage clothes?" I asked. "I am going to wear this," said Larry, pointing to the suit he was wearing. "Anything wrong with it?" There was nothing wrong with it. I thought: "How wonderful, just to walk on stage in your street clothes!"

Kit and Guthrie were taking another train; Bob Sherwood and the other members of the Playwrights' Company were coming later, in time for the opening. Larry, Margalo, Bobby Flemyng, John Williams and I spent the evening in the club car. There is something exciting and adventurous about bringing a new play to an unfamiliar city. Of course being young helps. The fact that you don't know whether the audience of strangers is going to like you adds a tang of hazard which no one mentions. Larry began to tell stories.

"I'd been playing Hotspur in England. I played him in a red wig. Once you've decided to wear a red wig you have to make up for it all over. My makeup, to live up to that red wig, took me about three hours. I had to get into my dressing room by five o'clock in the afternoon. At one performance, I was annoyed from the very beginning by a flamboyant commercial type sitting down front with a girl. He kept whispering to her all the time, especially after I made an entrance. The man became an obsession with me. I tried not to see him, but, do you know, I could see nobody else. Next time I came on he gave me a personal welcome. He said out loud to his girl:

" 'Well, here comes Old Ginger again!' "

"Love's Labour's Lost," said Margalo.

"Exactly," said Larry.

John Williams asked Larry how his son was.

"Tarquin?" said Larry. "Oh, he's all right. He's growing up."

"Don't tell me," said Margalo, "that you had the effrontery to pin a name like that on your son?"

"Why not?" said Larry. "I thought it would look good on the bills." He traced it out with his hand: "Tarquin Olivier. Is it bad?"

"It's not bad," said Margalo, "but it's impossible. The poor boy'll never be able to live up to it."

We asked the porter to switch off all the lights in the car to give the visiting Englishmen a sight of the famous U-turn the Pennsylvania train makes around Horseshoe Curve near Altoona.

We opened, appropriately enough, at the English Theatre, a lovely old house which reminded me of the Hollis in Boston. It must have been of about the same vintage and has probably disappeared by now, as the Hollis has. Because Kit was in the play the performances were all sold out before we arrived. Bob Sherwood and the rest of my colleagues showed up, as did Alexander Woollcott, a devoted friend of Kit's. The little contingent from New York did not alleviate the tension of appearing before a new audience; if anything, it heightened it. It was apparent to me, from the first, that Kit was nervous and insecure; it was the first time in years that she had played a straight comedy part. John Williams, who had a long scene with Kit, before Larry came on, played with authority and ease and made his effect in a strange laconic part. Larry walked on in his street suit. His playing was, from the moment of his entrance, so effulgent that the audience was startled and fascinated. Kit looked wonderful; she had her beauty, but beauty is a static thing. Larry had the most engaging and volatile good looks. There was a stir in the audience about him that lasted all evening. His authority and idiosyncrasy were so compelling that it put the play out of balance in a way; the other actors seemed a bit perfunctory. The only one who was imperturbable was Bobby Flemyng as Pym; he had a razorlike edge to his comedy-playing that nothing could

Laurence Olivier

dent. In the intermissions I heard people exchanging queries about who this surprising young man Olivier was and where had he been keeping himself all this time. When it was over I went to see Kit in her dressing room. She was crying.

"I let you down," she said.

I made light of it. "Bob and the others," I said, "think the play got over."

"Thanks to Larry," she said.

In our conference after the play, at which Aleck Woollcott put in an appearance to register how dazzled he was by Larry, I was conscious of the panic that afflicts managements on occasions like this: "Would Kit quit?" But the apprehensive ones did not know Kit. She did not quit. She stuck. She got better and better as she vanquished her nervousness. The company was her responsibility. She mothered it. They all blossomed under her ministrations. I made a discovery myself: the woman she was playing *was* Kit, though I had hardly known her when I wrote the part. She became surer and surer. By the time the company left Indianapolis it was an ensemble.

Our last stop before New York was Baltimore. On the last night I went into Larry's dressing room for a few words with him. He had just finished taking his makeup off. He put a few things into his suitcase. He was delighted that he had so little to carry. I asked him whether he wasn't going to buy a new suit for New York. "It would make me uncomfortable," he said. "I want to keep the feeling I've had in the towns we've just played. I've had such a good time." I could see that Larry's performances were like a stroll in the park for him.

In New York Brooks Atkinson wrote: "The cast is the most spring-like event that a sullen April has borne this season." Of Kit he said: "After two years of silence in New York, which does not enjoy the quiet, Katharine Cornell has returned in all her magnificence, playing comedy with effortless skill and personal sincerity." The company settled down happily for a run at the Ethel Barrymore Theatre. I have never known anything quite like the sympathy and warmth of that engagement.

I had to go to England to see Rex Harrison, who was to play the Olivier part in London. Kit gave a farewell party for me in her house on Beekman Place. I was in her dressing room at the Ethel Barrymore waiting for her and Margalo when Jean Giraudoux walked in. I hadn't seen Giraudoux since the evening, two years before, when I had tried to comfort him over the income tax that threatened him from *Amphitryon 38.* He now had a play he wanted Miss Cornell to read. Kit asked him whether he wouldn't like to come along to the party she was giving for me. He said he would be delighted. The three of us, Kit, Margalo and I, rode uptown with him to Beekman Place.

I cannot exactly explain why, but Giraudoux was not somehow — at least for us — cozy to be with. He was very polite. He wished to be friendly. Perhaps it was the language barrier; none of us spoke French. There was an aura of great distinction about him that gave the effect of austerity. Perhaps he was shy of his English. No one who knew his work — and we all did — could have been shy of him on that score, but he was shy-making.

It was a very pleasant party. It started in the garden and later moved inside, to the gracious Victorian rooms. There were several handsome and distinguished ladies, all agog to meet Giraudoux, an unexpected dividend. We watched the tall figure of Dolly Schiff, the publisher of the *New York Evening Post,* make her bid — in French. Giraudoux replied, very courteous, but he seemed to be distracted by something just beyond her shoulder. She departed, unnourished. Giraudoux stood, waiting for the next applicant. I sat with Margalo, watching the procession. Giraudoux, the head of a receiving line consisting of himself, was welcoming, affable and unresponsive. He was just a great man; he couldn't help it. I even thought I detected, around his sensitive nostrils, an expression of apology: "Forgive me for being Jean Giraudoux. It's not my fault. I didn't ask for it." Finally, deserted by choice, Giraudoux was left alone. He lit a cigarette, walked to the terrace, and stared at the tugboats plying the river.

I said to Margalo: "Why don't you try?"

"I don't speak French."

"Try the universal language — sex."

Margalo laughed.

"I don't think I any longer have command of that."

"Revive it. Help him look at the river."

Margalo got up and stood beside Giraudoux. She looked at the river. I watched them. Margalo said something. Giraudoux nodded and responded. Then they resumed looking at the river. Margalo spoke again. Her companion responded again. They returned to the tugs. Margalo turned abruptly and came back to me.

"Triumph," she said. "A bloody triumph. You try. After all, you adapted his goddamn play."

At this moment Margalo caught a glimpse of a girl, about whom she had been articulate before. No one knew this girl, nor could anyone account for her presence. Somebody must have brought her but no one knew precisely who. She was an overblown strawberry blonde overburdened with cheap jewelry.

Supper was served. I exchanged a few words with Dolly Schiff. "How did you get on with Giraudoux?" I asked. "Oh," she said, "he doesn't look at you. He keeps looking over your shoulder hoping to see someone he does want to look at. Nothing doing — not for me, anyway." She was very good-humored about it. After supper I walked out on the terrace to taste the fresh air. I watched the tugboats; you can get into a trance watching tugboats as you do when you sit looking at a fire. Margalo called me; she was motioning me to join her.

"There's something you've got to see!"

I followed her through the crowded drawing room and into the hall. Off the hall there was a cozy little writing room. The door was open. Margalo was very hush-hush.

"Look in there," she whispered.

What I saw was Giraudoux on a sofa, in a deep tête-à-tête with the blonde. They were engrossed in conversation. We couldn't hear what was said, but Giraudoux's halting English seemed no longer an obstacle. After a while the girl got up and left the sofa.

"Well," she said in farewell, "so long, Frenchie!"

The next day I left for London for my interview with Rex Harrison. It was the fateful summer of 1939. My talk with Harrison was satisfactory; he was keen to do the play. I also saw Binkie Beaumont, who was to produce it at the Haymarket. I liked Binkie's casting ideas: Diana Wynyard and Lilli Palmer. The Sassoons were away. So was

Laski. I returned home on a leisurely boat. The evening I got back I looked in at the Ethel Barrymore. Everything was going tidily. But when I went back to see Kit, I found her downcast. She told me awful news: Olivier was leaving. He was married now to Vivien Leigh, who had come over for a visit. Larry had plans for himself, plans for Vivien. He promised to stay to the end of the New York run. But he simply could not remain for the transcontinental tour that Guthrie had arranged for the following fall and winter. It was a heavy blow.

When it became apparent that England would soon be at war, Bobby Flemyng left too. He loved his part, he loved being in New York, he loved playing with Kit. But he felt he must go home and enlist. He had a varicose vein in his leg; he knew that this would disqualify him. He quit the play and went into the New York Hospital to have an operation on his leg. He sailed for home, qualified for enlistment, and served all through the war. He put in what the English describe as "a good war."

There were two doleful evenings when I went to see Bobby Flemyng for the last time and Larry for the last time. I went with Gertrude Macy, Kit's business manager and a great buddy of mine. Gert Macy was considered one of the ablest managers in New York. On both occasions Flemyng and Larry were at their best, which made the evenings more poignant. I condoled with Gert — she felt the way I did. Gert and I took Kit home. We mourned Larry. "It was so exciting playing with him," Kit said. "You never could tell what he would do. But whatever he did it was always right — some new facet, some new insight." When we left Kit, I said to Gert that I couldn't imagine the play without Larry but that Kit had to do more than imagine it: she had to play it. "That is exactly what she will do," said Gert. "She will play it. Moreover, she will keep it up. You'll see!"

Play it Kit did, till late next spring, on an immense tour that went from Boston to Seattle, with major cities in between, and from Seattle south through California and Texas, to New Orleans; from New Orleans north through the East to the final performance in Newark. From Newark I went to Kit's house where she was giving a farewell party for the company.

I loved Kit's house. I always felt in it that I was in a Chelsea house in London. It was comfortable, spacious and unpretentious. Everyone was pretty tired; the company had been touring hard for many months. Guthrie made me a little speech and gave me a present from the company, a silver cigarette box with a map of the United States on the cover with a red band marking every town the company had played. Gee Gee James, John Williams and Margalo, the veteran elite of the original company, stood around the piano and sang. The stage manager played the piano. It was all slow-paced and pleasant. I sat with Kit on a sofa in a corner, under a Burchfield painting. I thanked Kit for what she had done for me and for the play.

"The audiences enjoyed it," she said, "but I was never, not from the beginning, happy about my own performance. I have never been happy about my own performance — not in anything!"

I said that was nonsense, that she had been marvelous in *The Barretts of Wimpole Street.*

"I came nearest in that," she said. "That suited me. But you know . . ." She paused; she was gathering her thoughts. "I wanted to act when I was young. There was nothing I wanted so much. But I was never secure in it. I never . . ." She paused again. "I've always had to be cautious."

This quality in Kit — modesty in so great a star — was remarkable. She is one of the most distinguished and gracious women I have ever known. Some time after this party, Kit got together a company — with Margalo — and took it to Italy to give performances for the GIs. The GIs adored her. Margalo wrote a book about it. In it she reveals how admirably Kit carried off this demanding enterprise, and how thrilled the troops were to find themselves in close contact with this luminous lady of the theatre.

XIX

The Gershwin Years

I N Verona, Italy, the hometown of Romeo and Juliet, I was taken to see the house where Juliet lived. I was sure that this attribution was apocryphal, but I inspected the commonplace little cottage. From it came the strains, on a phonograph record, of George Gershwin's "The Man I Love." This was thematically appropriate; was the present occupant imagining the earlier tenant's last thoughts? But "The Man I Love" was followed, almost immediately, by another Gershwin, the *Rhapsody in Blue*. This was in 1938, about a year after George's death; it saddened me that I should be unable to report this little concert, on a Verona street, to the composer of both works. It would have amused and delighted him. I had heard him play, electrically, both works; I should have liked to tell the present tenant that I had known him and adored him. I walked away from the little house pondering the mystery of the incidence of genius. There is no mystery more incalculable, more tantalizing, than the emergence of genius from an ordinary, even coarse, social texture. I walked along thinking of the years I had known the Gershwins: from the early Saturday nights at the Lou Paleys' on West Eighth Street to the later grand nights at George's duplex apartment on East Seventy-second Street.

To a memorial volume published after George's death Ira has contributed a compact and lucid paragraph, describing the environment and early tribulations of the Gershwin family:

The Gershwins, Ira and George

My brother, born in Brooklyn, N.Y., September 26, 1898, was the second of four children of Morris and Rose Bruskin Gershwin. I was the oldest, then came George, then Arthur and last, our sister, Frances. Most of our early boyhood was spent on the lower East Side of Manhattan where my father engaged in various activities: restaurants, Russian and Turkish baths, bakeries, a cigar store and pool parlor on the 42nd Street side of what is now Grand Central Station, book-making at the Brighton Beach Race Track for three exciting but disastrous weeks. We were always moving. When my father sold a business and started another we would inevitably move to the new neighborhood. George and I once counted over twenty-five different flats and apartments we remembered having lived in during those days.

A great day in the Gershwin history was the arrival of a piano. It was a secondhand upright purchased on the installment plan. Mrs. Gershwin thought she ought to have one because her married sister had one. It was addressed to Ira as the eldest in the family. The moment it arrived George began to play by ear some popular songs he had heard.

Pleased to find a pianist in the house and relieved of responsibility, Ira returned to his thoughts and to the St. Nicholas Baths at Lenox Avenue and 111th Street, where he was then working. George found a piano teacher, and the two brothers went their own ways, without suspecting that soon their destinies would be inextricably welded. George left the High School of Commerce at fifteen to become "the youngest piano-pounder in Tin Pan Alley" for fifteen dollars a week. When he submitted a song of his own to his employers, he was bluntly told, "You're here as a pianist, not a writer." Little by little George demonstrated that he was indeed a writer.

Ira was literary. He sold a filler to the *Smart Set* for one dollar. Not long after, he tripled his income; he describes the process in his book *Lyrics on Several Occasions:* ". . . in my late teens I fooled around with French verse forms, such as the triolet, villanelle, and especially the rondeau — with its opening phrase taking on new meanings when repeated. I even sold one to the *New York Sun,* for which I received three dollars:

RONDEAU TO ROSIE

My Rosie knows the places where
One goes to lose all trace of care.
The ultra swagger cabaret . . .
The crystal chandeliered café . . .

And oh, she knows the waiters there.
Her wink will fetch from magic lair
A bottle of a vintage rare . . .
And potent beer? Hot dog! I'll say
My Rosie knows!

Without my Rosie, I declare
I'd plumb the depths of dark despair.
To her I dedicate this lay;
To her I owe my spirits gay,
My smiling mien, my cheerful air,
My rosy nose.

Ira was known to his family as "the floating soul." Unanchored, he took a job touring with a carnival show. On tour, from Pittsburgh, he wrote to a friend to thank him for clippings about George's successes as a rehearsal pianist for musical comedy celebrities; he wryly admitted: "I now belong, I see, to the rank of Brothers of the Great." It was a role Ira set for himself early and he remained contentedly within it for the rest of his days. Even now, when George is gone, Ira devotes himself to fostering his brother's memory. He had become a lyric writer of singular genius. His book *Lyrics on Several Occasions* is an enchanting volume, not only for his songs but for his numerous comments upon them. I said to him once, while I was reading this book with inordinate pleasure: "You know, Ira, you are every bit as good as George." He shook his head. "No," he said, "George was more original." At the Gershwin parties, with everyone spellbound around the piano, while George was playing and singing Ira's lyrics, I would steal a look at Ira, standing on the outskirts of the crowd, a small, benignant smile on his face, stirred to happiness by the effect his brother was creating. That they were his lyrics George was singing was, to him, peripheral. He was under the spell of his brother's over-whelming personality, as the rest of us were.

The fact is that in the Gershwin years there was nothing more thrilling than to hear George play the piano. It heightened the sense of being alive. How universal his effect was is attested to by Eva Gau-thier, the first singer to perform George's songs in a concert hall. In a piece she wrote for the Gershwin Memorial book, she remembers:

> After our London concert, which was a repetition of the New York and Boston programs, Lord and Lady Carisbrooke (cousins of King George V) gave a party for us. It was Gershwin's first meeting with royalty and it was as if he had always been there. With his charm and talent he made the party alive and interesting and had everyone around the piano as he sang and played all his latest song and dance hits. . . . In London he became the good friend of Prince George, now the Duke of Kent, who used to drop in at George's apartment while he played to him. Gershwin took great pride in a photograph inscribed "To George from George."

Those lucky enough to have the acquaintance of certain members of the proliferated Strunsky family in the early Gershwin years had, although they did not suspect it, a jump of many years on Lady Caris-brooke and the party she gave for Eva Gauthier and her accompanist. There were two Strunsky girls, Leonore and Emily. The former married Ira Gershwin, the latter, Lou Paley, an English teacher who wrote song lyrics on the side. He wrote with Ira and he wrote for George. The Paleys had an apartment at 18 West Eighth Street. On the first floor lived Mr. and Mrs. Howard Dietz. Dietz began to be an-noyed because on Saturday nights the chandelier in his living room began to have the shakes due to a rhythmic pounding on the floor above. One Saturday night he and his wife were going to the theatre. Just as they were leaving, Dietz decided to go upstairs and protest the tremors to his chandelier. "One of us might get killed," he said to his wife, "if that chandelier falls."

Dietz, who later became vice-president of Metro-Goldwyn-Mayer

and a librettist for revues and musical shows, himself has described
what happened on his trip to save his chandelier:

> I knocked on the door of the Lou Paleys'. Someone opened the
> door carefully and put his finger to his lips, cautioning me not to
> disturb the music. About forty people were sitting on the floor around
> the grand piano at which a dark-haired chap was playing and singing
> in a rich guttural, and vastly entertaining. I took a seat on the floor.
> My wife below got impatient waiting and came upstairs to find out
> what had happened to me. I went to the door, put my finger to my
> lips and motioned her to come in and sit beside me. We never got
> to the theatre and we stopped bothering about our chandelier. We
> became regulars at the Saturday nights at the Lou Paleys' to hear
> George Gershwin.

I have read numberless pages of musical analysis of Gershwin songs
and his more ambitious writings by experts — "diminished sevenths,"
"tonic triads," "broken chords." I don't understand any of it as I know
nothing about music. Gershwin's originality, they all agree, came from
his intuition for the dramatic and the colloquial. But when I first heard
him, and subsequently, I found that I had an intuition of my own — as
a listener. I felt on the instant, when he sat down to play, the newness,
the humor, above all the rush of the great heady surf of vitality. The
room became freshly oxygenated; everybody felt it, everybody
breathed it.

In Philadelphia, some time after my initiation, I met Josef Hofmann. He said of Gershwin: "He is a pianist. He has complete
command of the keyboard." One got this sense from him immediately:
command, mastery triumphal. I knew, from the first Saturday night at
the Paleys', that I was having the best time I'd ever had in my life.
Other composers played their stuff, but these were preliminaries. They
were all waiting to hear George play "That Certain Feeling," "Liza,"
"I've Got the You Don't Know the Half of It Dearie Blues." He
demolished rivalry. Later, on East Seventy-second Street, the audience
was augmented by Society and Finance. The old regulars from West
Eighth Street did not snub them. It was fun to show Doris Duke
George's paintings, those he'd done himself and those he'd bought.

For one thing, George was extraordinarily handsome, lithe and well built. Osbert Sitwell has described his looks in one of his books: "Streamlined," he says of his appearance. This was so; George was streamlined in all of his activities: as a composer, pianist, painter, golf and tennis player. Thinking over the people I have known, it strikes me that George stands almost alone among them for possessing an almost nonexistent quality: the quality of joy. Pessimism, melancholia, depression are a dime-a-dozen; joie de vivre is the rarest phenomenon in the world. George knew that he was something new; he was perpetually fascinated by the development of this novelty. A great many of the stories about him can be explained by this view he had of himself. Once when he was talking about his mother, he said: "You know the extraordinary thing about her — she's so modest about me." It was not that George especially valued modesty as a quality. It was that he wondered whether his mother appreciated fully the variations of what he was and that her modesty perhaps emanated from being half-informed. DuBose Heyward, the author of *Porgy,* said of George that his self-appreciations were beyond modesty and beyond conceit. He was incapable of insincerity; he didn't see why he should suppress a virtue or a talent simply because it happened to belong to him.

The popular composers are a race apart, like dancers and kings. The famous ones are canny and move about in a carefully spun cocoon of pretentious modesty. George Gershwin was neither canny enough nor calculating enough for that. He was just plain dazzled by the spectacle of his own career; his unaffected delight in it was somewhat astonishing but it was also amusing and refreshing.

He also had a knack for making enigmatic remarks. One of them I puzzled over for years without hitting on an explanation. I was walking up Broadway on a hot August night with George. The papers were full of the sensation of the moment: the announced engagement of Irving Berlin to Ellin Mackay. George and I were deep in it. He stopped suddenly, gave me an earnest look, and said: "You know, I think it's a bad thing for all songwriters."

George was becoming one of the most eligible bachelors in America; there was curiosity among his friends from the beginning as to who the girl would be. I began hearing about the "Dream Girl."

The Dream Girl was a Chicago physical culture teacher whom I never met. She gave George elaborate workouts, which he thought were good for him. Physical well-being led to infatuation. Perhaps some of us thought it was a bit naïve of George to enhalo his sweetheart in this way, but on the whole we didn't mind. We liked the concept; we believed in Dream Girls. It was a more guileless time.

We waited for a wedding announcement. It didn't come; it kept on being delayed. Years passed. One day Ira called me to tell me some devastating news: "Dream Girl" (we never referred to her in any other way; I never knew her name) was married! He hadn't the heart to tell George. He begged me to relieve him of this disagreeable chore. I took on the job. I went up to Riverside Drive, where the Gershwins were then living. I went up to George's room; he was working on the Concerto in F. He played me a passage; he completed a variation on it.

"George," I said, "I have bad news for you. Dream Girl is married."

His brown eyes showed a flicker of pain. He kept looking at me. Finally he spoke.

"Do you know?" he said, "if I weren't so busy I'd feel terrible."

The phrase "Music by George Gershwin" came to have an incantatory spell for managements; George White signed him up five times to write the music for his *Scandals*. His activities were incessant; his involvements in musical comedies did not stop while he was preparing the *Rhapsody in Blue*. The audience that assembled on that February afternoon to hear the *Rhapsody* included Walter Damrosch, Victor Herbert, Jascha Heifetz, Sergei Rachmaninoff, Ernest Bloch, Willem Mengelberg, Leopold Stokowski, Fritz Kreisler. The concert added a dimension to George's stature. Samuel Chotzinoff, music critic of the *New York World,* said that George had made "an honest woman out of jazz." Walter Damrosch commissioned him to write a piano concerto for the New York Symphony Society. My listener's intuition told me that the opening of the slow movement of this concerto was one of the loveliest, most poignant passages I had ever heard.

The two brothers wandered about in all directions: George wrote shows with other lyricists; Ira interpolated his lyrics wherever he could find an opening for them. He also wrote *Two Little Girls in Blue,* with Vincent Youmans and Paul Lanin. But one day it occurred to the musical comedy producers Aarons and Freedley to combine the brothers in a show written entirely by themselves. The result was *Lady Be Good,* which was a big hit and established George and Ira, who admirably supplemented one another to produce something unique — lyrics which matched the spontaneity and verve of the music. In it the brothers found each other; their wanderings ceased; they produced an unexampled series of musical comedy hits, and branched into folk opera — *Porgy and Bess* — and various films.

George knew that his own circle, his tried and true friends, took a deep, personal interest in him. He shared this interest. When he moved into his new apartment, the duplex on East Seventy-second Street, he invited Mabel Schirmer and Emily Paley to lunch. The girls were very excited. They wanted to justify the honor of being George's first guests and hoped to impress him. They spent the morning making themselves as glamorous as possible. At one o'clock they rang his front doorbell. George, who had put on a new suit he had bought in London, opened the door. He presented himself. "Well, girls," he said, "how do I look?"

In this apartment George began his work on *Porgy and Bess.* The Theatre Guild was producing the opera. I called on him one day with Theresa Helburn. He played sections of it for us; he played "Summertime." Our reaction delighted him; he was in a state of tremendous excitement. "You know, Terry," he said, "they tell me that the interest in *Porgy* is so great that just to be sure they'll get good seats, they're subscribing to all that stuff of yours." As among that stuff there was a play of mine that the Guild had just announced, I hoped the rumor was true.

The saga of stories about George and his self-absorption grew into a mythology. When any of them were repeated in front of him he laughed as heartily as everyone else. He laughed when I told him that my play was included in the "all that stuff" remark of his. "Just the same it's true," he said. "I was told that." He respected the truth. There is a famous story of his playing catch with his friend Harry

Ruby, the songwriter. Ruby threw very hard; George quit. "I've got to be careful of my hands," he said. "With you it doesn't matter." Ruby chided George for this remark. George listened hard and adjudicated the case impartially. "Well," he said, "it's true, isn't it?"

George's time was far too valuable for him to waste it on building up a pose of modesty. He was incapable of it even if he had had the time. He enjoyed his life and his work and he didn't see why he should muffle this enjoyment. George Kaufman complained that he played his stuff so much at parties that by opening night, when the audience heard the overture, many of them must have thought it was a revival. George's mother cautioned him about this; she begged him to quit playing his new songs at parties. George refused to be cowed. "You see, Ma," he said, "if I didn't play I wouldn't have a good time." Neither would the people at the parties.

George was engaged to play his concerto with the Pittsburgh Symphony. He invited Oscar Levant along so he could practice with him on two pianos. When Oscar got into their drawing room on the train George was already settled down in the lower berth, smoking a big cigar. Oscar resignedly climbed up into the upper. "Well, Oscar," said George, smiling up at him through a cloud of cigar smoke, "it's the difference between a small talent and genius."

Rouben Mamoulian, who directed *Porgy and Bess,* speaks of George's extraordinary modesty as a composer:

> It seems to me that this sense of exaggerated modesty in artists is highly overrated by people. It is made out to be a saintly virtue where frequently it is merely sanctimonious and actually nothing but masked vanity and conceit. Very often people who seem so modest about their work would all but tear you to pieces if you suggested cutting anything out of what they had written, considering every word of it as well-nigh sacred. Yet George, who loved his own stuff as much as he did, never hesitated to make any cuts that were necessary. *Porgy and Bess* as performed in New York was almost forty-five minutes shorter than the original score. He did this because he had no false vanity about his work and also because George was one of the best showmen I have ever known.

ii

The difference in the personalities of the two brothers was striking. If George was streamlined and propulsive Ira was reserved and scholarly. He was gently humorous. One sensed in Ira even at the very center of involvement, a well of detachment. George gave you everything at once; he was boyish, with an extraordinarily sweet character. He wanted his listeners to participate in the excitement of his own development. Ira was shorter than George, somewhat rotund. It took time to discover the pawky humor that irradiated him. He was diffident. He was too modest and too proud to want to coast along on the rapidly expanding reputation of his kid brother. To his early songs, which were intermittently inserted as "interpolations" in occasional shows, he attached the name of Arthur Francis, the first names of his younger brother and sister. When he came to write his book, *Lyrics on Several Occasions,* by Ira Gershwin, Gent., in his quiet way he let himself go. As an epigraph for his book Ira uses a quotation from John Aubrey's *Brief Lives:*

> How these curiosities would be quite forgott, did
> not such idle fellowes as I am putt them downe!

He prints the lyrics of the shows he wrote with George and others and comments on the exigencies that produced them; these comments confirm what the lyrics have already established, that Ira is one of the most authentic humorists of his time. A veteran in this field, P. G. Wodehouse, happens upon this book every year at Christmastime and writes to Ira annually to tell him the renewed joy he finds in it. At the first performance of *Of Thee I Sing,* during the torchlight parade for Wintergreen that opens the show, when I heard Ira's first lyric:

> *Wintergreen for President!*
> *Wintergreen for President!*
> *He's the man the people choose;*
> *Loves the Irish and the Jews.*

I knew that I was in for a first-rate political satire. It couldn't have been neater; without malevolence but sharp enough. Ira repeats this lyric in his book with the following comment:

> For some years Strickland Gillilan's "On the Antiquity of Microbes":
>
> > *Adam*
> > *Had'em.*
>
> was considered the shortest poem extant. But this record fell when someone (Anon.) came up with "Lines on the Questionable Importance of the Individual":
>
> > *I . . .*
> > *Why?*

Compared with both of these, the words of "Wintergreen for President" almost equal the length of an Icelandic saga. I imagine, though, that in Songdom "Wintergreen" is one of the shortest lyrics ever. Additional lines would have been supererogatory.

In 1928 the Gershwins went to London to see the closing performance of Gertrude Lawrence in *Oh, Kay!* — a salute to the benignity of the times — and then moved to Paris to settle down for a bit. George met the leading composers, Milhaud, Ravel, Stravinsky, Prokofiev, Poulenc, and worked on his tone poem, *An American in Paris.*

In 1930, the Gershwins made their debut in Hollywood: their first film, *Delicious,* for the Fox Film Corporation. As it happened, I was also working for Fox Films at that time. We had a happy reunion. I introduced them at once to the Hoveys, who had become, by this time, like my own family. Sol Wurtzel put Sonya on the Gershwin film; she worked on it with them and with Guy Bolton, who was to write the screenplay. The three Gershwins, George, Ira and Lee, took a two-story Spanish house at 1027 Chevy Chase in Beverly Hills. George's charisma and his piano brought people from far and near. Arthur Rodzinski led the Los Angeles Philharmonic in *An American in Paris.* George became a friend of Arnold Schoenberg, who used to come over to swim in his pool and play tennis with him. George painted him. In all this George had the advantage of having his sister-in-law as hostess. As I myself can testify, there is no more gracious hostess in the world.

In those days everybody was going to psychoanalysts. Herman Mankiewicz, an outstanding wit, wished all the patients of his own doctor (Semel) to have a huge S embroidered on their sweatshirts, to show that they had the courage of their special cult. George went to the same man; he also had a psychoanalyst in New York. Oscar Levant added to the gaiety of nations. Most of the habitués took seriously the injunction forbidding them to report on their séances; Oscar defied this injunction. He reported singing to his analyst George's song "Love Walked In," by which Oscar was enthralled. "The s.o.b." he complained, "is so unmusical that he didn't realize what a great song it is!"

In July of 1937 I had to go to New York to meet the Lunts to rehearse *Amphitryon 38*. They were to open in San Francisco. I went over to say good-bye to George. He played me some of his Shostako-vich records; he spoke of the Russian composer's addiction to short themes. He held forth a bit on this, as if it were a method he might himself apply. He suggested we go for a drive. I said all right. We drove, George at the wheel. There was something odd about him that day, something I had never noticed in him before. He was subdued, shadowed. I edged about in my mind, to account for this. I had heard that George had fallen seriously in love with a film star and that it had not been going well. George said nothing. Neither did I. He had been writing great stuff: "A Foggy Day in London Town" and "They Can't Take That Away from Me." I asked him to sing them and he did — in bits:

> *The way you wear your hat,*
> *The way you sip your tea,*
> *The mem'ry of all that —*
> *No, no! They can't take that away from me!*

The way your smile just beams,
The way you sing off key,
The way you haunt my dreams —
No, no! They can't take that away from me!*

I spoke of how marvelous it was of Ira to add singing off key to the list of the heroine's perfections, how it bathed nostalgia in humor. George agreed. We got together on how extraordinary Ira was.

George began asking me about *Amphitryon 38*. He couldn't wait to see it. I said: "You will. After two weeks in San Francisco we come to Los Angeles. I'll have seats for you opening night." George thanked me. All the time I wanted to break through and ask him if there was anything on his mind — he did not seem as carefree as usual. But I didn't do it. I felt that if he wanted to talk about whatever it was, he would do so. Still it was a beautiful day and a lovely drive. He dropped me at my own door in Beverly Hills. I confirmed our date: to meet him on July 5 at the Biltmore Theatre in Los Angeles, where *Amphitryon 38* was to open. He looked forward. I looked forward.

iii

From San Francisco, on the Friday night of the second week, I called the Gershwins in Beverly Hills. I got Ira. I told him I was returning the next day and hoped to see them that night. He said fine. He said that George had not been feeling well the last few weeks. When I asked what was wrong he seemed unable to give me a definite answer: it seemed to him to be some nervous ailment. I told him I was leaving seats for him and Leonore for Monday night and two for George also. He said he would tell George.

On arrival on Saturday I called up Sonya and Oscar Levant. We had dinner together. I tried to find out what was wrong with George. I could get nothing definite. Oscar said that the general opinion was that George had been frustrated by his lukewarm reception in Hollywood, and by the mild success of the films he had worked on. This

---

drove Oscar crazy, as he considered that George had never written anything better than the songs in his recent films. In any case George was in the hands of his psychoanalyst, Dr. Samuel, who was trying to cheer him up.

When Oscar said this I remembered an incident recounted to me by George Kaufman. "There are days," George said, "when I just feel awful and have to stay in bed. Beatrice [his wife] had been trying to get me for a long time to go to her analyst, Dr. Zilboorg, but I was stubborn and wouldn't go. On one of my bad days she looked in on me and offered again to call Dr. Zilboorg. I said, 'No, thanks.' She gave me a long look and said, 'You know, George, with you it may be partly physical.' " Hollywood was so preempted by the psychoanalysts that it was inconceivable that any ailment could on occasion be physical. Such a bizarre source of malaise never occurred to anybody even as a possibility. Whatever was wrong with you must be a mental aberration due to some disappointment connected with the film industry.

We went over to the Gershwins'. Lee and Ira greeted us. George was upstairs. Lee told us he knew we were coming and would be down presently. We waited in the living room. George came downstairs accompanied by a male nurse. I stared at him. It was not the George we all knew. He was very pale. The light had gone from his eyes. He seemed old. He greeted me mirthlessly. His handshake was limp, the spring had gone out of his walk. He came to a sofa near where I was sitting and lay down on it. He tried to adjust his head against the pillows. The nurse hovered over him.

I asked him if he felt pain.

"Behind my eyes," he said, and repeated it: "behind my eyes."

I knelt beside him on the sofa and put my hand under his head. I asked him if he felt like playing the piano. He shook his head. It was the first such refusal I'd ever heard from him.

"I had to live for this," he said, "that Sam Goldwyn should say to me: 'Why don't you write hits like Irving Berlin?' "

There was silence. He spoke of the *Porgy* tour, which had not been successful.

I asked him whether he would come to my opening Monday night.

He shook his head slowly. He moved his head around on the pillow. I took my hand away.

He looked at me with lusterless eyes. I had a sinking feeling: he is no longer one of us. He turned to the nurse and said he'd like to go back to his room. The nurse got him up. They went upstairs.

When he had gone I looked at Leonore.

"How long has he been this way?" I asked.

"For several weeks. He seems worse tonight. Maybe it's seeing you — reminds him of the past."

"Didn't you tell me he has trouble eating?" Oscar asked Leonore.

"Yes," said Lee, "he doesn't seem to be able to manage his food. I have to cut it for him."

We sat for a time not speaking. Oscar, Sonya and I rose to go. I asked Lee whether I should hold the seats for them for Monday night. She said certainly, that it would be a diversion for them.

In the car, Sonya, Oscar and I rode in silence. Finally Oscar said:

"You think George is very sick, don't you?"

"Yes," I said, "I think he is *very* sick."

The next day was Sunday. Sonya drove me out to her beach house in Santa Monica. I said to her that I thought something should be done about George. I was leaving for New York on Tuesday, and I felt I should take George along and get the best medical treatment possible for him there.

"You can't take the responsibility," said Sonya.

When I got back to Beverly Hills that night I called Ira. George had seen his analyst, Dr. Samuel. Dr. Samuel had conferred on the telephone with Dr. Zilboorg, George's New York analyst. They had decided that it would be wise to separate George from his family. He had been transferred to the house of a friend who had luckily left that day for New York. Ira was relieved by the fact that the two analysts had conferred and come to a conclusion.

The next afternoon I went to the Gershwins'. I saw Paul, George's Swedish butler, whom I had known in New York. He had driven George to his new domain. I asked him how George had behaved.

"He was all right," said Paul, "till we got to the house."

"What happened then?"

"He asked for a dark room. I darkened the room for him — pulled all the shades down — made it quite dark. Then he asked for a towel to put over his eyes."

When I heard this something snapped in my mind. For a long time I had been irritated by the pseudoscientific vocabulary that dotted the conversation of most of my friends who were involved with psycho-analysts. I had a special antipathy for George's New York psycho-analyst. He was boorish. Years later, when I came to read Sir Ernest Jones's life of Sigmund Freud, I came upon Freud's own fear of the psychoanalysts who might succeed him. He called them "wild analysts." I thought at once of this analyst. I was sure he was one of them. I called in Lee and Ira. I told them that I thought George was gravely ill. I asked their permission to call Dr. Abraham Flexner in New York to get his advice. While I was trying to get Dr. Flexner, Moss Hart, who was in analysis, came in. He didn't see why I was making all this fuss. "I myself," he said, "have had many suicidal impulses — I have been helped over them." I lost my temper somewhat with Moss. I said his suicidal impulses were not relevant to George's case.

I got Dr. Flexner finally — at his summer place in Canada. I described George's condition as briefly as I could. He advised that the Gershwin family should, as soon as possible, get hold of Dr. Dandy, an eminent brain specialist at Johns Hopkins. I tried at once to get Dr. Dandy in Baltimore, I was told that he was out sailing on Chesapeake Bay and could not be reached. By this time Lee and Ira were a bit scared. I told them to give up all idea of going to the opening that night, but to concentrate on trying to get adequate medical help for George. I went to the theatre alone. I sat in the balcony. By this time I knew the performance by heart. Watching Lynn and Alfred's exquisite interpretation, I couldn't help but think of George Gershwin lying in a strange house, in a darkened room, with a towel over his eyes. I hoped that the hours would go swiftly for him. I tried to postpone my departure, but I was urgently needed at home. I arranged with Oscar to call me daily when I got home. On his second call, on Friday, Oscar told me that George had been taken to the hospital and was in a coma. I had to talk to somebody. Who to call? I thought of one of George's friends, who was also a patient of Dr. Zilboorg's. I told him George was in a coma. George's friend took it lightly. "That coma," he said, "is self-induced."

The surgeon found a brain tumor. George did not survive the operation.

In the years since George's death when I have met new people whom I have especially liked, I invariably think: "If only I could introduce them to George Gershwin." I feel pain over the missed delight they would have taken in him.

Thinking back on George's career now, I see that he lived all his life in youth. He was thirty-nine when he died. He was given no time for the middle years, for the era when you look back, when you reflect, when you regret. His rhythms were the pulsations of youth; he reanimated them in those much older than he was. He reanimates them still. Fred Astaire said after his death: "He wrote for feet." A Gershwin tune has a propulsive effect still, all over the world. He was perpetually in pursuit of new horizons; he was ambitious to write serious music. In youth there is always time for everything; we all aged; George remained young. His own tempo was as propulsive as those of his songs; whether he was playing golf or tennis, or painting pictures, or collecting them. "Golf," writes a friend of his, "is supposed to be a leisurely game, but not for George. He ran from hole to hole. He was like a young colt." One can never know the truth about anyone — what their inmost motivations and feelings are, but George's life was lived so out-of-doors, so in the public eye, and these activities so absorbed him that he was always "too busy," he said, for introspective agonies. He told me once that he wanted to write for young girls sitting on fire escapes on hot summer nights in New York and dreaming of love. His memory is of a golden youth, of a young man who in a short time won all the rewards of acknowledged genius.

Leonore and Ira Gershwin are now settled in a handsome house on Roxbury Drive in Beverly Hills. It is a very livable, even palatial, house to stay in. It is also a Gershwin Museum, as untaxing as the Frick in New York. At the Frick the pictures are mostly all Duveens;

on Roxbury Drive they are all Gershwins, bought by George during his collecting years with the aid of a cousin whose name was often on his lips: "my cousin Botkin the artist." The paintings are post-Duveens, because George bought his pictures not to sell but to keep: Rouaults, Derains, Utrillos, Picassos, Kandinskis. There is George's piano and an immense oil by Siqueiros of George playing to a packed house in Carnegie Hall. An upper corridor is lined with posters of the European tour of *Porgy and Bess* — from Paris, Rome, Florence, Venice, Vienna, Budapest, Moscow and Leningrad. Leonore went on this tour; she practically managed it. Ira showed up in Moscow. When he was asked how he spent his time there he said: "They kept me busy." Who "they" were and what they kept him busy at, he did not specify. Leonore is more specific; she tells of a dinner party in Moscow where she found herself sitting next to Andrei Gromyko and that he was a humorous and sociable dinner companion. Ira has devoted his life to the preservation of his brother's memory; to the distribution of his manuscripts to the Library of Congress and various universities. He has put himself in charge of the Gershwin correspondence; he answers every letter from Gershwin fans all over the world who write to inquire about the minutiae of various Gershwin scores. When Ira didn't show up at a lunch party one day the host explained: "Oh, Ira is answering some letters from New Zealand." He is still being importuned by film companies to supply lyrics for musical pictures. I called him up one night from my hotel to say good-bye as I was leaving for New York. He told me he'd had a good day; he had managed to get out of doing a film he was being pressed to do (and it was a script he had really liked). "How'd you pull that off, Ira?" I asked. "I told them," he said, "that I had too much on my mind." He has. He keeps going over Gershwin manuscripts, notebooks, letters. He keeps adding to the huge library of Gershwin records. After dinner, he will reminisce with friends about the early days, his tour with the carnival, the tryout of his first show in Philadelphia. But he doesn't reminisce for long. After an hour or so he is drawn upstairs to his study, to indulge his passion for the history and etymology of words. He loses himself in the *Oxford English Dictionary* and in his cherished, carefully gathered reference works. He is a varied and esoteric reader. That is why he was able to toss off, in a song written with Jerome Kern, in 1944, "Put Me to the Test," lyrics like:

> *Test me — put me on my mettle!*
> *How would you like a snowball from Popocatepetl?**

But all that is behind him now. His days and nights are spent in reanimating the Gershwin years. They are the breath of Ira's present.

* Copyright 1944 by T. B. Harms Company. U.S. Copyright renewed. Reproduced by permission of the publsher, T. B. Harms Company.

XX

Esrigs* at I Tatti

SOME TIME IN 1944 I had lunch with William Shawn, an editor of
the *New Yorker*. I had been working for him, on and off, for some
time. To amuse him I told him an adventure I had just had in Palm
Beach. I was there as the guest of Nate Spingold, an executive of
Columbia Films. He introduced me to a friend who had written a book
on Lord Duveen which he had been unable to get published. When I
read it I saw why. It was a marmoreal panegyric on the late lord and
his clients. They were all Franciscan characters, living for Art and
Others. While I was satirically describing the rampant nobility of all
these people, Shawn interrupted to say: "Why don't you do Lord
Duveen and all these characters for us?" By the time the lunch was
over, my working life was preempted for, as it turned out, six years. I
hadn't worked on the book long when I discovered the pivotal position
of Bernard Berenson in Duveen's career. I brought Berenson in from
the beginning. I'd been working on the pieces for two or three years; I
had four of the six parts done, when I had another lunch with Shawn.
He said: "What would you think if you said nothing about Berenson
in the beginning of the piece? If you didn't refer to him at all and
then — say Part Five of the six — devote the entire chapter to him?"

I told Shawn what I thought. I thought that it would be great. I left
for Venice to see Berenson.

It. was to Venice because Berenson was there at the time. The visit

---

* In most reference works this word is spelled Ethrog. I spell it this way because that
is the way we pronounced it on Providence Street.

was arranged for me by a friend I had acquired in the course of my researches, John Walker, the director of the National Gallery in Washington. Moreover, Walker was going to be there, which was a windfall. Before I left Venice, Berenson said to me about Walker: "You will voyage far in the world before you come upon another biped as engaging as John Walker." Berenson divided the world into a variety of bipeds. There were well-dressed ones, slovenly ones, boring ones, stimulating ones, "life-enhancing" and "life-diminishing" ones. On the first night Berenson was not visible, which I appreciated because I was nervous about meeting him — it had loomed up rather as an ordeal for me — but I met Nicky Mariano, who as Walker had told me "makes B.B.'s life the delightful thing it is." I could see why. She made my life the delightful thing it was for that evening and for many evenings subsequently. We went to a symphony concert in the Doge's Palace on San Marco.

The meeting with B.B. was set for the next day for lunch on the terrace of his hotel; Miss Mariano, Mr. Walker and myself. B.B. was a bit late. There was a certain malaise; Miss Mariano's eyes were troubled; I felt that the Ship of State was somewhat off course. B.B. appeared: a tremendous appearance, a tiny Jove, moreover a Jove who, displeased about something, had hurled a thunderbolt, not in the least tiny. Providential turn: Berenson asked me whether I knew Sinclair Lewis who, he said, had been coming to visit him once a week. I said that indeed I did, that I'd had lunch with him a few days before he'd gone abroad. I said he'd been very funny about the breakup of his marriage. The lines around B.B.'s eyes crinkled; he sniffed gossip. I told how Lewis had described his life with Dorothy Thompson:

"She goes to Washington. She has breakfast with a cabinet officer, then she slips in a visit to Felix Frankfurter. Lunch: Lord Halifax. The French Ambassador fills in for her till she goes to tea at the White House. She gets home, and I have to listen to the whole goddamn thing." I described how Lewis gathered himself together to deliver his topper. I had met him a few days before at a first night. He was with a girl.

"Now, that little girl you met with me at the theatre the other night — *she* got a hell of a kick because I brought her backstage and introduced her to Donald Cook!"

I explained that Donald Cook was an admirable actor but not an iridescent one.

B.B. was on the same wavelength with me and bubbling to give me information I didn't have.

"He brought the girl to I Tatti. Also her mother, and shall I tell you what happened? Bertie Russell ran off with the girl and left Lewis with the mother."

I repeated this to Mark Schorer, who wrote the definitive life of Lewis, and he said he'd found nothing to confirm it. As B.B. was Bertrand Russell's once-upon-a-time brother-in-law and he stated it so firmly, I saw no reason to doubt it. It was just the kind of thing that might have happened to poor Lewis.

Several days passed before I saw Berenson again. He was ailing. I know now that it took a lot of doing before Miss Mariano and the engaging biped could persuade Berenson to see me, especially on a subject that was perhaps the most distasteful to him of any in the world. I didn't know this then of course; I have deduced it since. I think the argument that turned the trick was John Walker's; he said that someone was bound to write about Duveen, that it was inevitable. In this dire case it might as well be me. Berenson yielded to *faute de mieux,* as many less-favored people have to do.

Berenson was in bed when I interviewed him. With just his head showing, he looked gigantic. Certainly his looks were extraordinary; of the kind of looks they were, they were transcendent. The sentences rippled from him, at once casual and lapidary. One sentence that emerged, its balance and propulsion, I have never forgotten. It was thought expedient, for one reason or another, to omit it from my book. But there is no reason I shouldn't print it now. With no change in inflection or volume I heard him say:

"Duveen was at the center of a vast, circular nexus of corruption that reached from the lowliest employee of the British Museum, right up to the King."

It was beautiful but it rather shocked me. After all, he was describing his partner. When your partner is at the center of a corrupt nexus how then do you yourself keep free of centripetal suction? I have since then read everything Berenson has written, except his technical books. In his autobiographical books Duveen is never mentioned by name. Berenson does speak of him in his fascinating, posthumously published diaries, but always invidiously. But then I have developed a special theory about this immensely complicated man which, for what it is worth, I shall enlarge on in its place.

Something like six years passed after this Venetian visit. My Duveen book was finished and in the bookstores. I was in Rapallo visiting Max Beerbohm. I received a note from Nicky Mariano inviting me to spend the weekend at I Tatti. She cautioned me to bring a dinner jacket.

I was met at the train, in Florence, by Berenson's English chauffeur, Hugh Parry. I had been told about Parry, that in all the immense tours B.B. made to the museums of Europe, Parry never once entered a House of Art; he preferred to wait outside. This did not in the least prejudice me against Parry; it made him more companionable. He drove me to the door of I Tatti, where it was refreshing to be greeted by Miss Mariano. Nicky Mariano was one of the most beloved of contemporaries, and you didn't have to know her long to see why.

"Well," she said. "Welcome! How are you?"

"Fine."

"How very American!"

"Why?"

"No European takes such a good view. You ask B.B. how he is. He is never fine. He is always . . ."

Laughing, she made an ambiguous gesture, indicating a dank region between not very good and worse.

Iris Origo has described I Tatti far better than I could so I will let her do it. I know nothing about architecture, or styles of furnishings or the subtleties of landscape planning. I do know whether a house is warm or cold. I have suffered in English houses; I was to suffer in I Tatti. But Iris Origo is actuated by other considerations. She is outlining briefly the career of "the last true humanist perhaps of Western Europe." It is loutish to tear at the fabric of her beautiful style but the alternative would be to force me to describe this grand house, which would be light years beyond me. Iris Origo says:

> The books which first made him known — *The Venetian, The Florentine* and *The Central Italian Painters of the Renaissance,* and the monograph on Lorenzo Lotto — all appeared between 1892 and 1901, before he was thirty-six. Then came the profession of expertise and the partnership with Duveen; soon, in the great international art market, the value of an Italian picture came to depend upon its authentication by Berenson. With the very considerable profits, he transformed a rustic villa of the Quattrocento near Settignano into his famous villa, I Tatti — as pure and exquisite a quintessence of Tuscan architecture, art, and landscape as only a non-Tuscan could have conceived — and this, for the rest of his life, became his home.

I was ushered into my suite by a one-eyed giant and left to myself till dinner time. The walls of the parlor were lined in what looked like green silk and old paintings. A crystal chandelier bathed the room in a mellow light. On the commodious desk, which had the look of a museum piece, was a leather folder, stamped in gold. Inside, under cellophane, was a printed inventory of the paintings on the walls, with the names of the artists and their dates. I walked around, the guide in my hand, matching up. They matched. It was a courtesy of the imagination on the part of the planner to embrace the possibility of entertaining a guest who might not know one of these artists from the other. The little brochure gave me a feeling of security, at least in my own domain, and I was grateful to the teacher who had provided it. But what about the corridor through which I had just passed, studded with formidable paintings? I decided to trust to luck.

There were no thunderbolts waiting to be launched from behind B.B.'s forehead this time. He welcomed me to his house, all hospitality, all warmth and full of talk, full of animation:

"Your book is out in Italian: *Il Re degli antiquari.* Have you seen it? *Succès fou.* They sell it in the railway station."

I had brought Edmund Wilson's last Christmas card, a gay little production, spangled with gold flecks, because I wanted to show B.B. a poem of Wilson's in Hebrew, dedicated to Isaiah Berlin. B.B. gulped it in narrowly but said he'd have to look at it again. He had been, he said, as a matter of fact, translating another Hebrew poet, Jehuda Halévy's "Lament for Zion." He recited a threnody from it, in his translation. He handed me a copy of the current *Foreign Affairs.* "Have you read Gardner Patterson's article on Israel? Another threnody."

It could not have remotely occurred to anyone that this darting, encyclopedic, humorous mind was housed in a body that was pushing ninety.

I was introduced to an attractive Italian lady who had just come in. She spoke perfect English but I didn't catch her name. She was obviously a familiar of the household. B.B. took my arm as we walked into the dining room. He advised me to talk to this lady, that I would find it rewarding. "As for me," he said gaily, "I am an extinct volcano!" At dinner he talked about the chances for Israel. In spite of the doleful *Foreign Affairs* article, he was optimistic. Somewhat to my surprise he approved of the Young Turks in Israel, the militants, and deprecated what he called the "Parliamentarianism of Weizmann." He volleyed the conversation through three languages, French, Italian and German, with occasional dips into Latin. It was an implied compliment to me, I suppose, as if it would have been barbarous of him to assume that I wasn't at home in these tongues. But I did wish that B.B. had provided the linguistic equivalent of the guide in my chandeliered salon. At one point Berenson turned to me. "You remember Saint-Simon . . ." and made a little excursion, in French, into him. I couldn't remember Saint-Simon, as I'd never read him. This gave me a special twinge. I had always meant to read Saint-Simon but kept putting him off. Latterly, I had earmarked him for my old age, which I was then on the verge of. Now I am in it, full in it, and I've still never looked at Saint-Simon. I know now I never will. There is no more pitiful human illusion than that you can catch up on lost reading in old age. Old age is the busiest of them all. Things you used to do effortlessly take you forever, provided you can do them at all.

What with Saint-Simon and a myriad others, it was well after ten when we got back to the drawing room. I got a chance to talk to the lady who had evoked volcanic memories in B.B. and very sympathetic she was to talk to. She was a Florentine. "Florence," she said, "is a malignant city." I expressed surprise. She explained. "They live for gossip, the more malevolent the better."

"Don't we everywhere? Don't you notice how B.B.'s eyes light up when there's a hint of gossip?"

She laughed. "Oh, I agree! B.B. adores gossip. After all, he's a Florentine too, isn't he? He's lived here for half a century. Don't you think he may claim to be one of us? Or do you think of him — as American — a typical American?"

"Not run-of-the-mill," I said.

She was smiling.

"You see, don't you, how malignant we are! Myself included, I think myself especially."

She got up to go. I was sorry. But she said we would meet again.

After she left, Nicky asked whether I wanted to go to bed or would I mind listening to some music from Turin. "It's a rather special program," she said, "Brahms and Strauss."

I opted for Turin. Nicky arranged the cushions on B.B.'s armchair. We listened awhile, Nicky sitting close beside him. B.B.'s head began to nod. Presently he was fast asleep. His head fell on his elegantly shirted, tiny chest.

The *Foreign Affairs* B.B. had given me was on the table beside me. I determined to read it before I went to bed. I remembered an imitation of Weizmann performed for me by Isaiah Berlin. I heard Weizmann saying petulantly: "Berenson! That Berenson! What is he doing there in Florence — sitting there?" I remembered what the mothers on Providence Street in Worcester, Massachusetts, used to say of an unmarried girl. "She sits," they would say, as if, not being married, there could be no reason for her to get up. To Weizmann, any man, and especially a gifted man, no matter what marginal tasks he might be engaged in, was, if he was doing nothing to further the Zionist cause, merely sitting in a vacuum, purposeless and faineant.

The next morning I spread out my notes of work in progress on the exquisitely crafted desk. I tried to work but it didn't go. The surroundings were too elegant. I am used to American hotel rooms and bridge tables. I made the round of my selected painters again, guide in hand. I looked out of the window at twin rows of elegiac cypresses. There was a welcome knock at the door. It was Nicky. She said that B.B. wanted to take me for a stroll in the garden. He wanted to show me the limonaia. Without knowing precisely what a limonaia might be, I went along.

I walked with B.B. down the cypress allée. They had been planted very close together and had intergrown so that they now gave the effect of a monumental hedge — a massif.

"I planted this allée when I bought the place fifty years ago. I have raised a sturdy family, have I not?"

He stopped and looked at the cypresses as if he had never seen them before.

"It's rather awful to think, isn't it, that when I am pushing up the daisies all this will be an institooshun."

He was referring to the fact that he had willed I Tatti to Harvard as a seminar for graduate students.

We resumed walking — his eyes still on the trees.

"My Jewishness is an essential part of me. We should be proud, you know, we Jews, of our greatest creation — Jesus Christ."

Punily, I whipped up some pride. Perhaps B.B. felt I was not ready for conversion. He switched to a secular subject.

"How did you like our Florentine?"

"Immensely. And she's clever; subtle. I felt that not much gets by her."

"You are quite right. Nothing gets by her. I have always loved women. And I have never refused their love. In London — early in the century — the most radiantly beautiful of the great Edwardian ladies — when I went to see her after a great lapse of time — the saddest remark that was ever made to me . . ."

I waited to hear. B.B. seemed to be ruminating.

" 'Oh, B.B.,' she said, 'dear B.B. I have changed so dreadfully since first you knew me! It's gotten so that I am ashamed to undress in front of my lovers.' "

* * *

In Berenson's last diaries, *Sunset and Twilight,* he takes note of my visit:

"He . . . gets me to say, because of our common ghetto origin, what I seldom say to others." It was this walk and its culmination in the limonaia, that Berenson must have been thinking of. We *matched* ghettos.

We went under a great arch and then entered the glass-roofed limonaia, the plant house. We sat on a bench. The sun streamed in and a resinous breeze wafted through. I looked at the profusion of glowing, jeweled fruits, limes and lemons.

"What marvelous fruit," I said. "Limes, aren't they? And what superb lemons!"

"They are not lemons," said B.B.

"They certainly look like lemons. If they're not lemons what are they?"

"They are esrigs," said B.B. quietly.

"Esrigs! Succoth!" Succoth is the Jewish Harvest Festival.

"Exactly." His eyes were twinkling. He had successfully maneuvered a coup.

"Succoth, you know, or suka, in Hebrew also means a hut. Did you have one?"

"Of course. My father built it in our yard."

"You had a yard!"

"Yes, with a pear tree in it."

"You must have been very rich."

"Didn't you have a suka?"

"The ambiance of the North Station in Boston where we were shunted when we arrived from Lithuania did not encourage pleasure domes."

"Ours was very simple. The roof was made of fir branches, and Father hung pears, apples and oranges from it. We had all our meals in the suka for a whole week. The aroma of that suka . . . it smelt like — it smelt like this limonaia!"

"I am complimented. Indeed I am."

I looked again, incredulously, at the heavy fruit, the outsize lemons.

"I can hardly believe it. Are they really esrigs?"

"They meet every specification. In fact, I send them to Israel. It's an item in their export market, you know. Where did your father get his?"

"At the Providence Street Synagogue."

"And the Providence Street Synagogue got them from Israel."

"I had a tragedy with one once. A real tragedy. Another boy and I played ball with Father's esrig. I broke the stem."

"You broke the pittim!"

"I'm afraid we did."

B.B. shook his head in horror.

"That was indiscreet of you," he said.

"My father was furious."

"Justifiably. The pittim is the soul of the esrig. Also, probably a priapic symbol."

The pittim is the longish, thickish black stem of the fruit. It has, for the Orthodox, a profound liturgical significance. For my father it was a tragedy. I had emasculated the esrig.

B.B. got up, picked an esrig, and brought it over to me. He displayed it with pride.

"Look — this pittim whose ancestor you wantonly destroyed — isn't it superb? An oak might grow from it. Triumph of refined breeding. Yes, I am proud of my esrigs. Will you, one day, credit me with this? Will you add it to the list of my dubious achievements? Would your father have accepted this plant house as a suka? Would it have pleased him?"

"He would have been in ecstasy."

"Your father got his esrigs from Israel. Did he also get Palestinian earth — to be scattered over his grave?"

"Yes. How did you know?"

"While you were lolling about in your luxurious yard on Providence Street, I was looking up your father's Judaean peasant ancestors."

"Were they all peasants?"

"Of course they were. Who but a peasant would have a harvest festival? That's what Judaea was — a miniscule nation of peasants."

"Were the prophets peasants?"

"Of course they were — or the sons of peasants. When you think of the literature produced by this tiny group of farmers! Bergson says man is a machine for creating gods. These peasants did more. They created them and then had the imagination to re-create them, to make them more companionable. They destroyed the vengeful God who enjoyed tormenting Job and created the God of the Psalms, the merciful God, the Shepherd God who saw to it that His flock would not want."

"By the way, you've said nothing about the lulov."

The lulov was the palm leaf which was carried in the synagogue procession in one hand, the esrig in the other.

"That is very old. It was carried in religious processions in the Minoan civilization."

"Didn't they carry esrigs?"

"I know no record of that."

"Why did we have to add them?"

Berenson smiled. "Because we are a peculiar people."

Nicky appeared.

"We are a well-organized household," she said. "We serve lunch. And," she said, smiling at me, "in honor of our guest, New England boiled dinner."

The three of us started to walk back to the house.

"Not in *my* honor?" said Berenson. "Do you forget, my dear, that I am a New Englander too?"

"A New Englander," I said, "without a suka. He, in Boston, Mass., never had a suka, but I, in Worcester, Mass., had a ducky one."

"You may have had the suka," said B.B. tolerantly, "but *I* have the esrigs."

It was a gay lunch. Mr. and Mrs. Peter Viereck contributed greatly to it. B.B., reassured as a horticulturalist and an exporter, was in wonderful form. As for the New England boiled dinner, it was the quintessence of what such a dinner should be; you couldn't have remotely met its like anywhere in New England. Nicky enjoyed her triumph.

Harold Acton came to dinner. He had just come from Paris. He had seen — he couldn't remember for the how-manyeth time, Manet's

Olympe. He was in a dithyramb about it as if he'd never seen it before or as if Berenson didn't know it equally well. It was a delicious evening for me; it gave me all I asked — not to have to say anything, to just listen to these two talking about their foibles. I drank their conversation in, at least when they spoke in English.

So it went for the rest of the weekend, people at every meal and for tea. I asked Nicky how she stood it, to say nothing of Berenson. She said: "Oh, well, B.B. rails at the constant succession of people, but once, when I severely rationed him, he found that he missed visitors very much."

It turned bitter cold. I suffer from a chronic bronchial condition and cold is my enemy. I get a chill at the drop of a hat. I Tatti had in it some of the greatest masterpieces of Italian painting, one of the choicest private libraries in Europe, Bernard Berenson and Nicky Mariano, but no heat. Also, there wasn't a cigarette in the house. I asked Parry to drive me into Florence to buy chocolates for Nicky and cigarettes for myself. I have never known such penetrating cold as I felt that afternoon in Florence. Parry took me to Doney's for hot chocolate. Nevertheless, by the time I got back to I Tatti, I had a chill. Nicky provided a hot-water bottle. I went to bed with it and managed to pull myself together enough to dress for dinner.

When I came down I was handed a wire from Alexander Korda from London, telling me that he was going to Monte Carlo and asking me to join him there, as he had a project he wanted to speak to me about.

At dinner B.B. admitted that in the winter there was a punishing west wind at I Tatti, from which he and Nicky suffered also. I read them Korda's wire.

"Are you working on anything?" B.B. asked.

I said I was.

"Then go," B.B. said. "When you are working on something it doesn't matter where you are. Besides, you will be warm in Monte Carlo."

On Monday morning we said good-bye in the hall. Parry was waiting in the car to drive me to the station. B.B. smiled wanly as he shook my hand in farewell. He looked poignantly frail. Nicky moved close to him and encircled her arm through his to sustain him. Sitting with B.B., conversing, one didn't think of his age. At this moment I did. I could see that Nicky was thinking of it too.

For a farewell present B.B. gave me his book on Caravaggio, inscribed to me, and a recent paper of his, "A New Preface to the Italian Painters of the Renaissance." When he gave them to me he said: "When Walter Lippmann was here I gave him these. I've had a letter from him since. He said that what struck him was not so much the intrinsic interest of the material as that they were so well written."

I found this touching. I knew enough about B.B. (I am sure that so did Lippmann) to know that a word of praise for his writing was the one thing in the world that he would wish. The overriding passion of B.B.'s life was neither expertise nor scholarship nor being a "sight to see," but writing. It was all he thought about, it was all that he eternally reproached himself for — that he hadn't made a better writer of himself. I was glad that Lippmann had written him this; it gave me the clue for my own subsequent letter. I saw that it never remotely occurred to Berenson that Lippmann might have merely slipped an extra pat on the bread.

In the car Parry told me with pride that B.B. was planning to depart in several weeks with Miss Mariano for Tripoli. It was a formidable journey and I could see that Parry was happy that his master had the vitality to undertake it. It reassured him. As B.B. had told me that my Duveen book had appeared in Italian and was being sold in the station, I tested him out. It was there — *Il Re degli antiquari*. I bought it. For a moment I entertained the illusion that I was an internationally known author. Then I saw that the initials of my name were reversed. The illusion evaporated.

In Monte Carlo I found that Korda had not arrived yet. I put in a call to Nicky. B.B. had looked so frail. I wanted to find out how he was feeling. I also wanted to talk to Nicky.

My phone rang. Nicky!

But it was not Nicky. It was the operator, who said Miss Mariano was not available.

"Any message?"

"I've given you the message. Not available."

I sat on the side of the bed. This was disturbing. Could anything be wrong at I Tatti? I had a thought. I picked up the receiver again. I put in a call to Parry. Parry was the only one on B.B.'s staff who spoke English.

I was sure there was something wrong. I imagined the worst. With B.B.'s age, with his frailty, what could one imagine but the worst? I remembered the expression on Parry's face when he was driving me to the station in Florence, the pride, the triumph with which he announced that his master was going to Tripoli.

I walked around the room. I smoked. I began to be afraid I wouldn't hear from Parry either. The phone rang. It was Parry.

B.B. had been in a bad automobile accident. He was in poor shape. Nobody's fault. Miss Mariano was looking after him. The doctor was there. The doctor wasn't at all alarmed. He counted on Mr. Berenson's remarkable constitution. They were all counting on it. He promised to let me know how things were going.

B.B.'s constitution survived this gruesome accident by five years. Nicky survived by fourteen. She lived long enough to earn the gratitude of the Harvard Corporation, which congratulated itself on "Harvard's good fortune that the University could benefit from the interest and assistance of this remarkable woman." In the spate of books that followed Berenson's death, among them the biography by Sylvia Sprigge and Nicky's own memoir, *Forty Years with Berenson,* the most fascinating is *Sunset and Twilight,* Berenson's diaries from the age of eighty-two to ninety-three. Every morning the ruler of this "strange little kingdom," as Kenneth Clark calls the regime at I Tatti, sat at his desk and wrote up his diary. The range and the scope of it, the daring intellectual speculation, the incessant and probing curiosity about the world and people, the astonishing candor about himself, constitute a psychological history of an extremely complicated character through nine decades. He seems to have everything he has ever read — in Greek and in Latin and in Hebrew — at his fingertips. Miss Sprigge, in her biography, tells of a bicycle tour Berenson made with Bertrand Russell in Lombardy in 1894. Of that tour Lord Russell said afterwards: "I was amazed at his reading. He it was who first put me on to Fustel de Coulange's *La Cité antique,* for which I've always been grateful, and he first put me on to reading Ranke."

Iris Origo, in her introduction to Berenson's engrossing diaries, is impressed by Berenson's frankness. It is so. He is frank with the reader. He is not frank with himself. He accuses himself of every sin — except the sin of violence. We all of us do this — if not in print, as Berenson does, privately to ourselves. But, as the sins parade, they produce an effect of déjà vu. It is very difficult to be original in perfidy.

Berenson emerges from these diaries a tragic figure, Prometheus chained to the rock. He never got what he wanted, he never devoted himself to what he deeply wanted. He never — almost alone among his myriad friends and the countless sightseers — succumbed to his own myth. He felt it was hollow. He lists his accomplishments in art history, in expertise, to bolster the myth; but his inventories do not convince him. What he really wanted, what he wanted overmasteringly, was to write, to be accepted, not as an expert — he refers to "my disreputable profession" — but as a writer. That is what he wanted from youth to his dying day. Lamentations for the lost opportunity drop everywhere through these diaries like petals from a funeral spray. Iris Origo, in her preface to B.B.'s diaries, writes that he had "a nagging, driving need to fulfill himself in writing," and she goes on to quote him: "I am humiliated, exasperated at my impotence in finding words and phrases. . . . I never had one [a vocabulary] adequate to my purpose, and it has been a handicap." She comments parenthetically: "(This, strange as it seems in a man of such wide reading, was true.)" She might have added that he also had a fabulous memory. Iris Origo, herself an excellent writer, seems to have overlooked one small point: writing takes more (and less) than the acquisition of a large vocabulary; it takes a special talent. B.B. just didn't happen to have it. While still in college he fell in love, stylistically, with Walter Pater. He couldn't have done worse because had he been left to himself, he would have written like Walter Pater (in fact he often did), earning for himself, on his own, the epithet which Max Beerbohm applied to Pater, "sepulchral." The trouble with B.B. as a writer is that he lacks vivacity. Berenson was aware of this himself. He was a great talker. His diaries, because in them he is talking, have

marvelous passages; *Sunset and Twilight* is far and away his best
book.

Forty years ago, because I was interested in Berenson even then, I
asked a patrician Bostonian whether he knew Berenson. He did indeed. I asked what he was like. We were walking in the Public Garden
in Boston. My new acquaintance stopped in his walk for a muse. "Ah,
Berenson. He is so gifted that he might have become anything he
liked. He could have been God — he chose to be Mephistopheles." I
once asked B.B. whether he knew this man without, naturally, quoting
him. "Oh, yes," he said, "indeed I knew him. Edith Wharton adored
him — all the Boston ladies adored him. I could never stand him. He
was the wrong kind of homosexual." It was one of the strange line-
crossings which life insists on providing; could I have dreamt that
autumn morning in Boston that nearly half a century later I would be
inquiring of God-Mephistopheles himself, in his garden at I Tatti,
about his ambivalent friend!

I have always thought it strange that Berenson never mentions
Duveen in his autobiographical books; in *Sketch for a Self-Portrait* for
example. He does mention him in his diaries and, I believe, far more
revealingly than he was aware of. He is talking of Sylvia Sprigge, who
was to be his biographer:

> Impossible for her to conceive of my life except as a vulgar suc-
> cess story, the highlights of which are Mrs. Gardner and "Lord"
> Duveen, a personage who affected me negatively, if at all.

Here, I believe, Berenson is lying to himself, a necessary lie which
veils the heart of his mystery. Significant are the quotation marks
around the word "Lord." No one knew better than Berenson how
these things are done; by this suddenly invoked standard, quotation
marks might be ringed about many members of the House of Lords.
He finally broke with Duveen but he never got rid of him. I believe
that Duveen was the canker of his life, the core of his tragedy. It was
Duveen who had made him rich, made his princely style of life possible. In conversation with me about Duveen his expression would
change; benevolence vanished from it. Why? Many people liked

Duveen. Mary Berenson liked him; Kenneth Clark liked him; J. G. Constable, who, when I interviewed him, was curator of the Boston Museum of Fine Arts, found it invigorating to be with him.

Elsewhere in the diaries, Berenson expands on his aversion to money. He has, he explains, no aptitude for business, for dealing. His dislike of money is so indurated that he will not have any on his person. When they travel Nicky handles it all, does the tipping, pays all the bills. The transparency of this is almost touching. Whom was Berenson fooling? Surely he knew that you had to have an awful lot of money in order to be able to travel without it. In a much later entry he confessed to envying Duveen's money:

> And what has become of the Duveen fortune divided between his wife and daughter and possibly two or three assistants? I cannot help regretting all I could have done with money to do what I pleased with, according to my own ideas and judgment.

Were it not for Duveen, Berenson seems to be saying, he would have devoted his life to writing and might have become a first-class writer. If so, he never knew, the tragic man, from what a dangerous career Duveen had saved him.

XXI

W. Somerset Maugham

IN LATE SUMMER of 1938 Siegfried Sassoon invited me to Heytes-bury in Wiltshire to see the house he had finally found and to meet his wife, Hester, and his infant son, George. Before I took the train I went to a toy shop and bought a commodious Noah's Ark with a full passenger list. I dragged the big, neatly wrapped bundle on the train.

Heytesbury House, large and substantial, was set back from the road — the main street of the village — by a hundred yards of clear lawn. Mrs. Sassoon was lovely and gracious, but seemed subdued. In the front hall I gave them my present for George. Siegfried promptly dropped the package. It fell to the marble floor with a great crash. The ark broke. They were both horrified. I said to Hester that it was very characteristic of Siegfried, recalling some of his old clumsinesses in New York. But they were both comforted when they saw the immense variety of animals. They felt that George would be consoled. He was; the first time I saw him, he had a happy stranglehold on a giraffe. He smiled warmly at me whenever he saw me.

Siegfried looked well — tall and handsome. It was a comfort to hear his gentle voice again. He took me into the library. I saw the stately bound sermons of Tillotson and rows of books on cricket. Hester told me that the villagers, who hadn't mastered Siegfried's name, referred to him as "on a horse," as that was the only way they ever saw him, on his daily rides. "It's wonderful country for riding," Siegfried said. "I go out the first thing in the morning. It's glorious." Siegfried took me up to my room to change for dinner. There were to be two guests: Geoffrey Keynes, the brother of Maynard — an eminent surgeon and foremost authority on the manuscripts of William Blake — and G. M. Young. Siegfried briefed me on the latter. "A wonderful man — no one knows the physique of England as he does." I told him that I was greatly taken with Hester. "We must bring her out," he said, somewhat cryptically, and left me. He returned in a moment. He asked if I had, by any chance, a photograph of my infant son, David, about the same age as George. Chance was favorable. I had. Siegfried was rhapsodic over the joys of fatherhood. He told me that George's arrival had made him feel that he had not known hitherto what an extended sense of being life might offer. He indulged a fantasy: "Wouldn't it be wonderful," he exclaimed, "if David and George met — if they became great friends. They must meet — they must become great friends." He left, reassured that this prophecy would come true, eternalizing our friendship.

Hester presided over us at dinner, looking lovely in a black frock. She was mainly silent, contenting herself with telling Mr. Young and Mr. Keynes that Siegfried and I had become friends when he went to New York to lecture. Both men had grace of style. Mr. Keynes was older than his brother Maynard. Not as sharp as Maynard, less angular. Mr. Young was what a Broadwayite might instantly put down as a "honey." He was enthusiastic about Siegfried's acres. He had been over every inch of them. He loved every hillock, every rivulet. Addressing me, he dispensed a bit of information. "Behind this house King Alfred conquered the Danes." He made me promise that while I was there I would make the same *tournée* that he had; he only regretted that he had to leave in the morning and could not accompany me. He approved Siegfried's plan for planting the Jubilee Allée that would be tall when George was twenty. At this Hester ventured a remark: "Oh, Sieg, do tell them about E. M. Forster when you were taking the Allée walk with him!" Siegfried complied:

"I love Morgan Forster — I can't get him to come often enough. I walked him around the Allée and told him my plans for it. He seemed interested and happy when, suddenly, he burst into tears. He sobbed like a child. I tried to calm him, begged him to tell me what was wrong. He finally told me. He had had a quarrel with his mother, with

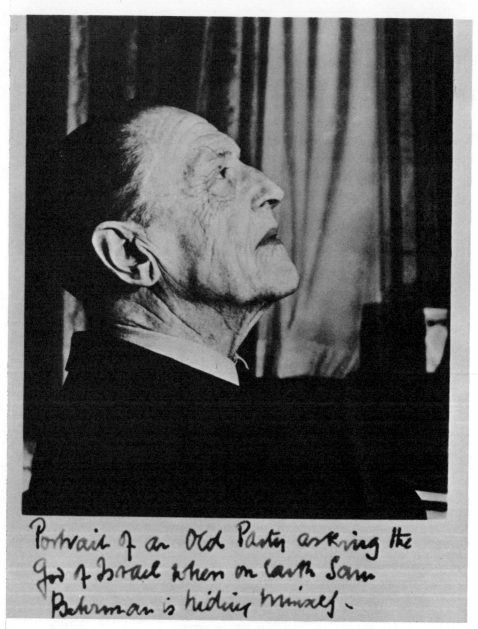

Portrait of an Old Party asking the
God of Israel when on earth Sam
Behrman is hiding himself.

W. Somerset Maugham

whom he lived, with whom, in fact, he had been living all his life. It was over a latch key. As he was over sixty, he felt he might ask for a latch key so he could get in and out of the house without waking anybody up. His mother was furious. She thought the demand an effrontery. It was their first quarrel; it had shaken him unbearably. Telling it calmed him down a bit — in fact, it did calm him down — but isn't it extraordinary? A man of sixty — over a latch key!"

"Let it be a lesson to you, Hester," said Young. "Give George a latch key to the Allée when he is ten!"

On Sunday afternoon the Sassoons had a stream of visitors from weekenders in the neighborhood. There were Lady Juliet Duff, Simon Fleet, Moura Budberg, Alan Searle and W. Somerset Maugham. The first to arrive was Moura Budberg, an ample woman of ample spirit who was then working for Alexander Korda as story editor. Siegfried took her upstairs to display George to her. I sat alone with Hester. I was attracted by Hester and, somehow, touched by her. She briefed me on Moura, described her extraordinary amorous history, beginning — "Imagine!" — with Maxim Gorky, going from him to Bruce Lockhart, and ending, currently, with H. G. Wells. I could see that for her it was unimaginably romantic. How could one be so free and easy? Siegfried and Moura came back. Moura was in a glow about George. She had a most pleasing voice and a contagious laugh. Lady Juliet Duff came with a young man, Simon Fleet, and then Somerset Maugham with his secretary, Alan Searle.

Maugham made a strange and powerful impression on first meeting. His features were strong and clearly cut. He was smallish but one felt great strength, enormous self-control. The expression on his face was hard to define, elusive in spite of the clarity. It conveyed a kind of punitive resignation, as if he expected very little from life, but that he meant to make up for that little by distributing petty revenges. We got together almost at once on a happy common subject, Harpo Marx. He described having gone to the theatre in New York, arriving early; the rows of seats in front of him were empty. Suddenly he saw climbing over the backs of those seats, like a gorilla, a strange creature, making for him. "I was scared, you know. I saw myself attacked by some

American fanatic. It wasn't till he slid into the seat beside me that I saw that it was Harpo. After that it was all cozy."

Moura asked Maugham about the huge work in which he was involved: an edition of world classics, cut by him, so that the reader could examine these works uncluttered by repetition. Not in the least on the defensive, Maugham answered all the criticisms that were soon to be leveled at him by this act of wholesale truncation. He was simply cutting the repetitions imposed on their authors by the necessities of serial publication. "For example," he said, "Thomas Hardy once published a novel with a different ending from the one published serially in the *London News*." As Hardy was not on his list, he was not forced to cope with that. He talked to me about American literature; he had unstinted admiration for *Moby Dick*. That, to his regret, could not appear on his list for copyright reasons. I asked him whether he knew Steinbeck. "Oh, yes," he said. "He is a leading American novelist now but how long will that vogue last for these limited characters?"

For some time now, Theresa Helburn had been urging me to dramatize "Jane," a short story of Maugham's. I had put her off because I felt that the climate of the time had changed greatly since the untroubled days when the story was written. I wondered whether Maugham knew about this. When he invited me, quite suddenly, to visit him at the Villa Mauresque at Cap Ferrat, I felt that perhaps he did. I said I would love to, that I would let him know as soon as I got back to America. Quite fatuously I asked, in an effort to insure the privacy of the mornings, whether I could get breakfast in my room.

Somewhat curtly Maugham answered: "That's the only place you *can* get it!"

He and Alan Searle left. It was called to my attention that Alan had been wearing an Eton tie to which he had no right.

My visit to the Villa Mauresque was in any case considerably delayed because, when France went to war, Maugham was forced out of his house and had to catch an overcrowded freighter to America. He had to go to great pains to sequester his pictures lest they catch the connoisseur eye of Hermann Goering. He described the ardors of this trip in a book that was published soon after his arrival in America. On my return from England I set about to finish my play *The Talley Method*.

Meanwhile, Terry Helburn kept after me about "Jane." I read the story again, an amusing anecdote about a frump of a provincial who comes to London annually to visit her close and fashionable friend who, as I made it turn out, is the divorced wife of Somerset Maugham. What bothered me greatly about dramatizing this story was that it occurred in a time when people could come into London and capture society. Jane did it by a refreshing habit she had of telling the truth. There was nothing much on society's mind, which made its capture a trivial acquisition. But at this moment there was a great deal on society's mind — its survival, for example.

Maugham called me up the morning after his arrival. He was staying at the old Ritz at Forty-sixth Street and Madison. He was in excellent spirits. He had spent a triumphant evening. He had played bridge and won twelve dollars from Charles Goren. He was very set up by this. I did not know who Charles Goren was. Maugham was distressed. "You do not know Charles Goren! Then you are not a member of civilized society. He is the greatest bridge player in the world — he has revolutionized the game." Nevertheless, he asked me if I was free for lunch. I wasn't. I had a date at 21 with Harold Ross. I asked Maugham to join us. He accepted at once, as he was a habitual *New Yorker* reader. It was a jolly lunch. I confessed to Ross that I was not a member of civilized society, since I did not know who Charles Goren was. Maugham repeated his victory over Goren to the tune of twelve dollars. Ross was impressed; he thought, in fact, that Goren would be a good subject for a profile and would I take it on? I said I was too ignorant and that Maugham should do it. Ross was delighted. Maugham said that he thought the central pieces in the *New Yorker* were running too long. Ross said he spent a lot of time cutting them. Maugham insisted they were still too long. He was stuttering badly; the conversation moved to the agony of his stutter. Ross asked couldn't anything be done about it? Maugham said that he'd been to a psycho-analyst. Ross asked whether that had helped. "All the psychoanalysis did for me," said Maugham, "was to increase my sexual desires." We were joined at that moment by Leonora Corbett, the lovely young actress who had just made a hit in Noel Coward's original and vastly entertaining *Blithe Spirit*. She was full of *The Razor's Edge*, Maugham's just-published new novel. "You must dramatize it," she said to Maugham. "I'd love to play the heroine." "Well, my dear," Maugham said, "you have the legs for it, haven't you?"

I flinched at this. In the novel Maugham makes a point of saying that the heroine was beautiful but that her legs were oversize. I saw that Miss Corbett got it. She kept on with her line for a few seconds, but she was dampened. I could see that she hated Maugham. She left us. I wondered why Maugham had felt it necessary to say this. It was gratuitous. I talked about it to Ross after we left. "It's his nature, I guess," Ross said.

I saw a good deal of Maugham before he left for North Carolina, where Nelson Doubleday, his American publisher, had built a house for him on his estate which Maugham occupied for the rest of his American stay. We discussed casting *Jane* — who would play Jane, who would play Maugham. Before setting pen to paper on it I offered it to Katharine Cornell. Her husband, Guthrie McClintic, was for her doing it but Kit shied off. Maugham was astonished at the immense difficulty of getting actors for plays. He had been one of the most successful playwrights in the world. At one time he had four plays running simultaneously in London. *Punch* ran a full-page cartoon showing William Shakespeare groveling before the billboards announcing the ubiquitous Maugham attractions, and biting his nails in anger and envy. In his day he wrote his plays for the American manager, Charles Frohman. They would decide whom they wanted and inform their chosen actors when rehearsals would start and where. No one ever thought of sending a script for approval. Maugham said that the effervescence of the mechanical arts had seemingly made it easier to get the president of U.S. Steel for a part than a leading actor. I told Maugham my worries about dramatizing his story in a parlous time like the present. He did not share my qualms: "It's only meant to be a light entertainment, you know." "Is this a time for light entertainment?" I countered. He brought up the example of Jane Austen. "Look at her novels," he said. "They were written at one of the gravest moments in English history, when we might have been invaded at any moment. Jane Austen is blithely indifferent to all that — never mentions it." The analogy was plausible but not convincing. You come into the theatre from the street tingling with headlines. It's different from going into a library for a quiet read. I made a private vow to introduce the headlines into *Jane.*

In Washington I met Alan Searle's predecessor, Gerald Haxton. He was quite different from Alan, who was very quiet. Gerald was outgoing, articulate and amusing. He was working then for some government agency. He was himself an American from San Francisco. When I reported the meeting to Maugham he said that he was greatly worried about Gerald's health; he was tubercular. Indeed, not long after, Gerald gave up his job in Washington and came to New York to be hospitalized. He was the love of Willie's life. They had spent years together in the South Seas, where Maugham gathered the material for bookfuls of stories and novels.

Maugham was a fascinating companion. He knew everybody and he had something personal and idiosyncratic to say about everyone. His memories of New York reached back to the early days of the century when the Vanderbilts reigned. He was their familiar. More recently, when Billie Burke married Florenz Ziegfeld, he had been chosen by Miss Burke to receive her when she descended the staircase at the grand wedding and to escort her to the waiting bridegroom. He told of a dinner and an evening with Rudyard Kipling in the nineties. He greatly admired Kipling, but he remembered that he had made a private resolve that if Kipling said "pukka sahib" one more time, he would throw a decanter at him. Winston Churchill was a friend of very long standing; they made a deal early on. Winston had discovered how adroit Maugham was in barbed response, having publicly exchanged several sorties with him. Winston proposed a lifelong armistice: that each of them should refrain from attacking the other. The armistice had held; Winston had been a frequent visitor at the Villa Mauresque.

Just now Maugham told me of a private disaster he had endured in New Haven. He had undertaken to deliver a speech at Yale. He chose as a subject "The Price of Liberty." He took the trouble to write up a grand peroration, enlarging on how costly the price of liberty was and on how necessary it was to pay it. He explained that he was subject to short bouts of amnesia, blackouts. He said that the speech had gone very well — he hadn't stuttered and was congratulating himself on approaching the end. "And do you know," he said, "all of a sudden I couldn't remember for the life of me what the price of liberty was. I'm usually pretty good at remembering what things cost, but the price of liberty just plain vanished from me. I explained afterwards to the chairman. I must say he was very nice about it."

I got a letter from a well-established publisher which I showed Maugham. It amused him very much. It was a proposal that I write a book about him in collaboration with Edmund Wilson. "There is no race in the world," Maugham said, "as stupid as publishers. Here is a man who has been slating me for years and they pick him to collaborate on a book about me." It is a curious example of Maugham's objectivity that he told me then that Nelson Doubleday had sent him a manuscript of *Hecate County* and asked his advice about whether to publish it. Maugham liked the first story in the book very much. He urged Doubleday to go ahead. I began to wonder whether, if Wilson knew about this, it might not ameliorate some of his strictures. I was perfectly certain it wouldn't. Mr. Wilson is objective too.

Maugham spent his summers in Cape Cod. He transferred Gerald to a hospital there. I saw Gerald once before he left for the Cape. He looked frail and emaciated, but he was vivacious and full of good-natured fun at the foibles of people, including Willie's. I got the sense, which I'd had before from him, that all this was an easy routine for him, a patter he had developed to use on outsiders like myself. There was never anything genuinely personal. It was like a document prepared by a cunning enemy in a war, a document intended to be captured. I would call up Maugham on the Cape and ask how things were going. He said it was a very monotonous life, as he went to the hospital daily to sit with Gerald. There were diversions. Kit Cornell had invited him to a clambake which he found overpowering. It was so ample it put him to sleep. He became a friend of Max Eastman's, whose company he greatly enjoyed. I had been told that once, while

London: a wartime ad

sitting by Gerald's bed, he had been forced to listen to a violent denunciation of himself spat out by Gerald in a delirium, a wild forecast of the fun Gerald would have after Willie's death. In his *Summing Up* Maugham makes a confession that people do not usually make: that no love he had ever felt was reciprocated. This story supplies a fearsome background to this confession.

I had begun my dramatization of "Jane." I put the current headlines in: for example, I allowed Jane to quietly defend Anthony Eden, who is being ignorantly and volubly denounced at a society lunch. Harold Ross had been asking me for some time to go to England to write a piece about London in wartime. Maugham thought it was a very good idea and encouraged me to go, especially as Binkie Beaumont was prepared to produce *Jane* in London. He had found a star for it, Yvonne Arnaud, a perennially popular English favorite. Maugham gave me letters to H. G. Wells and to his brother, Lord Maugham, the Lord High Chancellor of England.

London was cold, dark and gloomy. The V-2's were falling steadily, preceded by their gruesome whistles. I had just gotten into my room at Claridge's and was unpacking when one fell. It sounded just outside; the windows shook. I was so scared I thought of rolling myself under the bed. The telephone rang. It was Alexander Korda, who lived in the penthouse upstairs. "That was a fucking bomb, old boy," he announced pleasantly. I went up to have a cup of tea with him. He informed me that the bomb had done a good deal of damage but at quite a distance from us. "They always sound as if they were on top of you," he said. He encouraged me to go out for a little walk, to Grosvenor Square. On the way there, through the dim streets, I saw the skeleton of a house with one room intact, an elegant oval-shaped drawing room with a pale blue ceiling with a circular indentation where the chandelier had hung. That gave me the title for the piece I intended to write and which eventually appeared in the *New Yorker,* "The Suspended Drawing Room."

I went to see the Lunts, who were rehearsing passionately in their suite at the Savoy Hotel for a new play of Terry Rattigan's. They were in the grip of a marvelous idea Lynn had conceived for it. They told it to me in a rush of enthusiasm. They acted it out for me. When I saw

Rattigan he told me that the effort to elide it had shortened his life by a good many years. I went to see Olivier in *Richard III,* a thrilling performance. Larry told me in his dressing room afterwards that Churchill had been there the night before and nearly ruined him. He sat in the third row and mouthed every line of Larry's, but ahead of him. "He wasn't audible," Larry said, "but I saw his lips form the lines. I don't know how I got through that evening. It was ghastly. When he came back to see me afterwards, I didn't know what to say; I could only congratulate him on his memory." I met Noel Coward in Claridge's dining room. He told me that his theatre dresser had characterized Hitler, doing even better, I thought, than Churchill, who demoted Der Führer to "Corporal Hitler." Noel's dresser simply said: "That 'Itler, 'e's a fidget." Binkie Beaumont introduced me to Miss Yvonne Arnaud, perhaps the most popular star in England. She was Belgian, short, plump, spirited. She had been, before her theatre career started, a concert pianist. Binkie had told me that she refused resolutely ever to play the piano in a play. Our first meeting went very well and so did our subsequent ones. Miss Arnaud was as irresistible personally as she was on the stage. Her husband ran a pig farm and she made this occupation sound romantic.

I heard H. G. Wells was ill and I did not present the letter Maugham had given me to him. In Hollywood Ruthie Selwyn had told me that H.G. had taken her through his new house in London, of which he was very proud. She was astonished at the commodiousness and comfort of the servants' quarters. She commented on this. H.G. said: "My mother, my dear, was a servant." Wells was an abiding hero of mine. I had met him, briefly, the summer before the war, at Lord Allington's. He was sitting on the porch on a warm day, rather heavily caped. I told him how intensively he had been read when I was an undergraduate at Harvard. I asked him whether he was writing anything. "Oh, yes," he said rather grimly, "the diarrhea goes on." He had written a short book which he said he could not get published. This seemed hardly credible but he insisted it was so. The book was called *Crux Ansata* and dealt formidably with the Catholic Church. When I got back home I made inquiries about it. Bennett Cerf told me that it had been offered to him, but that he could not possibly publish it because Random House was a tenant of the Catholic Church at Fiftieth and Madison.

I did, however, present my letter to Lord Maugham and was promptly invited to lunch at his house in Cadogan Square, directly across the street from where I used to visit Arnold Bennett and Dorothy Cheston. Lord Maugham was not there — he was sitting — but his delightful wife and his daughter, Honour, were there. Honour, very unconventionally, was a passionate Zionist and went around making speeches for the cause. Lady Maugham was very amusing; she did wish that Willie wouldn't write her about the freshness of the eggs he got in Martha's Vineyard when it was so hard to get eggs of any quality in Cadogan Square. I spent the afternoon with Honour and returned later to have tea with the Lord Chancellor. He was much taller than Willie, gaunt and serious. He asked me what I was doing for the war effort. I said I had participated in several radio broadcasts to Germany. He wondered who listened to them in Germany. I couldn't tell him but said that at the Ministry they believed that a good many Germans did listen. He spoke of Willie's books, without ardor. He asked me whether Willie had mentioned to me a book of his own on the Tichborne case. I said no but this was not true. Willie had mentioned it. He said: "My family writes. They are fluent but not idiosyncratic."

In my absence, Gerald Haxton had died in New York. I called up Willie. I had sent him the first draft of my piece on London. I had lunch with him in the parlor of his suite at the Ritz. I looked for signs of grief in his face but they were not visible. He had his habitual composed and impassive expression. He told me with a certain pride that the cook he had broken in at Nelson Doubleday's house was now the best cook in North Carolina. He liked my piece, especially the idea I proposed at the end, that American civilians rather than the military should go to London. He was very interested in everything that had happened to me in England. He was especially inquisitive about my meetings with Yvonne Arnaud. Finally I said: "But Willie, you haven't told me. How was it with Gerald — at the end?" I was instantly sorry. "Please," he said in a broken voice, "don't ask me that."

He began to cry and left the room. It was the sudden demolition of a carefully built image.

With the possibly mistaken idea of cheering Willie up, I took him to the opening of a major production of the Playwrights' Company. The play was by a leading American dramatist and it had a fabled star in it. When it was over Willie said he was tired and wanted to get back to his rooms to read. He said nothing about the play at all. Finally I asked him what he thought of it. "Even the obvious," he said, "must be made plausible." Then he began to talk about his cook in North Carolina. She had been an untutored girl when she came. He had trained her. She was now first class. In the Ritz lobby I ran into Alan Searle. I invited him for a drink. I told him that it had been a mistake to take Willie to the play, that all he talked about in the taxi was how good his cook was in North Carolina. "She is, you know," said Alan, "she's marvelous. Everybody loves to come to dinner. Willie takes great trouble over things like that. Sometimes it's embarrassing."

"For instance?" I said.

"For instance? Well, one morning Clare Luce called up at the Villa and said she'd like to come to lunch. Willie said fine. He revised the menu because Clare was coming. He must have made a dozen trips to the kitchen that morning to consult with the cook. He's a great house-keeper. Well, Clare came — so did the first course. Clare looked at it, made a dab at it, and passed it up. The second course came with the same result. I saw Willie's expression and I felt nervous. I prayed that she would do better by the next course. She didn't. 'I see, Clare,' said Willie, in a quiet but dangerous tone, 'that you don't like my food.' 'Oh, no,' she protested, 'it's just that I don't eat at midday.' 'If you don't eat, why did you come to lunch?' said Willie. It was a very tense moment, I can tell you!"

The war ended. Willie returned to France to put his house in order and to get his pictures — a prime collection of nineteenth-century French Impressionists — back on the walls. He promised to meet me in London for the first rehearsals of *Jane*. I had to go to Venice to meet Bernard Berenson. Willie invited me to spend a night or two at the Villa Mauresque on the way to London. The chauffeur had to stop several times to find his way but the French peasants seemed to know Mr. Mau-gam's whereabouts and presently I saw his gates flanked by the cabalistic symbol which appears on all his books. I was greeted warmly by my host and Alan. There was a young man staying, a representative of Doubleday. He was tall, good-looking, under thirty. We sat in the courtyard before lunch having cocktails. Maugham was surprised that I had never been in Venice before.

"To Venice," he said, "you should go when you are young and in love and with the object of your adoration."

"It's nice work if you can get it," I said.

At lunch Willie made us an apology. "I have been invited to the annual fête in the village. You don't in the least have to go, but I am afraid I have to. It takes place in a canvas tent expecially got up for the occasion. There is music and dancing. It might amuse you, but I *have* to go."

We all chimed in that we would love to go and we did. We sat for a while with the mayor, who looked authoritative but wore no collar or tie. It was an inspiriting spectacle. The whole village was indeed there — young and old. We were at once attracted by a man who must have been eighty who danced — with tremendous agility and improvisation — with one young girl after another. Willie kept indicating various girls on the floor; they had all had extracurricular relations with some member of his past and present staff. The mayor didn't pay much attention to us. He was busy dancing. It was a very lively scene and great fun to watch.

We left about ten-thirty. In the car on the way back to the Villa, Willie said: "You know, I suppose, that everybody there, including the mayor with whom we sat, they're all Communists. This village is solid Communist."

The young publisher was troubled by this; it mystified him. He was hashing it over when we got back to the house.

"I don't understand, Willie — your saying they're all Communists. They're Catholic, aren't they? And what you say about their sleeping with everybody — it just doesn't make sense."

"It does to them," said Maugham. "They're Communists because they're poor and want to be rich; they're promiscuous because they are highly sexed; they're Catholics because they don't want to go to hell."

He was already on the stairs going up to his room.

"I am going to my room to read Chaucer. When I read Chaucer I think that everything's all right."

Willie called me when he got to London. He always stayed at the Dorchester. I invited him to lunch the next day as we had decided to go see a mutual friend, Sibyl Colefax, who was in the hospital with a broken leg. Alex Korda had gone to New York and had offered me his grand apartment at the top of Claridge's while he was away. I wanted Willie to see the style in which I was living, surrounded by terraces and Alex's Monets and Manets. The next day he came on the dot, twelve o'clock. He looked haggard; he said at once: "May I have a drink, please?" I went to Alex's well-stocked bar and poured him a stiff one. After he had swallowed it he relaxed a bit. He explained. He had just come from his eye doctor, where he had undergone a rather painful operation.

I protested: "For heaven's sake, Willie, why didn't you tell me? We could have postponed this."

"I don't like to cancel appointments," he said.

It was like him. I have never met anyone who had greater will-power, greater self-control than W. S. Maugham.

He went on to tell the history of his eminent oculist. He used it as an illustration to support his favorite theory, about which we were always arguing, that everything in life is due to accident. His doctor had been a poor boy in a Midlands city who took a job as a caddy at the local golf course. A well-known eye specialist came from London to visit his parents and took the young caddy on. He was greatly pleased with him, sent him to medical school, and encouraged him to follow his own specialty. The ex-caddy now had a position analogous to his mentor's. Did not this prove Willie's point? I said it didn't, that you couldn't tell what might have happened to the caddy unassisted. He always reverted to his own basic accident, his career as a playwright. In his day the London managers relied on a fixed coterie of playwrights, many of them French. Willie's plays attracted nobody. One of the coterie let a manager down at the last moment; in desperation he put on a comedy of Willie's that he had rejected. It succeeded and the flood began. "Sheer accident," said Willie. "Sheer poppycock," said I.

We found Sibyl Colefax in traction in her hospital room, one thickly wadded leg suspended high in the air. She was reading *Adolphe*. She was very glad to see us, as we were to see her. She had never, she said, enjoyed *Adolphe* as much as she did this time, had never seen so much in it. It was a favorite of Willie's too and they had a get-together on it. Not having read it, I couldn't contribute. Sibyl said she was so glad we had come in on this particular afternoon because Tom Eliot was coming. Not as meticulous about appointments as Willie was, Eliot's approach was delayed. We waited. He never came. Beverly Nichols came. After a polite interval Willie and I left.

In the cab Willie grumbled: "We were p-p-promised T. S. Eliot. We g-g-got Beverly Nichols!"

The next day at noon Binkie Beaumont, Willie and I went to hear the first reading of the play. Ronald Squire, a beautiful comedian, played Tower, the Willie Maugham part. The first act, which covered the main part of Willie's story, was what Sherwood might have called tidy. Miss Arnaud was perfect, funny and touching, and Ronnie Squire as cutting as Maugham himself often was. At one point the juvenile, a young and untried avant-garde writer, refers to Tower as a "glorified hack." I took a side glance at Willie but that keen, impassive face revealed nothing; he was merely listening. After the first act my troubles began. I had found that when Willie's anecdote was disposed of, I had to write a play. The story simply says that Jane captivated everybody by telling the truth. I had to dramatize that. By the time the second act was over, the actors were flustered and uncomfortable. Willie said to Binkie so that everybody could hear: "It's too long. It goes on forever." He then felt it advisable to reassure the company. He told them that I was an experienced dramatist and that he was sure I would do what had to be done. After the reading was over, Willie and I returned to Korda's suite. He said he was going back to the Villa Mauresque the next day as he had a big job, the editing and cutting and introduction-writing to the series of the great truncated novels. I asked him if he could come to Blackpool for the opening or to Edinburgh for the second week. He said that would be impossible; it was my play and he made it clear that he would have nothing more to do with it. He did speak of one scene, an unimportant one between the juvenile and Mr. Tower's daughter. He said it had grated on him as not being natural. I asked how he would do it. He asked for a pad and pencil and went to work on it. I was astonished at what happened. It was a scene I could have rewritten easily myself, leaving it to the fingertips. What startled me was that Willie seemed to be in an agony over it. He was creating viscerally, thrashing and turning in his chair. What he produced when he finally handed it to me was quite ordinary and colorless.

Willie and I had an engagement that night to dine at Juliet Duff's, a very old friend of his and a recent but warm friend of mine. In the taxi on the way there, he assured me: "You can't go higher in English society than where you are going tonight." It was a small dinner party, comfortable and cozy. Another American was there, Alan Campbell, Dorothy Parker's husband. At dinner Churchill was discussed. A titled lady said: "Let's face it — Winston has *not* had a classical education." I whispered to Willie: "What would Jane say to that?" He whispered back: "That is for you to discover." We left early as Juliet was working for the Red Cross and had to get up to drive a truck through the devastated areas. I drove Willie to the Dorchester. As we passed through the gruesome, ill-lit, half-destroyed streets, Willie said with feeling: "Isn't it heartbreaking?" He transported the heartbreak next morning to the Villa Mauresque. I did not see him again for a long time.

Theresa Helburn and Lawrence Langner came over to help with *Jane*. I cut and cut. I had time to wander around. I wandered into the Haymarket Theatre one day for a rehearsal of *Lady Windermere's Fan*. I saw the Wildean Beau Brummels and fashion plates shivering on the bitterly cold stage, furred up and muffled to the nines. I got the idea for another London piece: "It's Cold at Lady Windermere's," which also appeared eventually in the *New Yorker*.

I traveled to Blackpool and sat with Miss Arnaud on the train. She had an extraordinary calm about her, even serenity. She never, she said, suffered from opening-night nervousness. She felt that she could do far better than those sitting out front, so why should she be nervous? I wondered whether her security came from having mastered an art before she embarked on her second career. We talked mostly about music, about composers. Her favorite was Delius because, she said, he was a lyric poet. She still practiced the piano when she could, but she did it privately, as she imagined writers practiced privately.

I went with Terry and Lawrence to the opening. It was Christmas Eve. The house was full. Miss Arnaud was received rapturously. Binkie was pleased. I was pleased because a line I had written about Lord Frobisher, a newspaper magnate, got an enormous laugh. The line was: "He is a Labor peer and very self-conscious about never having been a workingman." I was reassured by that laugh. I had been told that English audiences expected a speech from Miss Arnaud after each performance. She made one — graceful and modest. She thanked them for their warm reception and spoke hopefully of the play's success in London.

I went backstage to see Ronnie Squire. That elegant man was swathed in heavy winter underwear, toweling makeup off his face. He reverted to his favorite theme with me: the awful food in England and the superb food in Basel, Switzerland. He escaped there whenever he could and stayed at the Drei Könige Hotel. He recommended a restaurant in Basel where you could dine really well, but the food at the Drei Könige was excellent also so you didn't really have to leave the hotel. I could see that the poor man was apprehensive that *Jane* would have a run and that his next escape to Basel might be indefinitely delayed. I was just leaving when he called me back. "When you get to the Drei Könige," he said, "don't forget, ask for rooms on the Rhine."

After the opening Terry, Lawrence and I had supper in the hotel dining room. Blackpool is a beach resort but it attracts winter visitors also, for no reason that I could discover. The dining room was decorated to extremity — a great papier-mâché battleship hung from the ceiling with MERRY CHRISTMAS blazoned on its hull. It was festooned in colored lights. It floated ponderously over the room. In every corner there stood forlorn Christmas trees, laden with colored

ornaments. In the middle of supper, Terry, overcome with nostalgia —
began to cry. "She misses Westport," said Lawrence, "and Christmas
at home."

I went on to Edinburgh because I wanted to see that beautiful black
and white city. Terry and Lawrence returned to London. It was the
terrible winter of 1946. When I complained to the clerk in the station-
hotel about the lack of heat in my room, he said genially: "Don't
forget, sir, we won the war!" I heard Yvonne's nightly speech; she
seemed to have a personal relationship with her audiences. The
Frobisher line went even better in Edinburgh. It had become for me a
test line: whether I had succeeded in acclimatization. Yvonne's serenity was undimmed. Ronnie Squire kept suggesting restaurants to me in
Basel. I did not go on to Aberdeen, the last stop before London. Terry,
Lawrence and I sailed for home on the *Elizabeth* on the morning of
the London opening. On the boat train the highballs we had ordered
to warm up with came frozen stiff in their glasses. The *Elizabeth* was
cold too. I sat before a lit radiator and wrote with feeling: "It's Cold
at Lady Windermere's." We got a wire of tempered optimism from
Binkie the day after the opening. The play ran a long time in England,
due to Yvonne Arnaud's hold on her public. It had a successful tour in
Germany too, with Kaethe Dorsch, the leading German comedienne.
Here, with Edna Best and Basil Rathbone, it did not succeed at all. I
had acclimatized to England more closely than to New York.

After I'd polished off Lady Windermere, I sat down to read Willie's
book on Spain, *Don Fernando,* which I'd bought in London. Graham
Greene says it is his most honest book. It contains a widely anthologized passage on El Greco. Indeed, Maugham says that he wrote the
book in order to give himself a chance to write about El Greco, who
endlessly fascinated him — by his mystery, by his perplexity. Defying
Fowler, he says that El Greco's personality is the most "intriguing" of
any painter. He indulges in a long, circular, almost Talmudic analysis
of him as painter and as man. El Greco, he concludes, is not a mystic;
in fact, he is devoid altogether of religious feeling. His magnificently
painted religious pictures seem to have derived from a "vague and
tormenting sensation that seems to oppress him." Finally, lost in the

labyrinth of his own often contradictory arguments, he comes across a suggestion, "made in a ribald spirit," that seems to clear up the mystery for him: El Greco was a homosexual. He enlarges:

I should say that a distinctive trait of the homosexual is a lack of deep seriousness over certain things that normal men take seriously. This ranges from an inane flippancy to a sardonic humor. He has a willfulness that attaches importance to things that most men find trivial and on the other hand regards cynically the subjects which the common opinion of mankind has held essential to its spiritual welfare. He has a lively sense of beauty, but is apt to see beauty especially in decoration. He loves luxury and attaches peculiar value to elegance. He is emotional but fantastic. He is vain, loquacious, witty and theatrical. With his keen insight and quick sensibility he can pierce the depths, but in his innate frivolity he fetches up from them not a priceless jewel but a tinsel ornament. He has small power of invention, but a wonderful gift for delightful embroidery. He has vitality, brilliance, but seldom strength. He stands on the bank, aloof and ironical, and watches the river of life flow on. He is persuaded that opinion is no more than prejudice. In short, he has many of the characteristics that surprise us in El Greco. It may be that in this abnormality lies the explanation why his pictures fail of that ultimate greatness which is release. They thrill; they do not give you peace. They excite; but do not satisfy . . . I think no religious painter expressed emotion so perfunctorily as El Greco.

About a year later the newspapers announced that Willie was going to San Francisco to celebrate his seventy-fifth birthday with Bertram Alanson in fulfillment of a promise he had made a half century before. I had met Alanson, a tall, distinguished man who looked like a Spanish grandee. Willie and Alan popped into town, the Plaza this time. Willie called up.

"What," I asked, "has Bertram Alanson got that I haven't got?"

"Money," said Willie.

We had lunch. After a bit I brought up the perplexing passage about El Greco; I rose to the defense of homosexual artists.

"I've been reading *Don Fernando*," I said. "You say that the homosexual artist can produce nothing but decoration and trivialities."

"Did I say that?"

"Look it up. Page 242. What about Michelangelo? What about Leonardo da Vinci? Did they produce nothing but decoration?"

"What about Shakespeare?" he added, reinforcing my argument.

As he was so generous in building up my case, I felt that he didn't want to discuss it. I let it go at that. I remembered his reference in *Don Fernando* to the "perplexing sonnets." I told him that a friend of mine in Boston, the owner of the Ritz-Carlton, was such a fan of his that he would willingly pay him twenty-five hundred dollars just to come up and spend the afternoon with him. He said that he'd had an offer of a similar amount from an American magazine if he would write a description of lunch at the Villa Mauresque with Winston Churchill. He had refused that offer and he was inclined to think that he would refuse this one. We talked about the theatre: he had been disappointed at the failure of the musical version of *Rain* in New York. He attributed it to the lack of singable tunes. That brought him to a proposal that had been made to me: to write the libretto for a musical version of *Of Human Bondage*. I had had conferences on it, arranged by Harold Freedman, with Richard Adler and Robert Merrill, both immensely successful musical comedy fabricators. I told Willie I had called up a producer friend for advice. He said: "It's the sort of venture, if you ever got it to Boston, you and everybody else will wonder why you ever got it there."

"Mr. Adler came to see me," Maugham said, "with his delightful wife — they were very disappointed you wouldn't work on it." I said I thought it was better suited to grand opera than a Broadway musical, that it would be awkward to project a lame juvenile — he couldn't dance, for one thing.

At this moment Eddie Cantor came over to our table to say hello to me. I think Willie was relieved. I introduced them and Eddie sat down for a bit. When he left, Maugham said: "He looks remarkably like himself, doesn't he?"

I asked Willie if Alan was going to San Francisco with him.

"No," he said, "I think Alan will be glad to have a rest from me. When I made this promise to Bertram Alanson I was twenty-five years old. I thought fifty years would give me a reasonable time to think it over. Well, they have passed. I am very fond of Alanson and San Francisco is my favorite city. I have to return quickly. I have contracts to sign."

There could not be a greater contrast than that between Alan Searle and Gerald Haxton. Thin, almost cadaverous, mercurial, Gerald was sardonic, at the ready with any word on any subject. Alan was plump and shy. He dressed soberly, in double-breasted, dark suits; there was something aldermanic about him. I took him to lunch. He seemed depressed, full of worries. Willie had departed the night before. He told me that the year before, on Willie's last birthday, Alanson had appeared unannounced at the Villa Mauresque. "It was quite a stunt," he said, "for Alanson to have pulled off; he was slightly older than Willie, his wife had just died, he was lonely, he decided to come to see us. It was very nice to have him. I said to Willie: 'You've been talking so long about that fifteen thousand dollars you gave Alanson to invest for you, that he's never said a word about it since; why don't you ask him now that he's here?'

" 'I wouldn't think of it,' said Willie. 'He's probably long ago lost it and it would embarrass him. It couldn't matter less, anyway.' Nevertheless at lunch on Alanson's last day Willie did ask him. 'Do you remember the fifteen thousand dollars I gave you in Hollywood to invest? It's probably gone and it couldn't matter less. I simply ask out of curiosity.'

" 'I remember very well,' said Alanson. 'It is not lost. I invested it carefully and have reinvested it ever since. It is now worth well over a million dollars.' "

I gasped. "What did Willie say?" I asked.

"Willie said: 'Fancy that,' and no more was said about it."

I asked Alan what was unnerving him.

"Lots," he said. "The future. What am I going to do after Willie dies? I asked Willie that. He said: 'Go into lodgings.' "

"I am sure Willie will provide for you."

"Very skimpy. Hardly."

"Really!"

"He said he'd change his will. He did, finally. I read it. There was a tiny increase for me. I read the phrase: 'if he is still in my service.' That hurt me — it really did." Alan explained to me that this phrase was applied in legal documents to servants. Alan's face reflected the depression that this slight caused him.

I tried to buck him up without much success. I was touched by him. Haltingly, he began to enumerate his grievances. "You don't know what this job is," he said. "I get no time to myself at all. I try to get a night off to go to Villefranche — where the American ships come in. Something always comes up to stop it. You remember the night Willie said, at the Villa, that I was naughty to have burned Lytton Strachey's letters? They were wonderful letters — full of literature. Willie made me burn them. He said: 'Bring down those letters.' He sat in front of the fireplace while I burnt them. I had held on to those letters. I thought: if something happened to Willie, I might sell them."

I asked Alan about his parents.

He said: "Well, they never understood me — they didn't want me to live with them. I left. I know what living in lodgings means. I've lived in them. Traveling with Willie we live in the highest luxury. How can I go back to living in lodgings?"

"If you will allow me," I said, "I'll speak to Willie about it."

There was a frantic look in his brown eyes. He clutched my hand.

"Don't do that," he said. "Promise me you won't. If you did that Willie would never see you again as long as he lived. I would never see him again!"

I left him, marveling at the mystery of these relationships. They could never be understood by an outsider. Where all the rivulets of impulse flow from a different current, it cannot be done.

Richard Adler called to ask if he could drop in to see me. He and his wife, a delightful English musical comedy star, were going to Europe and expected to put in an appearance at the Villa Mauresque. It would be so pleasant if he could tell Willie that I had changed my mind and would work on the musical comedy version of *Of Human Bondage*. He let drop that the Spewacks were interested in doing it. I congratulated him on getting two such experts as the Spewacks. I said I was working hard on Duveen and couldn't stop. I said I'd like to send Willie a present by him; had he any ideas? "You can't send Willie a present," Adler said. "He has everything." That seemed to be decisive. Still, after he left, I kept thinking about it and I thought of something I was pretty sure Willie didn't have. I called up an expert in such matters and asked him to buy me a set of phylacteries, the best the market afforded. They were delivered to me that afternoon. Phylacteries are worn by Orthodox Jews in their devotions. A small, polished square box containing the ten commandments in Hebrew is set on the forehead. From it depend leather bands which are woven around the arm. It is a precise and complicated ritual. I wrote Willie a note in which I told him that advices had come to me from high theological sources which said that his standing with the Lord was not very secure and that he'd better do something about strengthening it. It had relevance to a little joke between us. Willie was always saying that I was anti-Semitic, probably to circumvent a feeling he had that I thought he was. I called up Adler to tell him I'd thought of a present for Willie without telling him what it was. He promised to deliver it.

Presently a thank-you letter arrived from Willie. He said that indeed he hadn't had any phylacteries for a long time; he had felt there was something missing but he couldn't pinpoint exactly what it was. Now he knew! To make up for lost time, he put them on at once, according to the instructions and the diagram I was considerate enough to send him, and he said at the end of his letter: "I dressed, full fig, and went, properly attired, to the synagogue in Nice for the Friday night service. I felt that the tension between me and the Lord was momentarily eased. As you probably know, in our synagogues we segregate the sexes. At the end of the service, as I was going out, a middle-aged, grave lady came up to me. She had just come down from the gallery. 'Oh, Mr. Maugham,' she said, 'it's so nice to have you with us. Tell me — why don't you get married?' "

A few days after the receipt of this letter the newspapers announced that Maugham had issued a blanket request that all those, all over the world, who had received letters from him, should instantly destroy them. I cabled him: "Not mine, honey."

* * *

For the next few years I had to go often to Europe. As I had never met Duveen, I had to dig up people who had known him, Kenneth Clark, for example, who had not only known him but liked him. Alexander Korda encouraged us to write a filmscript about Duveen. It excited us for a bit but we never actually got to work on it. I went to stay with Berenson in Florence. He complained that though Maugham was often in Florence he never came to see him. I promised to transmit this complaint.

I went to Monte Carlo and invited Willie and Alan over to dinner. Alan told me on the telephone that Willie was in low spirits and wanted me very much to come to the Villa. I went. Willie seemed to have aged considerably; his new novel, about Machiavelli, had not had the reception to which he was accustomed. We had a long talk about this. I had never known him so desperately serious. He said that his whole life was devoted to his work. Formally he worked mornings but he never really stopped. "I keep thinking about my work in my bath and get out to put down notes." He said that he didn't have the advantage of the classical education other writers had — Aldous Huxley for instance. He'd had to make do on his own. He talked like a man who had to reconcile himself to failure. The fact that he was probably the most popular author in the world was no comfort to him. He was despairful, his face was seamed in agony. It was something new in my relation with him, which had been mainly humorous. Alan came in. I picked up an old joke between us: that Willie couldn't possibly have turned out the vast amount of work that bore his name; that Alan had written most of it. I reverted to this; I asked Alan how his product was going.

"Alan is written out," said Willie, and went upstairs to bed.

Alan asked me out for a drive. I was glad to go. I told Alan how astonished I had been by Willie's confession.

"Nothing can be done about it," said Alan. "Letters keep coming — fifteen a day from fans all over the world. It's all I can do to keep up with them. I think, really, what it is, is that he doesn't think he can live very long. His new Russian doctor tells me that he's good for ten years anyway. I'm really very worried. I don't know what to do."

"Why?"

"We take walks, you know. On the walks I hear from him the most violent curses. The other day I got scared. I thought the curses were against me. I never could make out the words, actually. I was frightened. I came back here. When he got back, he asked what had become of me on our walk. I said I'd heard these terrible outcries and thought they must be against me. 'They have nothing to do with you,' he said."

"What's all this nasty business going on between him and his daughter?"

Alan, usually mild, spoke fiercely: "I can't talk about that. Willie has forbidden me to talk about that."

I had known Liza Maugham when she was a little girl. I had seen her with her father. It was a family. It was all too perplexing. Alan went on.

"Willie has warned me. 'If I should die while we are traveling, you get back here as soon as you can. You will be up against the most ruthless and predatory people in the world. Get your own things and get them away as fast as you can.' "

We were back at the Villa. I went to my room and to sleep.

The next morning Alan came into my room and said I was wanted on the telephone. I went into Alan's office to take the call. It was from a New York friend — a meteorically successful manager — who was calling from Monte Carlo. He wondered whether we could meet. I said I would try to arrange for him to come to the Villa for lunch. He said he'd like that very much; he would like to meet Mr. Maugham.

The lunch ritual at the Villa was very pleasant. It started with cocktails in the courtyard under an awning. The terraced gardens were visible, and the sea. Willie seemed to be in a relaxed mood. I said how much I was enjoying it. Willie recalled that in the twenties he had met Edna Millay in New York. He found her very agreeable and invited her, if she were ever in this part of the world, to come over to see his place. One morning she called up. "I asked Gerald to receive her and show her around. As it happened, Noel Coward and Cecil Beaton were lunching here that day. We were sitting here having drinks just as we are sitting now. Edna Millay, palpitating with excitement, her arms outspread, rushed in: 'Oh, Mr. Maugham,' she cried out, 'it's fairy land here!'

"There wasn't a hint of innuendo in her exclamation. It was all girlish enthusiasm, but Noel and Cecil were just a bit taken aback."

At lunch we talked about Arnold Bennett. I told Maugham how greatly I had liked him.

"You know," said Willie, "it's odd about A.B. He made a speciality of worldliness and I don't think I have ever known anyone so utterly unworldly. He called me up one day to tell me he was going to be married and could I receive him and his bride. I said of course I would. There was never any wedding because there was never any bride. He hadn't yet asked the girl. Now he had and found that she wasn't in the least bit interested. She had gone out with him because he was a famous author. Arnold I've known since our early days in Paris together where we were both writing away to lay the groundwork for great careers. I said to myself: 'Poor A.B. He, for one, will never make it.' One day he sent me the manuscript of *The Old Wives' Tale* and I had to say to myself: 'You're quite wrong. He *has* made it!'"

By the end of lunch I remembered the telephone call from my friend in Monte Carlo. I told Willie about him. I said he was a resplendent New York manager and that it would be very pleasant for me if I could invite him to lunch.

Willie said: "It might be pleasant for you. What would it be for me?"

I got up, went to my room, and began to pack. Alan came in. He was in a panic. "You mustn't go," he said. "You mustn't. He feels terrible already. He won't sleep tonight. I beg you — don't go."

"I won't stay here another night."

"Please. He says these things. When I think of the people who come here! I think he wants to talk to you and perhaps that's why he said it — so as not to be disturbed. He can't help it. He just says them. He particularly wants you this time. He begged me to bring you. It will be terrible for him if you go. For me too! Please!"

I yielded to Alan. He helped me unpack.

* * *

That night at dinner, to keep things neutral, I spoke of an article I had read by Alec Waugh about the effect of Maugham's novel *Cakes and Ale* on Hugh Walpole. I accused Willie of being a lethal novelist. Alan leaped into the conversation. He detested Hugh Walpole; they both did. Alan said that Walpole was very slow about picking up a restaurant check. Willie found nothing good to say about him. I gathered that they both felt if *Cakes and Ale* had helped to dispatch him, the book had succeeded beyond Willie's hopes. "Oddly enough," said Willie, "I did write one novel that helped to kill a man and that was a man I very much liked. That was the novel I wrote about Gauguin, *The Moon and Sixpence.*" The unintended victim was the chief editor of all the Hearst magazines, Ray Long. "I suppose that Ray was the highest-paid magazine editor in America. He was very kind to me, took everything I sent him, except one story about incest — he said that that was farther than he cared to go. But when he read the Gauguin novel, it destroyed him. He decided that he must do as Gauguin did. He resigned his job with Hearst and went somewhere in the Pacific to give himself a chance, at the age of fifty or over, to express himself. He'd always wanted to paint and he painted. He went on painting till one day it dawned on him that he was not a painter. He threw away his palette and brushes and killed himself. That was a death I did not intend."

After dinner we went into the chandeliered drawing room to smoke. Alan excused himself. He had to work, letters to answer. I looked over piles of new books, sent by publishers, on a round table. I picked one up, took it to a sofa, and started to leaf through it. Alan had turned on the gramophone before he left; the room was full of a Mozart symphony. I looked up to spot Willie. He was standing, his back to me, before a sunburst mirror hanging on a wall. I saw him make an extraordinary gesture. He stretched his arms out wide, flexed them, and stretched them out again. It might have been a calisthenic but it wasn't. It was a gesture of despair, a gesture of trying to burst unbreakable fetters, to escape from the unescapable. His arms fell to his sides. He stood there a moment, limp. It came over me that Willie was the most miserable man in the world. I felt for him. He turned, walked back to the center of the room, and sat near me.

"Alan is well instructed, you know — in furniture and house decoration. He has good taste. He worked, for a long time, in a prison. He has told me many stories that have been useful to me. He has some nice things in his room that he bought himself — that belong to him."

I remembered how Alan had also been well instructed to protect these precious objects in case of sudden death on tour. Alan had told me that Willie wanted to talk to me. I waited. He talked.

"No doubt you have read in the newspapers all that has been going on — in the courts of law — between me and my family."

I said I had and that I found it very perplexing.

"It is the business of lawyers — especially French lawyers — to make things perplexing. Would you mind, please, shutting the phonograph off?"

I put a stop to Mozart.

"I liked Liza's first husband very much. Her present one I cannot endure. He is useless."

I had met Liza's husband and found him charming but did not think it my place to contradict a maturer opinion. He went on speaking very quietly, as if he were telling me a new idea for a novel.

"When I was writing *The Razor's Edge,* I felt it necessary to go to India to complete my research on Eastern theology. I was going, of course, with Gerald. We sat here, our boxes packed and ready to go, when word came from London that I could go all right but that Gerald couldn't. It was very awkward. It took a very long time — it took weeks — but I finally managed it — the ban on Gerald was lifted. We were received everywhere, unofficially — by the maharajahs and so forth — but there was no official recognition of our presence in India." There was a freighted pause and then in a voice that stabbed like a knife thrust, he explained the official neglect. "The Viceroy was Lord Linlithgow."

There was, in the last words, an ultimate concentration of hatred. Lord Linlithgow was Liza's father-in-law. I was startled; I tried to gain a foothold. Was Lord Linlithgow responsible for the ban on Gerald? Was he continuing the ban while Maugham and Gerald were in India? Did Willie think that Liza was an accomplice? Why should

Maugham care so deeply about being excluded from official celebrations? Why, instead, wasn't he grateful?

The vituperation continued. He was embalmed in hatred. His face was contracted with anxiety. I began to feel that Maugham didn't care whether I was listening or not, so long as he could continue to pile up the mound of imprecations. But then I saw that he *did* care whether I was listening. He wanted to persuade me, as he was trying to persuade himself — though knowing all the time that it was a fantasy — that his daughter was not his daughter, that he was being dissolved in a treacherous sea. The denunciation included his wife, now dead, along the lines of the venomous piece he later wrote about her, which his friends deplored. I had met Syrie Maugham once and found her gay and delightful. Now her ghost was being grilled and excoriated. Why could she not be allowed to remain in oblivion?

I had reached the point where I felt that I could endure no more. I saw he was watching me. He said: "Am I tiring you?"

I admitted that I was a bit tired.

"Go up to bed. I'll sit up — wait for Alan."

I rose to leave.

He said: "I'm very glad you didn't leave today."

I saw his lips moving silently as I left the room.

I went upstairs to my room, so beautifully arranged for guests who liked to read. Although the table was stacked with fascinating books, I didn't read. I looked out of the window at the caressive night rustling the leaves in the garden. I felt suddenly that I must leave this place; its beauty compounded the sense of malaise. You felt it was malign, that you had to get out of it to escape what it might at any moment reveal. I couldn't bear to watch Willie. Whether suffering is illusory or substantiated, it is still suffering.

It was all so maddeningly incomprehensible. I had known Maugham for so many years. During all that time he had been a fascinating companion. What had happened to him? Was it old age? But his hatreds had all the vitality of youth. Sitting in a chair, trying to ravel out the heart of the mystery, I remembered suddenly a novel by Christopher Isherwood, *A Single Man*. It tells the story of a teacher in a California university whose male lover has been killed in an accident before the story opens. He is driving along the freeway to his class when he passes a block of newly built apartment houses. As he thinks of all those un-gay squares who will occupy those buildings, he gives vent, in his mind, to a sustained aria of applied sadism: what he would like to do to all these people; not only does he want to do away with them but he revels in the tortures to which he would like to submit them. It is like Willie's pedestrian execrations, only these transpire in quiet communion at the wheel. He wants to boil his victims alive, fry them, dismember them. He reduces them slowly and pleasurably to mincemeat. Is this how they really feel about us? I couldn't help asking myself — is this what they'd really like to do to us? And then I thought of Mr. Isherwood himself, with whom at one time I had a very pleasant acquaintanceship. This personal knowledge did not, at any point, cohere with the aria.

The next morning I improvised an important appointment in Rome and asked Alan to drive me to the airport in Nice. Willie was asleep in a chair under the great Zoffany painting of comedy and tragedy. I looked at him, an exhausted old man in an unreposeful sleep. I would not let Alan wake him.

On the way to Nice we didn't talk much. I was pretty sure that Alan felt that my Rome appointment was nonexistent. I felt also that he understood my wish to get away. I did allow myself one query. I told him of Willie's bitterness at the Viceroy of India, that he had not invited Willie to any official receptions while he was there. I said that this mystified me, that I should have thought Willie would be grateful to be let off such hollow demonstrations, especially considering how he felt about Lord Linlithgow.

Alan thought a minute. Then he said: "What you don't realize is — Willie wants to be respectable. He has always wanted to be respectable."

My last visit to the Villa Mauresque was some years later. Duveen was behind me. I was in Rapallo, Italy, visiting Max Beerbohm. I was in touch, on the telephone, with Alan. He urged me to look in on Willie. "Will he know me?" I asked, since I had heard that he no longer remembered people, even old friends. "I think he will," said

Alan. "Anyway, come. He'd like you to." Max urged me to go; he had great respect for Maugham's "brain," for his power of invention, a power which he himself, he felt, conspicuously lacked. Max was revolted by Graham Sutherland's recently published portrait of Willie. "He looks," Max said, "as if he'd been tortured." Remembering my last visit to the Villa, I said to myself, "He has been."

Alan met me at the airport in Nice. He was full of troubles, oppressed by the weight of litigation in which he and Willie were entangled. Willie's wish to adopt Alan had met legal opposition. To lighten things up, I asked Alan whether he'd seen the *Punch* cartoon: the irate mother to her lackadaisical son: "I suppose you're hanging around just waiting for Somerset Maugham to adopt you!" Alan had seen it; he didn't think it was very funny. He had only the week before been through a crisis. Willie had permitted him, after months of day-and-night service, to go into Nice for dinner. On his return, about ten o'clock, he found the staff in an uproar. Willie had disappeared. He had been last seen walking barefoot on the Lower Corniche, looking for Alan. Alan was terrified. Willie had presumably forgotten that he had permitted Alan to go out. The idea of Willie shuffling down that road in the heavy traffic was insupportable. It was a great relief when the police brought him back. He said to Alan: "I've been looking everywhere for you."

Alan warned me to speak loud, as Maugham had gone very deaf. The butler let us in. Presently Maugham came in; he knew me all right and embraced me. For want of anything better to say, I shouted at him:

"HAVE YOU SEEN WINSTON?"

"Yes," he said, "last week. If you think I'm g-g-ga-ga, you should see W-W-Winston!"

He went with gusto into an account of Churchill. He was living on the Onassis yacht in the harbor at Monte Carlo. "Winston loves to be photographed. He is being constantly photographed with Onassis, who sends these c-c-clubby photographs to his subsidiaries. Onassis needs bolstering, financially, at this moment." By this time we had walked into the drawing room. He faced me. He was looking rather disheveled, very unusual for him. "Well," he said, "it's obvious that I can't live very much longer."

Alan then urged him to accept a proposal from London that he go on the air on his 90th birthday to greet the British public. Maugham said he couldn't. Alan tried to enlist me to urge him. I made an effort but it failed. Maugham repeated his refrain: "It is obvious that I can't live very much longer."

But he seemed to revive. With a flash of his old humor he told me of going down in the lift in his hotel in Athens — an American woman got on and buttonholed him. " 'You don't know me,' she said, 'but I know you. You are Mr. Maugham. I recognize you from your newspaper photographs.'

" 'I was hoping,' I said, 'that I am more attractive than my newspaper photographs.'

" 'Oh, no, you're not,' she said, 'indeed you're not!' "

Willie asked about Max. I said he was, in spite of his disabilities, enchanting. I had been urging Willie for a long time to visit Max. He had indeed done so. I gathered that his visit had not been too successful.

"Well, you know Max," said Willie. "He lives entirely in the past. So we spoke of the past — of the people we had known in our younger days. But he has a cult, hasn't he, among the highbrows?"

I refrained from telling him what one highbrow, Edmund Wilson, had said to me of Max: "He's worth a hundred Maughams."

Willie said to Alan: "Show Sam the medal I got in Heidelberg."

"Oh," said Alan, "it's so heavy. Dinner's just been announced."

"Oh, has it? Let us then have dinner."

We marched into the dining room. Alan winked at me. I could tell that he was very pleased at the way his charge was behaving. Indeed, except that he was looking very aged and was deaf, Willie gave an impression of his old form. At dinner he told me that he had been honored at Heidelberg, the first foreigner who had been so honored. It had been an endless day; the mayor came and presided; the rector of the university, the chancellor — the room was packed. It was hot. The ceremony started in the morning; there was an elaborate lunch and then the speeches continued. "It was all I could do," said Willie, "to keep awake. 'Will it never end?' I thought. It did end. The great plaque was presented. Alan took it. He could cope with it. We walked out into the open air."

"I had to carry it!" said Alan.

"But tell Sam," insisted Willie, "what the rector said when he gave it to you."

"He said: 'Would you mind, when Mr. Maugham dies, returning this plaque to us? We went to great trouble with it and considerable expense. We want it as a memorial — of this glorious occasion!' "

"What could I do?" said Alan, "I promised."

"That is a promise," said Willie fiercely, "I order you to break. Never give it back to them — never. Promise — in front of Sam."

"I promise," said Alan. "Shall I give it to Sam?"

On the way out of the dining room, Alan clutched my arm. He was smiling. He had never hoped that things would go so well.

I went up to my old room; it was as gracious as ever. The books stacked on the table had been changed so that guests could keep up with the times, in literature and in thought. There was a new book by Lord Beaverbrook. I opened it. It was affectionately inscribed to Willie — just a few days before. I began to read it but I didn't know enough about English political history and cabinet shufflings to make it understandable. I picked up Cyril Connolly's *Enemies of Promise,* which had been there before, and went at that again. There is a warm passage about Willie in it. I reflected that perhaps a good deal of the denigration of Willie by the "highbrows" was caused, not only by his vast success, but by the fact that critics like Connolly, who could not be brushed aside, appreciated him.

The next day I walked down to lunch and was delighted to find Dadie Rylands there. He was an old friend of earlier London days. I had visited him in Cambridge, where he was a don. We embraced each other. Dadie asked about Max. I told him that he was as dear and amusing as ever, interested in everything but shadowed by awareness of impending dissolution. I described how he looked with distaste at the brown splotches on his hand resting on the arm of his chair. "How ugly they are!" he said. I told Dadie I'd had a look at Lord Beaverbrook's new book but hadn't gotten very far.

"Who," said Willie suddenly, "is Lord Beaverbrook?"

"Why," said Alan, "he came here to lunch last week!"

Willie couldn't remember. Dadie, unhurried, patient, embarked on a chronology of Beaverbrook's career. But it was obvious that Willie was bored by this history. Dadie gave it up. We went in to lunch. Dadie told about the new plays in London, the books that had interested him. It was difficult to say how much Willie took in. At one point, he mumbled: "The future of literature belongs to homosexuality." It was almost inaudible but I heard it and Alan heard it. I could see that it shocked Alan. On the way out he whispered to me: "He never mentions things like that!"

John Foster, an old and warm friend of mine, joined us in the garden. He had a very attractive English lady with him. Foster is very tall and impressive, not easily missed in any gathering.

"Who is this gentleman?" said Willie.

"He's your lawyer!" said Alan.

Willie accepted this fact without absorbing it. Indeed, I knew that Foster, in the vast legal scaffolding surrounding Willie, had a niche.

"You'd better go up for your nap, Willie," Alan said. "I'll stay here and talk to Sir John."

Without a word Willie shuffled out. Foster's friend wanted a look at the place, and I volunteered to show her around. We walked up through the garden terraces to the beautiful pool at the top with the classical sculptures at the head and bottom of it, which Willie had bought in Rome. We sat on a bench looking over the series of gardens, the Villa, the road leading up to it and the wooded area between it and the sparkling Mediterranean. It was breathtaking.

"And to think," said the English lady, "from books — from nothing but books!"

I did not see Alan again till he came to New York after Willie's death. He had a suite at the Drake. He kept up the style to which Willie had accustomed him. He was plumper. He wore a grand new suit of heavy dark cloth. Now he looked like a Lord Mayor. He had come out very well in the final settlement. He had taken an apartment in Monte Carlo. He missed Willie. He was lonely.

He described the last harrowing days. It would have served Willie very well as a set piece for the macabre. He brought Willie back to the Villa from the hospital so that he could die in his own room, in his own painted bed, beneath the photograph of his mother — with her great compassionate eyes — whom he had adored. The servants had all left. They had also transported Willie's carefully tended pride, his wine cellar. Alan had a pretty good idea who had taken it but he thought it inadvisable to get entangled with the French law again. He described his journey to Marseilles to have Willie cremated, a job which took many hours and was very badly done. He shipped the remains to London, where Willie was buried, on the grounds of his old public school.

Alan had been in London and he told me about the people he'd seen and the time he'd had. I asked him whether he had seen a mutual friend of ours, a vastly rich widow who had also been a friend of Willie's. He shot me a sly look and smiled as if he were sure that what he was going to say would amuse me.

"Oh, yes, I've seen a lot of her," he said. "She's after me for my money."

XXII

Climate at 77

SOME TIME after I had passed my seventieth birthday I began to work on this book. I worked on it steadily for a year, writing at random from memory. In August, after a summer in town, I went with my wife for a brief holiday to my sister-in-law's beach house. A beach house is not intended for writers; it is meant for visitors who leave their rooms first thing in the morning and lounge about in the ample living room, on the ample verandah or the ampler beach. I spent all day in my tiny bedroom — into which a bridge table had been inserted — working. I worked in this closet, quite happily, for several weeks, until I was interrupted by a mysterious occurrence. I went to bed on a Friday night, after a long day's work, felt restless, and decided to get up. I couldn't. I fell out of bed and lay on the floor, pinned between a heavy armchair and the bed itself. I called out for help but my wife, sleeping in the next room, could not hear me. Help finally came, and a doctor, at two A.M. I was lifted back into bed; the doctor said I'd better be hospitalized in the morning. I asked: "Is it a stroke?" He said: "We call it an episode," making it sound like a romantic coaching accident in the nineteenth century. Next day at the hospital, my own doctor said it was a blood clot and told me not to worry. He said he thought it would be all right. I knew something about blood clots. A warm friend of my wife's family had suffered a blood clot in his leg about two years before, and had been confined to a wheelchair ever since. I had been told that he would probably be in one for the rest of his life. Blood clots didn't have a good reputation: it was said of them that they kill you or paralyze you. I was kept for a month in a hospital room teetering between these two alternatives — my left side already felt weakened; I couldn't manage walking without help. In my night thoughts I hoped it would be the former of the two alternatives. I had reason to believe it might be quick and silent: it might, I hoped so, happen in my sleep. There was an element of relief in the prospect.

I thought and thought about it. I tried to imagine what it would be like afterwards. But it is impossible to imagine death. The act of imagination is a high function of living and life is removed from death. An old saying says: "Where life is, death is not; where death is, life is not." My nights were spent in cramped, concentrated abstracts of my past, insulated mainly in self-reproach: mistakes made, opportunities missed, remembered gaucheries, remembered crudities, reaching back to childhood. I remembered a little sister whom I did not remember. I remembered only that she was killed by a streetcar in front of our house in Worcester. I remembered her being carried in; I could not bring back what she looked like. I could remember only my mother's face and her silence; she was silent for a long time after this happened. Years later I returned to Worcester, with my brothers, for my mother's funeral. At the cemetery we saw the half-headstone for our little sister — my oldest brother, who had known her, who remembered her, wept over it.

About ten years before I was interrupted by this episode I had made a new friend. He was Fred Kohlmar, a producer at Twentieth Century–Fox. I had met him in the studio barbershop. We began to talk and this conversation continued more or less steadily for ten years. It was not a professional relationship; I never worked for him. He was a dear and loving man; we simply liked each other. His father had been a well-known character actor whom I'd seen in the Worcester Theatre, supporting David Warfield in *The Music Master*. It was to Fred's father that Warfield quavered the famous lines: "You von't take her —I take her. You don't vunt her — *I* vunt her!" Fred called me up weekly from Hollywood and we met in New York whenever he came, which was sometimes fairly often. He sent me the scripts he considered filming and I was frank with him about them. I sent him mine — he was equally frank. The last four summers Fred had been filming in

Paris. I went over to spend several weeks with him the last summer he was there. When I went to the hospital I asked my secretary to write to his secretary. My secretary told me later she'd had a letter from Kohlmar's secretary saying that her boss had gone to the hospital too and that it was quite serious. My secretary told me this when I came home from the hospital, when I'd given her the hackneyed instruction: "Get me Mr. Kohlmar on the telephone." A few days later I read in the *Times* that Fred had died. I missed talking to him. At seventy-seven there are fewer people that you long to talk to; there are fewer available. I have been reading W. H. Auden's *Commonplace Book*. He quotes a brief passage from Virginia Woolf's diary for May 1932:

". . . since we came back, I'm screwed up into a ball: can't get into step; can't make things dance; feel awfully detached; see youth; feel old; no, that's not quite it: wonder how a year or so perhaps is to be endured. Think, yet people do live; can't imagine what goes on behind faces. All is surface hard; myself only an organ that takes blows, one after another; the horror of the hard raddled faces in the flower show yesterday; the inane pointlessness of all this existence: hatred of my own brainlessness and indecision; the old tread-mill feeling, of going on and on and on, for no reason: Lytton's death; Carrington's; a longing to speak to him; all that cut away, gone . . ."

She longed to speak to Lytton Strachey; I longed to speak to Freddy Kohlmar.

I was, my doctor told me afterwards, somewhat disoriented in my first days in the hospital. Among the chronic self-reproaches that returned to plague me during those merciless nights, which I thought would be my last, was that I had spent too much time in Hollywood. I should have devoted that time, it came to me with an illusory clarity, to studying Latin and Greek, to give myself some semblance of a classical education. I felt that I had wasted my life because I cannot understand them; Greek passages drive me altogether crazy. Reverting to this self-accusation after I got home, I saw that there was another side to this indictment. In the first place I probably should have learned neither Latin nor Greek; I should probably have written another play. Had I never gone to Hollywood I should have missed some irreplaceable people: the Hovey family, Ernst Lubitsch, Sam Hoffenstein, George Cukor, Greta Garbo.

I cannot recall my friendships without including that of four ladies I have never met. With this quartet I have kept up a lively and enlivening correspondence for many years. It began with fan letters on pieces I had written in the *New Yorker* on my early days in Worcester, Massachusetts, or on meetings with Max Beerbohm. The letters were so intensive that they had to be answered in kind. My correspondence with these unknowns continued till they became intimates. One is the widow of an American university president; one the wife of a Chicago industrialist; one the divorced wife of an American professor who lives in a thatched cottage in an English village; the fourth the widow of another professor, from the University of Oklahoma. With the exception of the Chicago lady, who is worldly, I seem to run to academic wives, widows and divorcées. From the lady in the thatched cottage I have had the most extraordinary letters, taking me into the widely proliferated lives of her children, living in London, Paris and California. One Christmas I got from her a large package, containing a gamut of carefully packed greens from her garden, no two colors alike, subtly modulated from shade to shade. The fragrance from them filled my room; I was close to being in Surrey. I wrote to thank her for sending me the New Forest.

Now who would think, that from a lady living in Stillwater, Oklahoma, I would get an introduction to one of the most distinguished men in England, Sir Sidney Cockerell? My Stillwater friend had written about me to Cockerell; as a result I received an invitation from him to come to see him, should I happen to be in London. I saw to it that I was in London. I imagine that Mrs. Martin wrote about me to Cockerell as if she knew me, as I write about her now. Cockerell, when I went to see him, was nearing ninety. He had been for some time valetudinary; I found him in bed, in conversation rich and lively. In his youth he had been secretary to William Morris and to Ruskin; he had remade the Fitzwilliam Museum at Cambridge; he had suggested St. Joan as a subject to Bernard Shaw. At Shaw's funeral he read aloud a passage from *Pilgrim's Progress,* the only service there was. I brought the conversation round to Max Beerbohm. (I was then writing about him.) He was a great admirer. He began to remember the first time he had ever seen Max. I edged my chair closer to his bed. What he told me gave me a special close-up of Max that I could have gotten from no one else. It helped me materially for the work in hand. I owed it all to Grace Martin of Stillwater, Oklahoma.

We talked about Grace. Cockerell said that he was very fond of her, that she had a passion for writing and was well read, especially in English literature. He said that she had a beautiful speaking voice, low in register, melodic. I said that she had it in her letters too.

I wrote to Grace on my return (it had taken some time, but we finally got to calling each other by first names in our correspondence) to thank her for having made possible my visit to the entrancing Sidney Cockerell. I did not fail to mention what he had said about her voice.

Years passed. My book on Max was finished. Cockerell died. Grace and I exchanged consolatory letters. In her letters to me Grace always said that I needn't bother to answer; she deferred always to the pressing and deeply demanding work she imagined me to be doing. But I always did write. I noticed a longish lapse in reply to the last letter I wrote her. It worried me because she had always been so prompt. A letter finally came with an Oklahoma postmark. But it was not Grace's handwriting. It was from her niece, telling me that Grace had died. She enclosed obituary notices from the local papers. I tried to find out whether Grace had received my last letter. I couldn't. I developed a fixation about this. Had she died thinking I hadn't bothered to write, that the correspondence had begun to bore me? It would have been horrible had she thought that. I sat thinking about her. I tried to accommodate myself to the pitiless fact that Grace Martin was no longer in this world. I'd have given anything if I'd had someone to write to about her. I'd written to her niece, of course, but her letter in reply had been very reserved. If only Cockerell were alive I'd have written to him. As there was no one, I began rereading her letters. Of Cockerell's death she had said that since he had wanted to die she could not feel sorry for him, only for herself, and that his passing left her "diminished." Grace Martin's passing left me diminished.

I have been reading the Holmes-Laski correspondence, a fascinating book — except that the two volumes are spitefully studded with Latin and Greek. In one letter Justice Holmes says that as he ages, he feels that the walls of the room in which he is sitting are narrowing, that he is being hemmed in closer and closer. In another he writes:

> . . . I don't know whether it is the extra pressure of the atmosphere on some of these damp days or the knowledge that I am near the end that makes me rather gloomy. I was going to say indifferent when I remembered that half an hour ago I was fidgeting over a question of investment and that I still want to write and read (solid books, not novels) if it is worth thinking about. One would like to have a glimpse of the meaning, or I know not what transcending meaning of the universe before one dies, but one who thinks as I do perceives that he has no right to make the demand, but should shut up and go under quietly like a good soldier . . .

Erik Erikson speaks of dying with integrity. I don't really know what that means. Surely no man lived a life of greater integrity than Oliver Wendell Holmes. Did the knowledge of this widen for him the narrowing room? But I know what Holmes means when he finds that he takes time off to consider investments. I have been terribly upset by the Vietnam war and feel a general malaise about the situation in this country now. I grew up with a resplendent feeling about the glory and generosity of the United States. I am the only member of my family who was born here. We were an immigrant family living in deep poverty and yet my older brother and I were helped to secure the best American educations: my brother at Yale and I at Harvard. But I have, of late years, been conscious of a deep change. The country has taken on a frightening aspect. It seems to have become a plutocracy, cruel, capable of atrocities, which has darkened its image all over the world. I say to myself: Why should I care? In a short time I will know nothing about anything. But I do care. I care deeply. An incident related to me by an old friend has made a profound impression on me: it has clouded for me the climate of seventy-seven.

My friend is a playwright who has written some brilliant comedies. His brother whom I also know and whom I have found very likable is an industrialist who lives in the Southwest. My friend and his wife travel south for a reunion every year. They had booked to go down the day after President Kennedy was killed. My friend was so upset that he felt he could not go through with it. His wife persuaded him to go; she said it might take his mind off the tragedy. They went. His sister-in-law arranged a dinner party, as she usually did. My friend was appalled by the fact that the dinner party went off to the customary jollity; the assassination of the President was never mentioned. A point came where he couldn't stand it. He addressed the whole table. "Look here! How is it that no one has mentioned the President?" The hostess put her hand on his shoulder:

"Please, dear," she said, "no politics."

What strikes me as I look back is that I have known few contented people. I have known very busy ones, rich ones, triumphant ones, but few who have been contented. I have had quoted to me a remark made by Mrs. Oliver Wendell Holmes to her husband: "I beg of you, do not yield to the luxury of despair." It lies in wait, this luxury, behind the ambush of busyness, of immediate obligation, of scrutiny into the unanswerable. Maugham once said to me, in a self-assured moment: "I have made the ghastliest mistakes in my life and yet, somehow, they have all turned out very well for me." That is the way it seemed to him then; we are bouldered in by time; consciousness is the creature of time; it is discrete, volatile, mortal, as our bodies are. The ghastly mistakes come to be seen as ghastly mistakes.

There is a way of looking at it that could make it seem that I have had a successful life. Certainly, other people think so, but I have never been persuaded. In London once, where I had a successful play running, I met a charming and very attractive woman who had once been married to Ernest Hemingway. There is something about theatrical success which impresses people. "How does it feel," she asked me, "to be at the very top?" On the way home I asked myself: "If I am at the very top where is Ernest Hemingway?"

I spent a great deal of time with Max Beerbohm during the last years of his life, seeing him every day near the end. He was quietly great, great without assertiveness. He admired Maugham. He said Maugham had a powerful brain and seemingly limitless invention. "I myself," he said, "am weak on invention." What struck me was that he had no envy of Maugham's inventiveness, he had no wish to be inventive himself; he was content with what he had done. I was then seeing three celebrated old men: Max, Bernard Berenson and Somerset Maugham. Max, who had nothing, was the only one of the three who had contentment, even serenity. He knew his limitations precisely and had no wish to go beyond them. Berenson was eroded by being a failed writer; Maugham by not being a great one. Speaking to me one day about the Order of Merit, he explained humorously his never getting it: "It's the Order of Morals, you know." The first day I met Max he showed me, with great pride, a statement from Knopf, with a solid line of zeros under the Receipts column. He put the twin ogres, Success-Failure, in their proper places. He would not be cowed by a zero.

As I look back on it, I experienced one unalloyed felicity in my middle life, which compensated for the grievous misses in the hugger-mugger of the theatre. This was in the friendship and collaboration of two great editors: Harold Ross, who founded the *New Yorker,* and his successor, William Shawn. There could not be a greater contrast than between these two. Ross was not particularly well read; he was what might be called lowbrow and devil-may-care; but his instincts were impeccable. Wolcott Gibbs, a keen and subtle writer, loved to be edited by Ross. Gibbs told me once, "When Ross writes opposite a paragraph a simple query: 'Is this really interesting?' first I get mad as hell and then I read the paragraph and I see that it really isn't very interesting — I rewrite the paragraph or cut it." Isaiah Berlin, whom I saw fairly often in those days, admired the *New Yorker.* He wished to meet Ross. I arranged it. We met for lunch at the Algonquin: Ross, Shawn, Isaiah and myself. Berlin started off at high velocity. He is a talker who never has to limber up — he plunges in and, wherever he

Harold Ross

finds himself, he is at home. He inundated Ross in a freshet of in-Oxford speech. Ross asked whether he might change places with me, to be nearer the source of the Oracle. I yielded. Ross shifted, but I don't think it did him much good. When lunch was over, I walked back to his office with Ross. Somewhat bitter, he exclaimed: "I didn't understand a goddamn word your friend said but he can write anything for us he likes."

Some time later I was called upon to arrange another lunch party for another Englishman who wanted to meet Ross. This was Harold Laski. Ross was all slicked up to meet Laski; his hair was nicely combed. Somehow Ross had picked up a stray volume of Herbert Spencer's *Autobiography*. It seemed to him that this offered a nice opening for a conversation with a professor. He offered it. Laski's eyes gleamed behind his glasses. He sized up Ross as a Herbert Spencer man and began to dilate on various aspects of Spencer's work. It dawned on Ross that Spencer had written other books besides the *Autobiography* and that, embarrassingly, Laski had read them. Ross began to muss up his hair. I steered the conversation away from Spencer. The lunch went fine after that. It ended with Ross getting a promise from Laski to do a book review for him.

The difference between Ross and Shawn was easily seizable but this was superficial. Essentially they were alike: they shared an inbred humaneness. This constituted the symbiosis between them. When Ross caused a sign to be posted in his office, directed at those on his staff who had achieved national celebrity: "DON'T BE A GENIUS AROUND HERE," it was to deflect arrogance and to modify self-complacency. The atmosphere created by the *New Yorker* was humane; it was a warm Republic of Letters. Recently, a new contributor to the *New Yorker*, Professor Reich of Yale, in a public statement, said that the experience of working with the editors for a long time over a piece he had written, *The Greening of America*, had given him a glimpse into a civilized atmosphere that he hoped might one day come into being in the world at large. I know what he means. I worked with Shawn over many years. I did the same with Katharine S. White. For Mrs. White I wrote the ten pieces of reminiscences which later appeared as the book *The Worcester Account*. I wrote four books in the *New Yorker*. I worked often with Shawn late into the night arguing over a phrase, a word, a punctuation. Each piece was treated with care and vigilance, as if it were the only piece to appear in that particular issue. The friendships I have had with various members of the *New Yorker* staff, with Wolcott Gibbs, with St. Clair McKelway, who has written some of the most moving stories as well as innumerable funny ones, have been lit in varying degrees by the same quality I have found in the editors. I look back on this period as one of the happiest in my life.

XXIII
At Rise

EVERY PLAYWRIGHT IS HEMMED IN, in space and in time, by the
first words he has to write at the beginning of every play: AT RISE,
SCENE, TIME. Once you have risen you are committed till you are able
to write: THE FINAL CURTAIN FALLS. Those first two words are the
most fateful in the language: more fateful than "I thee wed" or "I
Will and Bequeath." In the first case there are remedies for disaster;
in the second, the bequeather, by the time his gifts are delivered, is
himself beyond disaster. These words, at the beginning and end of
every play, form the parentheses in which life itself is bounded: the
rises and falls within our lives, the innumerable rebirths and renewals,
from the mock deaths of depressions to the plateaus of self-belief, the
diminuendos and crescendos of the psyche. The falls and rises of non-
playwrights, of the anonymous stumblers, are no less momentous for
them, even when they are neither heroic nor tragic, even when they
are merely banal.

I keep filling my notebooks, which have been lifelong companions,
with ideas for plays which I shall never write. In my last years these
jottings have been preempted by a major ambition: to write a play
about Montaigne.

I had early become addicted to Montaigne. I wrote down a sentence
from him: "We are, I know not how, double in ourselves, so that what
we believe we disbelieve and cannot rid ourselves of what we con-
demn." The idea of pluralism in personality, of duality, fascinated me.
My first play was on this subject. I had a sense of plagiarism, some

years ago, when I found that W. H. Auden had used the sentence just quoted as an epigraph for his book of poems *The Double Man*. My play about Montaigne was to be called *The Many Men* and was to be a dramatization of a passage in which Montaigne speaks of the many men resident in every man. The warring selves within the self has always beckoned to me as a theme, because I have always had to cope with it myself. One uncomfortable manifestation of it has been indecision. I no sooner decide on a course than I repel it. It is my being victimized by these perpetual tournaments that drew me early to Montaigne. Over the years I have gone far with the idea for the Montaigne play but not far enough. I wrote the At Rise and that is all there is of it, except for a sizable crammed notebook.

When you are absorbed in a project people seem to turn up to help you. This happened to me. I met Professor Donald Frame, of Columbia, the biographer and translator of Montaigne. I have been told by other scholars that he is the foremost authority on Montaigne in America. I feel that the meeting was psychic; that my interest in his favorite subject was so keen that we were bound to meet. He has been immensely kind, has sent me his special writings from learned journals, illuminating recondite phases of Montaigne's career. Were I younger, had I the strength, I should have asked this gracious man to collaborate with me on a Montaigne play. I suggest to some future playwright who might engage in this difficult task that he couldn't do better than to introduce himself to Donald M. Frame.

Montaigne lived in a barbarous time, somewhat like our own. His friend, Henri of Navarre, the future Henri IV, was, on St. Bartholomew's Day, a prisoner in the Louvre. He looked out of the window and saw Catholic women drinking the blood of freshly slaughtered Protestants. I have read extensively for years about this era, an era during which Montaigne kept a level head. He realized that all he had, all he could cling to, was himself. He expressed himself, his various selves, and this expression has given him an ever-fresh immortality.

Stefan Zweig, at the end of his autobiography, says that he is planning to write a novel about Montaigne. But he committed suicide in Buenos Aires. In any case, to write a novel (especially if you are a

Michel de Montaigne

novelist) is easier than to write a play. Montaigne gave up the life of action for the life of thought; the former is easier to dramatize than the latter. I thought to resolve this difficulty by dividing the play between Montaigne and Henri of Navarre, who was fairly active. For a time Montaigne worked with him and Navarre enjoyed coming to see Montaigne for discussion and advice. Heinrich Mann, in his novel *Young Henry of Navarre,* touches frequently upon this relationship. The Scottish scholar M. M. Robertson, in his book *Montaigne and Shakespeare,* gives chapter and verse for the immense borrowings made by the latter from the former. My notes call for, in scenes between Navarre and Montaigne, dialogue with casual remarks in it by Montaigne, which Shakespearians would recognize. I conceived also that the idea for the Grand Design (the sixteenth-century adumbration of the League of Nations) should be suggested to Navarre by Montaigne. I dreamt of a scene in which someone should tell Montaigne that a talented young English playwright devoured his essays and used ideas from them in his plays. But who? In G. P. V. Akrigg's *Shakespeare and the Earl of Southampton,* I thought that perhaps I had found a link: this was Florio, Southampton's Italian language teacher, a hot-tempered fellow who got around.

I kept in my room an engraving of Montaigne, the frontispiece of one of the editions of his essays. He was short, inclined to rotundity, bald, grave-looking with a Mandarin moustache and a Vandyke beard. Who to play him? In every cast of every play — mine and others — I looked for Montaigne. It is a moment I shan't forget, the instantaneous thrill of recognition, when I first saw Oskar Karlweis. He *was* Montaigne. I think, had he lived, I would have put steam on and written the play.

I went home and wrote the At Rise. I hope that some future playwright may use it. To him I will and bequeath all my notes and the only part of the play which is written:

AT RISE: *A circular turret library in a small château in the environs of Bordeaux in France. The tower, with this room at the top, is the retreat of Michel de Montaigne, Mayor of Bordeaux. The Mayoralty of Bordeaux was an office Montaigne did not want but he yielded to the entreaty of his friend Henri of Navarre. It is the winter of 1581. The room is lined with books, choice editions, tooled volumes, red, brown and gold. In this library are the books left him by his dearest friend, Etienne La Boétie. In a frieze over the books, running around the circle of the walls, is written Montaigne's tribute to his dead friend: "Inasmuch as he desired that there should be some unique memorial of this most sweet, most dear, and most close companion, than whom our age hath seen none better, none more absolutely perfect, Michel de Montaigne, unhappily bereft of so beloved a guardian of his life, mindful of their mutual affection and of the kindly feeling which united them, hath set up, since nought more expressive could be found, this learned shelf, a special laboratory for the mind, in the which is his delight."*

On the rafters above the frieze are aphorisms culled by the Mayor of Bordeaux from his intensive reading: "Who knoweth if what men call living be not dying?" "The for and the against are both possible"; "Rejoice in those things that are present — all else is beyond thee"; and, from Terence, "I am a man and nothing human is alien to me." But the dominating motto is "Que scais-je?"

When the curtain rises, Montaigne, in black, is talking to his intellectual disciple, Marie de Gournay. She is wildly excited, because Henri of Navarre, the Mayor's guest, is about to arrive. Montaigne tries to calm her; the King, he is saying, "is, after all, only a man . . ."

Index